WHAT YOUR COLLEAGUES ARE SAYING . . .

"How many times have you heard 'a picture is worth a thousand words'? Visual, graphic information is important because human brains are hard-wired to attend to images. The challenge is that students still have to read words to achieve success. In this text, Lapp, Wolsey, Wood, and Johnson make a vital connection between reading words and the role of graphics. They demonstrate how teachers and students can blend the two such that great learning occurs in every classroom, every day."

—DOUGLAS FISHER
Coauthor of *Rigorous Reading*

"Lapp, Wolsey, Wood, and Johnson have written a book that will become *the* resource for using graphic organizers across disciplines! With careful attention to the details teachers crave in order to design meaningful lessons, the authors guide teachers on a journey that takes them far beyond the traditional uses of graphic organizers—jotting notes and organizing information—and show teachers how these visual tools lead students to independent thinking and inquiry, as well as support the Common Core reading and writing standards. What I love about this book is that it fosters original thinking among students as they design graphic organizers that enable them to unpack meaning from complex texts and develop arguments for essays."

—LAURA ROBB
Author of *Vocabulary Is Comprehension*

"Professional books have long urged teachers to use graphic organizers, but most of these books are dreadfully short on specifics. Diane Lapp and her colleagues have addressed this problem in an admirable fashion. They examine with care the kinds of organizers available to teachers, together with when and how to use them. And by showing how organizers transcend disciplinary boundaries, the authors pave the way for a school-wide focus for professional learning. Educators endeavoring to meet the challenges of the Common Core should mark this title as a must-read. This engaging book is long overdue and I recommend it enthusiastically!"

—MICHAEL MCKENNA
Coauthor of *Assessment for Reading Instruction*, Second Edition

"For educators looking for ways to implement graphic organizers in their classrooms, this is the resource for you. The numerous types of graphic organizers, the research behind them, and the how and why to use them with students are all at your fingertips. I envision this book being especially helpful for teachers new to the field just learning about graphic organizers."

—LESLIE BLAUMAN
Author of *The Common Core Companion, Grades 3–5*

MINING
COMPLEX TEXT

GRADES
6–12

*We are fortunate to work with so many exemplary middle grades
and high school teachers. We learn so much from them every time we visit their classrooms.
This book is dedicated to the teachers it has been our privilege to know.*

GRADES
6–12

MINING
COMPLEX TEXT

Using and Creating **GRAPHIC ORGANIZERS**
to Grasp Content and Share New Understandings

Diane Lapp / Thomas DeVere Wolsey
Karen Wood / Kelly Johnson

CL CORWIN
LITERACY

FOR INFORMATION:

Corwin

A SAGE Company

2455 Teller Road

Thousand Oaks, California 91320

(800) 233-9936

www.corwin.com

SAGE Publications Ltd.

1 Oliver's Yard

55 City Road

London EC1Y 1SP

United Kingdom

SAGE Publications India Pvt. Ltd.

B 1/I 1 Mohan Cooperative Industrial Area

Mathura Road, New Delhi 110 044

India

SAGE Publications Asia-Pacific Pte. Ltd.

3 Church Street

#10-04 Samsung Hub

Singapore 049483

Publisher: Lisa Luedeke

Development Editor: Wendy Murray

Editorial Development Manager: Julie Nemer

Editorial Assistant: Emeli Warren

Production Editors: Olivia Weber-Stenis and
Melanie Birdsall

Copy Editor: Sarah J. Duffy

Typesetter: C&M Digitals (P) Ltd.

Proofreader: Victoria Reed-Castro

Indexer: Wendy Allex

Cover and Interior Designer: Scott Van Atta

Marketing Manager: Maura Sullivan

Copyright © 2015 by Corwin

Printed in the United States of America

A catalog record of this book is available from the Library of Congress.

ISBN: 978-1-4833-1628-4

This book is printed on acid-free paper.

14 15 16 17 18 10 9 8 7 6 5 4 3 2 1

CONTENTS

Visit the companion website at
www.corwin.com/miningcomplextext/6-12
for downloadable resources.

ACKNOWLEDGMENTS

A special thanks to the following teacher consultants and lesson designers extraordinaire:

Doctoral Students in Curriculum and Instruction at the University of North Carolina–Charlotte:

Joyce Farrow, UNCC and Mooresville Graded School District, NC
Rebecca Kavel, UNCC and Charlotte Mecklenburg Schools, NC
Kyle Kester, UNCC and Davie County Schools, NC
Kim Heintschel Ramadan, UNCC and Charlotte Mecklenburg Schools, NC
Brian Williams, UNCC

Master's in Reading Education Students at the University of North Carolina–Charlotte:

Jennifer Harahus, Cabarrus County Schools, NC
Lindsay Merritt, Hope Academy, Concord, NC

Five more masterful educators:

Debbie Abilock, NoodleTools
Danielle Knight, High School Special Education English Language Arts, NJ
Stacy Miller, Patch American High School, Stuttgart, Germany
Melissa Olsen Provost, Portsmouth Middle School, ME
Traci Tarquinio, Programa de Aprendizaje de Lengua Extranjera, Universidad de Guadalajara

GRAPHIC ORGANIZERS

MAKING THE COMPLEX COMPREHENSIBLE

Graphic organizers, mind maps, knowledge maps, concept maps. Whatever you call them, chances are you've used them or created them to support students' learning. They are a powerful tool for visually representing one's understanding of information and concepts. This makes them terrific tools for assessment also, because they clearly show what students grasp—and what they don't yet fully understand.

Yet in the midst of momentum for increased depth and rigor in instruction and higher expectations of what students must be able to do in regard to complex text reading, writing, and thinking, do graphic organizers still have a role? How can a single-page tool, made up of simple shapes and a mere sprinkling of words, possibly take students where they need to go?

In this book we answer these questions by addressing why and how graphic organizers have more relevance than ever before in supporting secondary students' understanding of challenging content. We discuss why students need these tools to deeply comprehend complex ideas and present them. We explain just how these visual displays help students analyze a topic or idea by separating the constituent parts or elements. These visuals allow students to look closely at the key parts of a fairy tale, the chief trade artifacts of early Americans, the rain cycle—virtually any body of information, to analyze how the parts fit together. We explore the ways graphic organizers help students support their thinking as they work to absorb content, giving them a vehicle for writing and arranging their understandings, which they can then share with others.

We also explore how graphic organizers serve as weigh stations on the road to extended writing, further reading, and discussion. We have worked with teachers throughout North America, and we bring to this book their depth of insights regarding how to engage students in using and creating their own graphic organizers. In our research and observations in classrooms, we find teachers use graphic organizers most often to

- support students' comprehension of a text,
- promote students' oral sharing of information and their ideas,
- elevate organized note-taking while listening to information and, as our colleagues Fisher and Frey (2012a) suggest, note-making while interacting with complex texts,
- scaffold students' narrative and informational writing throughout the process,
- move students to independent thinking as they learn to create their own organizing, note-taking, and note-making systems.

Two consistent findings from our classroom observations are that teachers wonder how to help students understand why they have to construct or complete a graphic organizer, and how they can better support students to independently craft graphic organizers that fit their individual learning purposes. Students often don't appreciate the connections between a graphic organizer and their thinking and learning. Once this link is made, they realize the power of graphic organizers for note-taking, note-making, organizing, and presenting information. To support you in making this information apparent to your students, the lessons and strategies throughout this book include classroom examples from teachers that demonstrate the following:

- planning sufficient classroom time to allow students to complete or develop a graphic organizer
- modeling the process for using visual tools to support thinking, inquiry, and thorough understanding of information
- sharing the intended purpose and outcome for using the graphic organizer
- engaging students in whole-class, small-group, partner, individual, and independent work using and crafting organizers
- checking, assessing, and evaluating students' work for clues to identify their understandings, confusions, and next steps

HOW TO THINK ABOUT STANDARDS ALIGNMENT

In the next section we address the Common Core State Standards, and throughout this book, you'll find specific Common Core standards referenced, so in that sense our lesson ideas are completely aligned. However, we are well aware that just about any professional resource published after 2012 is going to tout these alignments, and we feel that the specific standards kind of "grey out" if all we do is show the literal match-up and stay at a micro-level. Thus, before we discuss the academic goals in the next section, let's consider how graphic organizers help students learn the ways of thinking addressed by the Common Core State Standards or other state standards.

These four considerations are meant to help you both use the lesson scenarios in this book and generate your own lessons that will meet the Common Core's call for depth, collaboration, and students' independent application of understandings. For each organizer, we help you consider the following:

1. **why** a particular graphic organizer works well to support content learning
2. **when** to use various graphic organizers to support various learning situations
3. **how** to deliver dynamic demonstration lessons that will teach students to select and use graphic organizers independently
4. **what** to tune in to when assessing students' work in order to pinpoint strengths and needs and then plan subsequent instruction that deepens their thinking, writing, reading, and speaking

HOW TO HELP STUDENTS MEET THE STANDARDS

The Common Core consists of 32 anchor standards that are grouped into four sections that address the literacy processes of reading, writing, speaking and listening, and language behaviors. Of these English language arts and literacy (ELA) standards, at least 18 that can be achieved with the support of various graphic organizers. Let's look at each of these four ELA sections, and then we'll think about them in an integrated fashion.

To begin let's consider reading anchor standards 1 and 10 of the Common Core State Standards (CCSS; Common Core State Standards Initiative, 2010b).

CCSS.R1.

Read closely to determine what the text says and to make logical inferences from it; cite specific textual information when writing or speaking to support conclusions drawn from the text.

CCSS.R.10.

Read and comprehend complex literary and informational texts independently and proficiently.

Notice that these two standards state that students are expected to be able to read increasingly complex texts. Doing so involves a host of thinking processes, including analyzing, comparing, and evaluating. Graphic organizers support each of these processes.

Now let's consider the 16 other ELA anchor standards for which we think graphic organizers are particularly well suited. As you read each standard, see if you agree with the type of graphic we would craft; there is no one right answer. We pose some questions to get you thinking about custom creating your own.

Selected Common Core **Reading** Anchor Standards Calling for Graphic Organizers

CCRA.R.3.

Analyze how and why individuals, events, and ideas develop and interact over the course of a text.

A graphic organizer would allow students to add information to it throughout the reading. Can you envision how its design would support students noticing the interactions and evolution of people, events, concepts?

CCRA.R.5.

Analyze the structure of texts, including how specific sentences, paragraphs, and larger portions of the text (e.g., a section, chapter, scene, or stanza) relate to each other and the whole.

Do you agree that this standard also calls for a visual that supports the reader in seeing the parts of the whole?

CCRA.R.7.

Integrate and evaluate content presented in diverse media and formats, including visually and quantitatively, as well as in words.

Readers, are you seeing a chart graphic being used here?

CCRA.R.8.

Delineate and evaluate the argument and specific claims in a text, including the validity of the reasoning as well as the relevance and sufficiency of the evidence.

Here again, this could be a graphic that helps learners establish, develop, and support an argument. Given that evaluating texts is a sophisticated skill secondary students find difficult, how might you devise the organizer to be developmentally appropriate for your students?

CCRA.R.9.

Analyze how two or more texts address similar themes or topics in order to build knowledge or to compare the approaches the authors take.

Yes, this graphic organizer might be a compare-contrast diagram. How might you use language and graphics to help your students consider both similarities and differences?

We encourage you to communicate to your students that they don't have to wait for you to hand them a graphic organizer—they can create one on their own. Over time, students get more adept at knowing which type of organizer might help them best display their thinking.

Selected Common Core **Writing** Anchor Standards Calling for Graphic Organizers

When we turn to the anchor standards for writing, it's easy to envision how graphic organizers support all the behaviors involved in composing work in various genres across the curriculum. Whether writing an argument, a book review, or a literary work, organizers support secondary students as they develop their ability to sequence and organize their details/text evidence and line of thought. Once again, we share our thinking about the graphics we might select or create in order to accomplish the tasks identified in each standard.

CCRA.W.4.

Produce clear and coherent writing in which the development, organization, and style are appropriate to task, purpose, and audience.

Graphic organizers that include structure and scaffolding shapes would help students organize sentences and paragraphs. How would you prompt students to consider task, purpose, and audience as they complete the organizer?

CCRA.W.7.

Conduct short as well as more sustained research projects based on focused questions, demonstrating understanding of the subject under investigation.

Because this standard calls for students to focus their research, it would be ideal to craft graphic organizers that included questions to help students tightly frame their research so that it's manageable. How might you design the organizer so that it also helps students organize their ideas as they write about the content? Would including writing prompts help guide them to fully demonstrate their knowledge?

CCRA.W.8.

Gather relevant information from multiple print and digital sources, assess the credibility and accuracy of each source, and integrate the information while avoiding plagiarism.

This would call for a graphic that invites a comparison of information across texts. How might you tailor this—and any organizer—to the age and stage of the students you teach?

CCRA.W.9.

Draw evidence from literary or informational texts to support analysis, reflection, and research.

This organizer would nudge students to go back in to the text to support their responses, so it would need to include areas that represent initial information and growing reflections. How might you set it up to remind adolescent learners of the types of evidence to use (e.g., key facts, character quotes, dates)?

Selected Common Core **Speaking and Listening** Anchor Standards Calling for Graphic Organizers

Being able to organize information to share orally is central to the Speaking and Listening Standards. Again we invite you to think about the dimensions of a graphic organizer that would support students as they organize information and understandings and shared them with others.

CCRA.SL.2.

Integrate and evaluate information presented in diverse media and formats, including visually, quantitatively, and orally.

This graphic would need to support students' analysis across text types. How might you prompt students to both select information and evaluate it?

CCRA.SL.4.

Present information, findings, and supporting evidence such that listeners can follow the line of reasoning and the organization, development, and style are appropriate to task, purpose, and audience.

This graphic might be a chart showing how a complex idea is developed over time. Might you also include a checklist that helps students effectively present information?

CCRA.SL.5.

Make strategic use of digital media and visual displays of data to express information and enhance understanding of presentations.

Illustrating information through multiple mediums will certainly promote comprehension of the information. Is there an existing graphic that does this or will you need to redesign an existing one or create a new design to accomplish this?

A variety of graphic organizers shared in this text support organizing one's ideas and information through formats that are comprehensible. Many can accomplish these identified ELA anchor standards, which of course are addressed across the grade levels through ascending or increasing levels of complexity. We urge you to teach your students to not stop with just the organizers we have shared. Their independence results from thinking on their own about the information they are attempting to organize or share and then crafting a graphic that helps them do so. Invite them to use ours as models for their own creations. Once they understand why they are using graphic organizers, encourage them to take the lead in selection or design. Their selections or creations will provide you with rich insights about their thinking.

Selected Common Core **Language** Anchor Standards Calling for Graphic Organizers

In the following language anchor standards, notice that here, again, there is an emphasis on students collaborating with peers and communicating with others. Graphic organizers lend themselves to partner and small-group work, and we encourage you to think about a variety of ways students can contribute. For example, students might be responsible for completing particular sections; each student might complete one and then bring it to a small group to compile ideas into a final version. Students can assume roles as text researchers, writers, presenters, and so on.

CCRA.L1.

Prepare for and participate effectively in a range of conversations and collaborations with diverse partners, building on others' ideas and expressing their own clearly and persuasively.

This graphic would need to involve the space for a student to collect his or her own ideas and also a section that invites comparison. How might you encourage collaboration? How might you ensure diverse partners and good quality of conversation?

CCRA.L.2.

Integrate and evaluate information presented in diverse media and formats, including visually, quantitatively, and orally.

Students share information through multiple media. How might these be displayed? Would there need to be space for graphs, photos, and data?

CCRA.L.4.

Present information, findings, and supporting evidence such that listeners can follow the line of reasoning and the organization, development, and style are appropriate to task, purpose, and audience.

This standard calls for a graphic that illustrates the organizational development of an idea or thesis. How might the information best be displayed for the intended audience? And might you develop an organizer to be used by those listening to the presentation?

CCRA.L.5.

Make strategic use of digital media and visual displays of data to express information and enhance understanding of presentations.

Creativity should be the subtitle for this standard since it invites one to resourcefully share information through a graphic supporting multiple media. How might graphic organizers support students' creativity as they prepare to share ideas across the disciplines?

TIPS FOR USING GRAPHIC ORGANIZERS DYNAMICALLY

We are excited that so many of the ELA anchor standards immediately invite ingenious presentations of information that push beyond traditional ways of tracking, showing, and sharing student learning. A first point we want to make is that for graphic organizers to significantly contribute to student learning, they have to become an essential element of learning. Students need to be engaged in selecting and devising them. Conversations about them need to occur before, during, and after learning. Without that commitment, graphic organizers weaken in their effect, becoming something to photocopy, something students dutifully complete and turn in—but not something that has truly helped them deepen pathways of thinking and creating.

Here are a few points to consider as you present a lesson involving a graphic organizer that will help you use it dynamically:

• As much as possible, invite students to help you select or create a graphic organizer. When students are involved in thinking about the *why* behind a particular organizer as it relates to curricular content or a task, it builds that critical metacognitive awareness— they're learning how to learn. One of the best gifts we can give our students is the awareness that although reams of information abound at the click of a mouse, it's each person's job to fully comprehend the *intent* of the information he or she is reading, discussing, or writing about.

• Think out loud as you select an organizer so students have a "script" of your decision making. Encourage students to join you in first identifying the purpose of the information they want to organize or share. For example, if the graphic is to support note-taking while reading a selected text, teach them to preview the text to determine the structure (story, cause/effect, etc.) the author used, and then look together for an organizer that seems a good fit. If one doesn't exist, support students in creating it.

- When you want students to ultimately share information in an oral presentation or written piece, lay the groundwork at the outset of the lesson. For example, discuss and help them name their audience and purpose. Then help them select or create a graphic organizer design that suits their purposes, their audience, and their vision for how the information is best displayed.

HOW TO MEET EIGHT INTERTWINED ACADEMIC GOALS

A second point we want to make is that even though we have just shown the potential for graphic organizers to address individual standards, in the day-to-day of the classroom, you'll be naturally bundling several standards. Reading, talking, writing, thinking, and presenting information are interwoven. So as you use the graphic organizers found in this book, remember they are designed to address several ELA standards at once.

Now, let's consider why it's important to group standards in a lesson. Think about it: When teaching we seldom address one isolated literacy practice in a lesson. As you'll see in each example shared, we suggest bundling standards to address the many literacy processes students are accomplishing in each lesson as they read, speak, listen, and write. Learning across the disciplines is directly correlated to the strength of students' literacies. Graphic organizers promote the development of these literacies by helping students chunk, organize, comprehend, and share information more effectively. Figure 1-1 shows some of the organizers you will find in this book. The following eight areas or big ideas illustrate the connection between literacy learning and graphic organizers.

FIGURE 1-1

Some of the Graphic Organizers You Will Discover in This Book

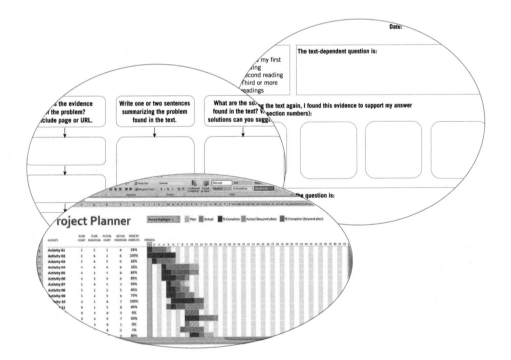

1. **Acquire and use academic language appropriately.** One aspect of the Common Core standards is that students can acquire and use academic language, including vocabulary, to become conversant with content. Academic language is different in many respects from the language students (and their teachers) use in most day-to-day literacy activities, such as conversation. Academic language focuses on more specialized knowledge of academic disciplines and concepts and often requires different language registers and vocabulary (see Townsend & Lapp, 2010). Academic language features discipline-specific terms and syntactic structures as well as terms that students would not generally use in conversation, such as *abandon* or *clarify*, that cut across disciplines.

How graphic organizers help: Organizers help students visually map their thinking about content onto a single, focused page, and both the written directions and the spheres themselves have academic language embedded. Think of the popular Venn diagram: two interlocked circles and directions that ask students to *compare and contrast* something using terms that are new or used in a new way. As they create and use these organizers and the information they contain, students have opportunities to use and improve their academic language proficiencies.

2. **Make connections.** In some ways, making connections is the essence of learning. Neurons connect with each other to produce powerful new learning (see Zull, 2002). Readers connect what they know of how texts are coherent, how one text connects with that of another (Hartman, 1995), or how texts connect with the world as they know it (see Harvey & Goudvis, 2000).

How graphic organizers help: Organizers allow students to see, almost at a glance, how one idea relates to another or how one process is contingent upon another. Our experience tells us that students do not need to have things simplified so much as they need to see the big picture before they can look at the details. We liken this to looking at the box showing the final product of a jigsaw puzzle before spending time assembling the parts into a whole.

3. **Comprehend complex processes or events** (e.g., sequences). A recurring theme throughout this book is that sometimes it is necessary to make things simpler than they may first appear. Learning occurs when problems, events, concepts, and processes present a challenge to our thinking. Learning simpler constructs can lead to greater understanding of complex concepts, just as learning complex constructs might be made more comprehensible with the support of an organizing schema.

How graphic organizers help: As with other academic goals, students are frequently challenged to understand information and ideas that are complex and sometimes complicated. *Complexity* takes into account nuances and details, while *complicated* sometimes means that the steps can be confusing, in our view. Graphic organizers, in the hands of a skillful teacher, have the potential to make the complex comprehensible so that the details and nuances can be integrated into a richer understanding. They also offer the opportunity to make the complicated comprehensible as students grapple with new learning.

4. **Understand five types of informational text structures.** Five general, or top-level, structures of text are often found in informational material. When students know the five structures of cause/effect, problem/solution, compare and contrast, descriptive, and sequential, they have a greater chance of making the complexity of a text more comprehensible (Meyer, Brandt, & Bluth, 1980).

How graphic organizers help: Though top-level structures, such as descriptive or cause/effect, seem obvious, applying them as a reader or writer is often a challenge given the complexities of the texts students are reading and those they compose. Graphic organizers give students the visual support to discern what those top-level structures are and thereby concentrate their efforts on understanding the content.

5. **Understand content.** Students use a graphic organizer most frequently in the process of trying to learn and organize information, be it a science concept, the truth found in a work of fiction, a mathematics problem, and so on. They are trying to learn discipline-specific information.

How graphic organizers help: Graphic organizers help for a couple of reasons. The obvious reason is they help students make notes and thereby create a placeholder for facts and other information. Students develop understandings in the midst of reading and learning, making recall and analysis a bit easier. The less obvious reason is that different types of organizers work better with some students than with others and that they are tools that can be used on an as-needed basis with a select few students. In fact, when they are assigned to every student as a kind of catch-all, and when teachers' assumption is that all students' automatically understand the content and benefit from the visual organizer, results are uneven. It turns out that students seem to learn best when graphic organizers are used strategically, and as they come to know them, they can choose ones that work best for them or create ones to illustrate their thinking. It's imperative to consider the organizational patterns different students know and respond to well. There are also students who don't like to use them at all for certain purposes; those who do not need them should be invited to create other ways to organize information. In many instances, these may become personally created graphic organizers.

6. **Explore a concept and determine the nature of inquiry.** In our experience, students learn well when they have something intriguing to investigate or a problem to be addressed. Learning is naturally a process of wondering and inquiring into many topics.

How graphic organizers help: Knowing content is one thing, but figuring out broad concepts and how those relate to an inquiry stance is quite another. Children in Grades 6–12 are fabulously curious and can become content experts on rainforest life, trucks, butterfly species—you name it. But what the CCSS ask teachers to do is "flip" or apply the knowledge into interconnected investigations (e.g., How is camouflage in the rainforest connected to survival? How does preserving rainforests relate to improving human conditions in and near the rainforests?). Even students in the primary grades can engage in these bigger quests if we scaffold learning with graphic organizers, so recording, comparing, contrasting, and so on become more concrete processes.

Inquiry is often informed by the discipline involved. Scientists approach a question they have in a particular manner, writers of fiction grab us with a hook or question, and historians may choose timelines and photographs. Graphic organizers can help students understand what they need or want to know, but also how to form a framework for thinking about their inquiry even if they later propose something different than a traditional approach. Knowing *how* it has been done is often the lever (Gardner, 2006) that leads to creativity.

7. **Synthesize multiple sources.** Though students often become used to working with a single text, much learning occurs when students compare and contrast the ideas found in several sources. Synthesizing a number of sources of information while reading, during discussion, and through composing appears to be a key skill expected in rigorous standards and in the digital age when many sources are readily available.

How graphic organizers help: Working with multiple sources of information is a key criterion for college and career readiness, but as any K–5 teacher knows, it can be a daunting task for young students. Graphic organizers provide a means of managing many diverse sources, and looking for confirming evidence for a given opinion, disconfirming evidence, and commonalities. Though teachers may choose to provide an organizer for such purposes, students are well served when they are able to recognize their own needs for an organizer and select or create one themselves. Though younger students are not always conversant enough with content and the way it is structured, teachers can help them by calling attention to the organizer and how it relates to the text they will read. As students move into higher grades, they will be better prepared to make their own choices or modify graphic organizers for specific purposes.

8. **Use reliable sources to form and write arguments.** Jumping to an opinion often short-circuits deep thinking. Everyone, it seems, has an idea about why something is the way it is, what it means, or how things should work, but effective opinions that lead to deeper understandings and conversations are based on well-considered evidence, and they are subject to refutation or disconfirming ideas. (See our companion book for younger students, *Mining Complex Text, Grades 2–5*, which explores in more detail how students might use graphic organizers to scaffold and promote skills with opinion and how they can become more independent at crafting their own thinking and their own student-created organizers.)

How graphic organizers help: Graphic organizers provide structures so that secondary students can more easily collect evidence, sort that evidence, and put it to use in written work or other multimodal composition tasks.

WHAT LIES AHEAD IN THIS BOOK

A structured overview is a type of graphic organizer that shows broad connections between and among related topics. It helps readers, listeners, and viewers of content understand how narrower topics relate to larger concepts. Typically, the teacher (or text author) prepares this in advance as an overview. We provide one here to give you a broad view of what lies ahead.

Throughout the book, we include marginal notes that refer to the eight academic goals or big ideas we described above; in organizing this book, we were mindful of the Common Core State Standards and related rigorous goals as well as college and career readiness outcomes. We illustrate through example how to use graphic organizers to help students engage with and comprehend timeless text types and also use and craft organizers as they think and write in genres that are evergreen as well as those that are newer, such as those found in digital environments.

Chapter 2: Thinking on the Page: The Research Behind Why Graphic Organizers Work. This chapter shares the research base illustrating how the cognitive processing of information can be supported by using graphic organizers. Also noted is how graphic organizers provide learning scaffolds, assessment options, and promotion of differentiated learning.

Chapter 3: Using Graphic Organizers to Acquire Academic Vocabulary. Here we demonstrate how graphic organizers can promote comprehension and use of academic language. Beginning in kindergarten students are immersed in academic language that comprises words essential to understanding content (e.g., *sink, float, community, insect, migration*) as well as words that describe the processes involved when reading, writing, discussing, and crafting a multimodal composition (e.g., *same, different, compare, contrast, sequence, evaluate, infer*). At the end of the book, you will find a glossary of terms that may be helpful as a reminder about the way we have used terms such as *academic language* and *academic vocabulary* throughout this book.

Chapter 4: Graphic Organizers Support Literary Text Reading and Writing Tasks. Works of fiction and informational genres of text share many qualities. However, they also differ in significant ways. This chapter shows how graphic organizers help students understand major text patterns specific to literature and help learners both read and write narrative.

Chapter 5: Graphic Organizers Support Informational Text Reading and Writing Tasks. This chapter zeroes in on how graphic organizers can extend and deepen students' thinking about expository or informational genres as both readers and writers.

Chapter 6: Graphic Organizers Support Students' Reading Proficiencies. This chapter supports teachers' objective to improve students' reading proficiency. The Common Core State Standards emphasize this goal (Common Core State Standards Initiative, 2010a). Graphic organizers that direct students' attention to specific information in a text can help them organize, analyze, summarize, and evaluate complex ideas in the "four corners" of the text (Coleman & Pimentel, 2012). In the elementary grades, special attention to top-level organizational structures and their interplay supports comprehension. As students become increasingly proficient with these and more fully understand how they work together in the secondary grades, they also become more capable with composing tasks. Secondary students will know the structures, but they may struggle with the increasingly complex nuances of the text.

Chapter 7: Graphic Organizers Boost Questioning and Responding. No effective teacher ever said, "Gosh, I wish my students did not ask questions about what we are learning or reading!" However, students in secondary grades are not yet experts at learning as a process or with content knowledge. In this chapter we show how graphic organizers can help students know what questions to ask, how to ask them, when and where to ask those questions, and how to respond to other students and members of the community who pose questions about learning tasks and content knowledge.

Chapter 8: Graphic Organizers Foster Understanding and Writing Arguments. Understanding and constructing graphic organizers are a cornerstone of writing tasks for secondary students working with the Common Core and similar standards. But just what constitutes an effective and informative argument? How might middle or high school student write or otherwise express an argument that others, who may not be of like mind, want to hear or read? Graphic organizers are on the job, again; they have the potential to help students think about what an opinion is and how it might persuade or convince others who do not quite think the way they do. (See our companion book for elementary teachers for more on how opinion and graphic organizers work together.)

Chapter 9: Graphic Organizers Support Collaboration. Most people agree that to be ready for college, career, the next grade level, or just getting a task done requires communication and collaboration. Who is going to do what? When will this occur? What class meetings did we have and what did we decide? Wait—there's a graphic organizer for that! Organizers that support collaboration are shared in this chapter.

The goal of this book is for students to learn the importance of organizing the information they are reading or presenting and, in doing so, to become confident in selecting or constructing graphic organizers to organize and share information and their ideas.

STRUCTURED OVERVIEW: GRAPHIC ORGANIZERS IN THIS BOOK

A structured overview is a type of graphic organizer that shows broad connections between and among related topics. This shows the book's content so you can see how narrower topics relate to larger concepts.

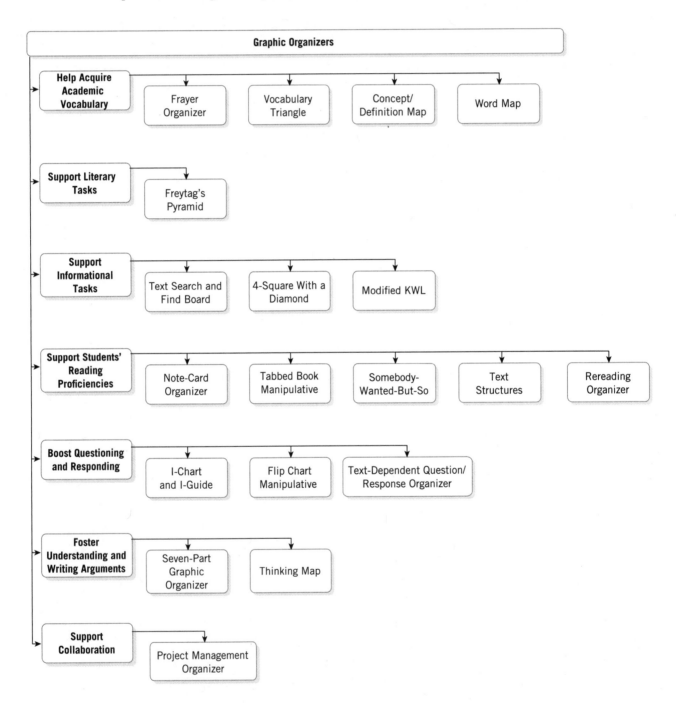

THINKING ON THE PAGE

The Research Behind Why Graphic Organizers Work

We Googled "graphic organizer business" and up popped more than 14 million results! No wonder graphic organizers are popular in classrooms—they are a tool that works in the world, helping people in all sorts of fields solve some of the very same problems that students often face. For something to be that popular, it must align with how humans think, decide, and function, but more about that in a minute.

*Comparing and contrasting, predicting and planning, organizing, identifying important attributes—*these are just a few of the thinking processes graphic organizers help us do. To do this cognitive work, we require our brains to process information in particular ways, and in layperson's terms, this thinking not only takes up space in our brains, it plays out spatially. Neuroscience in recent years has made advances in brain imaging, and we can now see just where vocabulary and other linguistic information is stored, where spatial and visual images reside, how emotions are encoded and stimulated, and so on. Put simply, our brains are uniquely wired for two main functions: making sense of language and making sense of the visual cues that are received. In addition, scientists have discovered the following:

- The more connections the neurons make, the more likely it is that learning will occur and creative ideas will result.
- When brains perceive connections between visual information (say, a picture) and language, learning seems to increase.

Now think about a graphic organizer. It has both words and visuals, so it reflects both of the processing centers of our brains. In addition, a graphic organizer helps us make connections between linguistic and visual information. When our brains confront challenging topics, the layout of an organizer helps make the connections apparent to us. We can more easily spot the connection on the organizer, or our interacting with the organizer helps us arrange and spread out facts and ideas in our heads so that we are better able to have that "Aha" moment of connection.

A good way to illustrate this idea is to conduct a little experiment. Ready? Read this excerpt from an online book produced by the U.S. Army describing the U.S. Civil War battle at Gettysburg.

> As Buford had expected, Hill ordered Heth's entire division to advance on Gettysburg at first light. About 0700, troopers from the 8th Illinois Cavalry, posted three miles west of Gettysburg on the Chambersburg Pike, spotted shadowy figures nearing the Marsh Creek Bridge to their front. According to tradition, Lt. Marcellus Jones borrowed a sergeant's carbine and fired the first shot of the Battle of Gettysburg. He then fired several more rounds at skirmishers from Brig. Gen. James J. Archer's brigade, the lead element of Heth's division. Jones immediately reported the contact; in short order, Buford learned not only of the mounting threat along the Chambersburg Pike, but also of enemy activity along roads to the west and north of Gettysburg. He immediately sent brief but informative assessments to the rapidly changing situation to Mead at Army headquarters and to Maj. Gen. John F. Reynolds, whose I Corps had encamped the previous night just a few miles south of Gettysburg. (Reardon & Vossler, 2013, p. 19)

(If you would like to read the rest of the account, you can visit www.history.army.mil/html/books/075/75-10/CMH_Pub_75-10.pdf.)

Now, without looking back, can you illustrate in some way the landscape, the positions of the commanders, and just where Lieutenant Jones was when he fired the opening shot in the Battle of Gettysburg? The task is a difficult one. First, it is necessary to remember who all those people are: Heth, Hill, Buford, and so on. Then, you must know and remember for which side each commander led his troops. Also, keeping track of the abbreviations, such as "Brig. Gen." might not be so easy if you are not familiar with these sorts of accounts. As you read, you must construct in your mind some idea of the lay of the land and the sequence of events, and keep all that mentally handy as you continue to read.

If only there were some ways to make this difficult and rigorous text more comprehensible. A picture or map, perhaps, with a timeline might do it. If you could pair up the complex text you just read with some visual information—a graphic organizer—that gives you some idea of the relationships of the ideas, it just might help. Depending on what your purpose for reading is, a graphic organizer that is already constructed might be best. At other times, partially completed graphic organizers that you fill in as you read might also work. In some cases, you might want to really work with the ideas and create your own organizer. Interactive graphic organizers might include two very different visual elements: a timeline and a map.

For an example of this latter type, you can visit http://storymaps.esri.com/stories/2013/gettysburg to take a look at the interactive visual "Decisive Moments in the Battle of Gettysburg." Best of all, you can point to different places on the timeline and see which troops were moving and the direction they attempted to move. If you hover over points on the map, you will see who commanded the divisions. In some places, the timeline and map are supplemented with additional photographs and concise text. Notice how the information on the timeline is organized in sequence and linked to the information on the map—it's organized visually. By putting the interactive graphic organizer with text, the battle about which you are reading is much more comprehensible and perhaps a bit of fun, too.

PICTURE THIS: VISUALS QUICKEN AND DEEPEN TEXT LEARNING

These brains of ours are fairly amazing, and smart approaches lead to better learning. Psychologists have an idea, a theory, that our brains tend to store or code information in one of two forms (Sadoski & Paivio, 2004). Information can be coded in our brains as linguistic, or language-based, knowledge, or it can be stored as imagery. Some time ago, one psychologist proposed that imagery might include physical sensations including smell and sound, among others (Richardson, 1983). For our purposes in this book, however, we generally stick with imagery in terms of visual information—a picture or chart, for example.

A term teachers often hear is *nonlinguistic representation*. Marzano, Pickering, and Pollock (2001), in their touchstone text, say that nonlinguistic representation refers to the imagery mode brains use to encode information that emphasizes that format. For example, you might encode a photograph of the battlefield at Gettysburg primarily in imagery mode because the information is presented as an image. Information you receive from reading this paragraph would be encoded primarily in the linguistic mode because language is the way the information is being conveyed. Typically, graphic organizers make use of nonlinguistic information and linguistic information from written text or spoken words; thus, the terms *nonlinguistic representation* and *graphic organizer* are related but not synonymous.

That is fairly straightforward, but there is more to it. Some generalizations from our own work in this area may help as we continue our exploration of what graphic organizers are and how they work to improve learning.

- When learners are asked to transform information in some way (say, from linguistic mode to imagery), the strength of the learning tends to increase.
- When learners are asked to pair information in imagery and linguistic mode, learning tends to increase.
- When learners are asked to create new representations, through application, analysis, evaluation, or creation (Anderson & Krathwohl, 2001), learning tends to increase.

Marzano et al. (2001) suggest that nonlinguistic representations should elaborate on knowledge. Keeping in mind the idea that graphic organizers usually blend nonlinguistic and linguistic information, we can put that notion to good use. Simply put, graphic organizers are best suited (not always, but usually) to generating knowledge or making sense of knowledge by building on the three generalizations above. How teachers construct tasks that ask for graphic organizer skills and how students learn to use and create graphic organizers is a primary focus in this book. Our goal is to help you teach your students that if a graphic organizer doesn't exist that supports their purposes, they should craft one that does. We hope that as you and your students analyze and use the ones presented in this text, they will develop the skill and craft that supports this independence.

GENERAL TIPS: HOW TO USE GRAPHIC ORGANIZERS WELL

Let's turn from the *why* to the *how*. Here are several general ideas for integrating graphic organizers into your teaching and students' learning.

Be Explicit

As with most any instructional routine or tool, students need to know how a graphic organizer operates. Without sufficient teacher modeling, young learners often assume it's a matter of simply filling in the blanks and moving on. It is very important that they know why the graphic organizer is part of their learning and how it contributes to what they might know or be able to do. As a teacher, the *why* may come from the skills embedded in a specific standard; the important thing is that you explain to your students in simple terms what it is they are being asked to do and how the organizer is going to help them. Throughout this book, we provide ideas for helping your students see the relevance of various organizers, and we often name the particular skills featured.

Use Graphic Organizers to Focus on Key Attributes and Concepts

No matter what the age, young learners have to assimilate an awful lot of new information and ideas coming at them. Graphic organizers put a frame around what kids are trying to read, or trying to write, or trying to comprehend. And in a parallel manner, organizers invite teachers to chunk academic content and processes into "small frames," helping them be more intentional about the focus of their instruction, which might focus students' attention on the key steps of writing a fact book, the three essential math concepts students need to take away from the unit, or the pros and cons of an issue. In this light, the graphic organizer is an instructional planning tool. At the risk of oversimplifying, if you can envision a student's thorough understanding fitting comfortably on a single-page organizer, with just a few boxes or circles and arrows, then chances are you have a good focus on key attributes and concepts. And as we said in Chapter 1, organizers help make challenging tasks comprehensible, not just simpler (though there are times when simplifying is appropriate or as a first stage to greater understanding).

Use Graphic Organizers to Help Students "Slice the Surface" of a Text

When what is to be learned is new, it can be a confusing array of information. That array of information may make it difficult for the novice learner, or the novice with specific content, to understand just what the key features or main ideas are. In these cases, graphic organizers can be used and revisited at each phase of a student tackling a challenging text, from skimming/previewing to after-reading reflection.

Try this. Unless you are a particle physicist, navigate to http://home.web.cern.ch/about/physics/standard-model (see Figure 2-1), a website of the European Organization for Nuclear Research (CERN). Read the page to understand the standard model of particle physics. Click the links if you like, and read what you find there. When you are done, close your browser and come on back to this page. Go ahead—we'll wait.

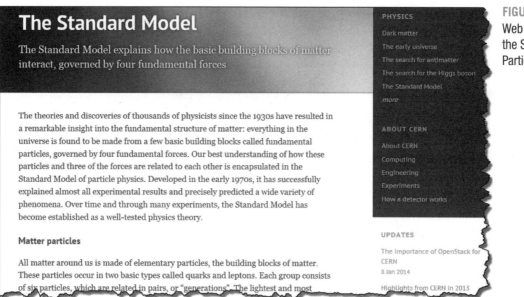

FIGURE 2-1
Web Page Describing the Standard Model of Particle Physics

Source: Screen capture is reproduced courtesy of the CERN Press Office, Geneva, Switzerland.

All done reading? Now, if you know something about particle physics, this should be a piece of cake, right? But if you are like us, particle physics is fairly complex from a conceptual standpoint and a topic about which you know very little. The web page you visited was written for a general audience, not scientists who work in this field. For those without specific prior content knowledge on which to draw, this information seems dense and overwhelming. The cognitive task is not just to simplify what is on the web page; rather, the task is to make it comprehensible. Sometimes two or three graphic organizers are needed for different purposes. Let's say that to begin understanding particle physics we think it might be a good start to visually organize the terms or vocabulary as they were encountered in the "Matter particles" paragraph. Figure 2-2 is our organizer that puts all the terms found in that paragraph in a visual order with a space for further questions. For example, we might wonder what the difference is between leptons and quarks and predict that we will learn more about that as we read.

FIGURE 2-2

Graphic Organizer for
"Matter Particles"

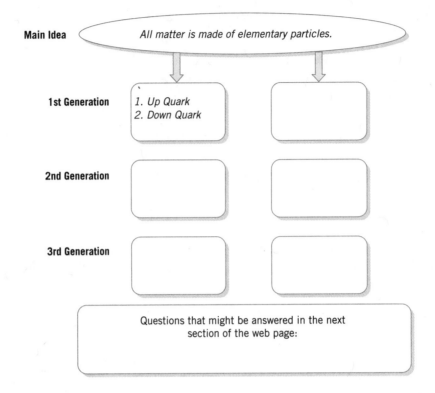

Main Idea — *All matter is made of elementary particles.*

1st Generation
1. Up Quark
2. Down Quark

2nd Generation

3rd Generation

Questions that might be answered in the next
section of the web page:

Next, if your purpose is to really understand the information from CERN, you might go back to the web page and reread the material closely. As you read, you might add details to your graphic organizer, such as a vertical line showing how first-generation particles are more stable than second- and third-generation particles. The key here is that the organizer was not the end product; instead, it served as a guide for reading and for close analysis of the text under study. Sometimes students think filling out the organizer is the point of the activity, but most often the organizer is just the visual learning tool that led to learning.

Use Graphic Organizers to Differentiate Instruction

How might that learning be scaffolded using graphic organizers? There are several approaches, but to help you get started thinking, here are some ideas.

1. Provide the organizer in Figure 2-2 to students who have little knowledge of the content and might struggle with the vocabulary or word-level reading tasks.
2. Modify the organizer to include some of the key words and a sample question for students who seem to have some applicable background knowledge of the topic or how it is organized.
3. Challenge students who are close to meeting the content standard to create their own graphic organizer for the passage. This may be more appropriate for students who have used several organizers and can make choices about which is most appropriate (see Haggard, 1985).

How learning is measured depends on the content and literacy outcomes and standards, a topic to which we return later in this book.

Use Graphic Organizers to Help Students Learn in Each Discipline

Students working with graphic organizers are typically trying to make sense of some content. It could be a science concept (as in our example above), a cause-and-effect sequence from social studies, a novel with complex characters and plot, and so on. In a sense, the content area doesn't matter: The challenge of understanding something new or at a new level of complexity is the same. For this reason, use any organizer flexibly, as you see fit. That said, occasionally we refer to disciplinary literacy (Moje, 2007; Shanahan & Shanahan, 2008), a way of thinking about literacy tasks that differ from one discipline to another. For example, as teachers we may sometimes show students how to think like a historian or a scientist. The idea is that historians and scientists look at text in their disciplines, whether they are reading or creating it, in different ways.

Use Graphic Organizers Digitally or as Hard-Copy Handouts

As you have seen thus far in the book, we like to use both digital graphic organizers and paper organizers that might be hand-drawn or copied for students. Which type you use naturally depends on the grade level you teach and on your school's access to technology.

At times it may not matter whether students work on paper or in digital environments (includes tablets, laptops, wearables, desktop computers, and other devices that are often connected to the Internet). At other times, it might be useful to consider the affordances of each. All of the authors of this book are proponents of technology as a means of constructing knowledge, sharing ideas, and making a place in our connected world; however, sometimes we like good, old-fashioned paper, too. What does paper offer?

- **Paper is expandable.** Pieces of paper can be connected together or manipulated. One neat graphic organizer is just 3 × 5 cards laid out on a table in one pattern for a while, then reshuffled and organized a different way. Using large pieces of paper, such as butcher paper, is a good way to track large projects or organize complex ideas with many intricate parts.
- **Paper can be folded** to form an almost infinite variety of organizational patterns. There is something about the kinesthetic task of physically folding paper that appeals to us and to many of the students with whom we have worked over the years. In this book, we sometimes refer to manipulative organizers, by which we mean organizers that students fold up to help organize their thinking on a page or two.

What are the advantages of digital formats?

- **Digitally created graphic organizers are easily shared.** An organizer created digitally can be shared with other students, parents, or other audiences readily using email, blogs, wikis, and course management systems (e.g., Canvas, eCollege).
- **Digitally created graphic organizers offer creative options** to mash up or include other content via links, embedded media, and the like.

- A variety of tools are easily adapted for digitally created graphic organizers. Presentation software, word-processing programs, and drawing programs may all be used to create digital graphic organizers. Of course, many programs are specifically designed for creating graphic organizers as well. The popular Inspiration software is one example.

TIERED ORGANIZERS: SCAFFOLD STUDENT PROGRESS

Throughout the rest of this book, we share organizers we have found useful and encourage you to see how powerful they are as a tool for differentiation (McMackin & Witherell, 2005). This differentiation can be in the form of using them to understand different modes of discourse, for example, the texts students read (Griffin, Malone, & Kameenui, 1995), the texts they compose (e.g., a report), or the "texts" they create through peer and class discussion of challenging ideas and concepts. And as you will see in the Examples of Tiered Graphic Organizers section later in the chapter, tiered graphic organizers can be used to differentiate learners working at different levels of proficiency or command of content. Across the disciplines, they boost knowledge acquisition and independence before, during, and after students encounter challenging texts:

- reading complex texts (see DiCecco & Gleason, 2002), including word problems in mathematics (Braselton & Decker, 1994)
- writing from sources (see McLaughlin & Overturf, 2013)
- discussing challenging ideas and concepts (Wolsey & Lapp, 2009)

Remember, not every student needs the same graphic organizer at exactly the same time during any instructional sequence. Think about your teaching purposes just as you will later teach them to reflect on students' purposes for using or crafting a graphic. For example, do you want students to make broad-stroke connections? Do you want to help them get an initial overview at the start of a new unit, or comprehend an article on new content? Do you want students to use an organizer to make nuanced connections once they have a handle on a topic? Do you want to share an organizer so that students can use it as a precursor to explaining a topic or idea to others? These are the types of questions to consider, and always be mindful of how much students already know, the level of detail they need to know, and how deep a connection you want them to make. All this is background for selecting or using tiered organizers:

- **Advance organizers** (attributed to Ausubel, 1960) are a means of helping students see connections before they engage with a concept or specific material. These organizers are useful when students are engaged with material they are taking in, or receiving. A useful tool, a type of advance organizer, is the structured overview. Suppose that students are entering a class for the first time. The instructor has graphically displayed how the various concepts in the course are related. As a result, students do not see the content as a disconnected set of ideas, but rather as a coherent whole with each idea associated to others. Instead of individual jigsaw pieces, the learners see the whole picture before they begin assembling the puzzle.

- **Partially filled-out organizers** are those in which the teacher has provided a basic structure but also some of the information that helps students see what goes where and why.

- **Blank graphic organizers** provide the bare-bones structure of the ideas, reading material, or other content such that students can see what direction the big picture is taking. However, students must do most of the work of making sense of the material.

- **Student-created or -modified organizers** allow students to make choices, based on their past work with graphic organizers and study guides, about what shape their organizers might take and how they might use them. These are often most useful for students in fifth grade and beyond, who are working on complex composing tasks (e.g., a written product, a multimodal project) or who have a good sense of the general organization of content or reading material.

- **Modified levels of complexity or depth organizers** create a step-wise means of adding depth or complexity to the organizers, which helps students dive more deeply into the content. Later in this chapter, we provide an example of how this modified, or tiered, organizer plan can work.

- **No organizer.** Yes, that's right. Not every student needs to use a graphic organizer just because some or most of their peers may be doing so. In some cases, students have an alternate way of organizing their thinking (and teachers should press students to explain this alternative) or they are familiar enough with the general organization of the content that the organizers become busy work instead of a helpful guide to learning.

Use Graphic Organizers to Promote Independent Thinking and Use

A proficient reader is able to visualize the structure of the text and use this organizational understanding to more deeply comprehend the information the author is sharing. As students become familiar with available graphic organizers, they can immediately make a match between the information shared in a text they are reading and a visual that supports their note-taking as well as later presentations of their related ideas and arguments. Students may need to craft or revise an existing structure to accommodate their intentions.

For example, in a seventh-grade class engaged in closely reading and discussing a text about orbital debris, Emmanuel noted that the author was identifying both a problem and a solution. Isabella chimed in and suggested that they should craft a problem/solution graphic organizer to take their notes while reading and conversing about the text. James added that they would have to add sections to include all of the possible solutions because some had been tested and others were just being hypothesized.

These students were able to engage in this type of thinking and learning independence because they had been introduced to the value of using graphic organizers to support their visualization of information and data. Doing so had become such a natural process for them that intuiting the structure of a text was a significant feature to consider as a part of their text analysis. They were able to move beyond what had been presented to them and create graphics that supported both their learning and presentation of ideas. As this example illustrates, the goal of introducing students to features of various graphic organizers is to support students' independent use and creation of them.

Use Graphic Organizers as Formative Assessment Tools

Graphic organizers provide many assessment opportunities. Dirksen (2011) demonstrates how graphic organizers may be used to provide formative feedback to students as their understanding of academic topics increases. Formative feedback is what the chef does when he tastes the soup (Stake, as quoted by Dirksen, 2011). Once the customer tastes the soup, that's summative assessment. We want our students to have the information about their performance that they need to adjust things as they go instead of waiting until the end to find out how they did. Graphic organizers provide just the venue for students to adjust their own thinking with feedback from the teacher and the organizer itself to know where new learning and ideas can take hold. Because students are novices at the learning—that is why they are students, right?—they need the guidance of experts who know how to question, nudge, prod, or point out what is worthwhile and helpful. We think graphic organizers can help guide students as they construct understandings and make new connections when teachers use them judiciously. We want to help students know when to taste the soup and whom to ask if they are not sure the soup is turning out as expected.

Teachers can best use graphic organizers as formative assessment while the learning is going on, not as a collection of digital or paper organizers turned in after the learning has occurred. What can teachers do?

• First, graphic organizers are often better suited as activities that help students work toward achieving outcomes and standards, and not so much as a gradebook item. They often present a low-risk means of helping students understand without the penalty associated with getting it just the way the teacher wants it.

• Second, graphic organizers are most useful when what students are learning is new, unfamiliar, or in a second language. For that reason, they are guides, not yardsticks.

• Third, in our careers as teachers and professors who work with teachers, we have had the privilege of working with so many fantastic teachers. We have noticed that the most effective teachers are always looking around the classroom, observing, coaching, and nudging. They never "walk and stalk." The moments when their guidance is necessary, planned or unplanned, are where the teaching and learning happens with graphic organizers as one way to make these magic interactions occur.

EXAMPLES OF TIERED GRAPHIC ORGANIZERS

Differentiated instruction meets the needs of all levels of learners in a classroom. Instruction can be modified in content, process, or product (Tomlinson, 1999). The *content* of instruction can be modified to give various levels of learners individualized instruction. The *process* of instruction can be differentiated by grouping students in homogeneous groups so the teacher can instruct the groups based on needed skills. By tiering the *product*, a teacher can plan a lesson and teach it to all students, but modify the way that students show understanding of the content. Teachers cannot feasibly plan small-group or individualized instruction for each lesson; therefore, modifying the product can help meet the needs of individuals if used strategically. Tiered graphic organizers are intended for all types of learners and challenge students' cognitive demand in any subject area.

Example: Science

One adaptation of tiered graphic organizers is giving students a choice of how to represent information they've learned. Students choose a concept map to represent the information collected. In 1972, Novak "developed" concept maps while he was researching ways to help students understand science (Novak & Musonda, 1991).

Students create or can be given content vocabulary cards, which they then organize on a table. Then, students draw this representation on paper (see Figure 2-3). The teacher can assess students' analytical and synthesizing skills. For instance, the teacher can assess students' conceptual understanding of whether the water cycle is linear or cyclical. Another option would be to give students a choice of graphic organizers by previously modeling each organizer's use and providing copies of various organizers during or after a lesson.

Example: Social Studies

A more structured way to use tiered organizers, instead of giving students free choice, is to group students into groups of students who share a common need. Each group receives a graphic organizer that is tiered to the group's overall needs. In social studies, for example, students may collect facts about the Roman Empire. One group might

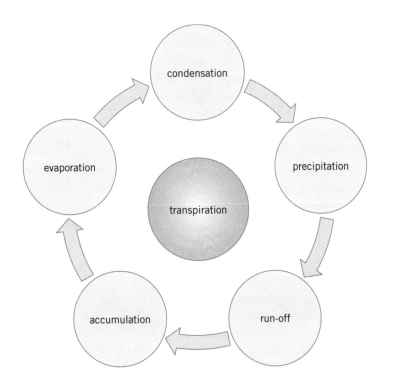

FIGURE 2-3
The Water Cycle

FIGURE 2-3
(Continued)

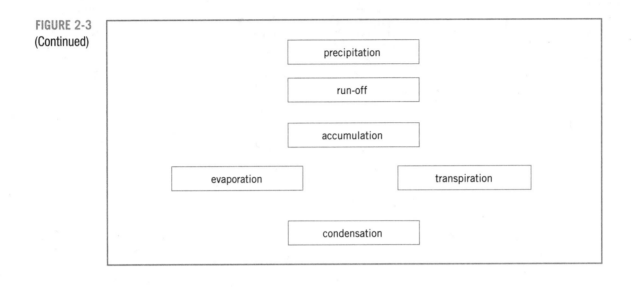

be responsible for completing a circle map of the culture (Figure 2-4). An intermediate group might complete a timeline. A high-achieving group might complete a herringbone organizer, showing the main characteristics, as well as details for each (Figure 2-5).

FIGURE 2-4
Circle Map

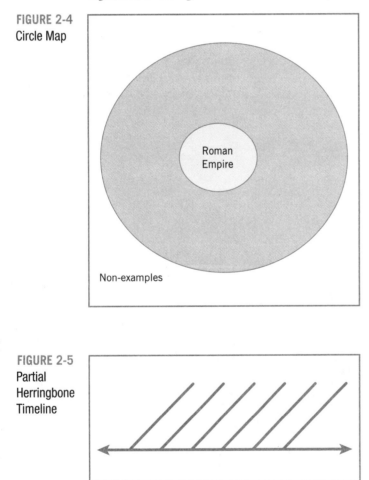

To extend this activity, students from two groups could compare graphic organizers to discuss the benefits and challenges of using each type. This will help students begin to choose appropriate situations in which to use each type of organizer. Another extension might be to teach about another culture, such as Greek culture, and have students use tiered organizers that illustrate understanding about new and previously learned cultures. For example, students with the circle map group could complete a double bubble map, comparing and contrasting the two cultures. Students in the timeline group could complete a double timeline. And students in the herringbone group could complete a double herringbone to compare and contrast. This could then extend into a discussion about the common characteristics of the cultures, their similar strengths and weaknesses, and situations contributing to each (Clarke, 1994).

FIGURE 2-5
Partial Herringbone Timeline

ADAPTING GRAPHIC ORGANIZERS FOR TIERED LEARNING

- Choose a skill, strategy, or concept you plan to teach.
- Determine the desired outcome for all students after receiving instruction.
- Consider students' level. Instruction should not be too easy or at a level that will cause frustration.
- Starting with your advanced students, design a graphic organizer that will help them think more complexly about the strategy.
- Using the same desired outcome, create two less cognitively challenging graphic organizers.
- Using previously collected data, group your students into achievement groups closely related to the skill you are teaching. Consider using a pretest or a formative assessment to help create the groups.
- Give each group the appropriate graphic organizer.
- Assess students' work and encourage them to advance to a more complex organizer when they are ready.
- Encourage students to add dimensions that support any ideas they may have that extend beyond the features of the existing graphic organizer.

A SAMPLE TIERED LESSON

Arguments and Opinions

CCSS.ELA-Literacy.RL.4.1

Refer to details and examples in a text when explaining what the text says explicitly and when drawing inferences from the text.

CCSS.ELA-Literacy.RL.4.2

Determine a theme of a story, drama, or poem from details in the text; summarize the text.

CCSS.ELA-Literacy.RL.4.3

Describe in depth a character, setting, or event in a story or drama, drawing on specific details in the text (e.g., a character's thoughts, words, or actions).

THIS SAMPLE LESSON ADDRESSES THESE STANDARDS

Graphic organizers can help make an abstract idea like inferring more concrete and, therefore, easier for all students to understand (McMackin & Witherell, 2005). Often, our students struggle with the difference between an argument and an opinion. Ms. Gourdin knew her students found this distinction difficult, so she asked them to read several editorials from a national newspaper. In each, they were asked to make inferences about what they might know or need to explore in order to understand the editorial. Students who were more comfortable with the editorial format could work with the advanced organizer as they examined the inferences required, the evidence provided, and the new information they might need to fully understand the piece. Students who felt comfortable with some aspects of editorial writing used the intermediate organizer, and those who were still unsure of the writing style of editorials and how they draw on sources or fail to do so used the introductory organizer. While Ms. Gourdin allowed students to determine their choice of organizer, she worked with them to realize that organizers did not necessarily make the task easier. Rather, each one scaffolded student learning so they were constantly challenged but always growing in their understanding.

Students' graphic organizers can be tiered by asking the more proficient students, given the content and text type, to make more inferences and cite more text evidence to support the inferences. Struggling students have fewer requirements for making inferences and citing textual evidence. Notice how the organizers in Figures 2-6, 2-7, and 2-8 differ in structure.

At this point, the teacher can collect the graphic organizers and assess each student. Alternatively, inferences and textual evidence can be shared on a class graphic organizer and students can add spaces to their graphic organizers. Be sure to encourage students to support their inferences from the text. Making text-to-graphic connections promotes students' independence as they begin to visualize how their ideas can best be represented and displayed.

FIGURE 2-6

Introductory-Level Graphic Organizer for Making Inferences

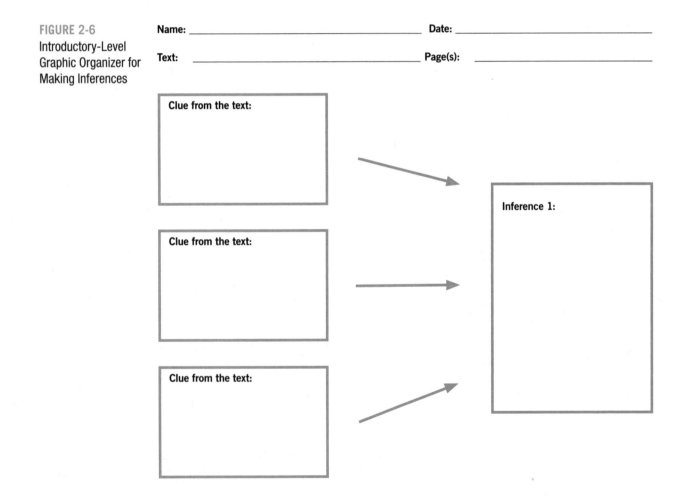

Name: _____   Date: _____

Text: _____   Page(s): _____

Clue from the text:

Clue from the text:

Clue from the text:

Inference 1:

Name: _____   **Date:** _____

Text: _____   **Page(s):** _____

FIGURE 2-7

Intermediate-Level
Graphic Organizer for
Making Inferences

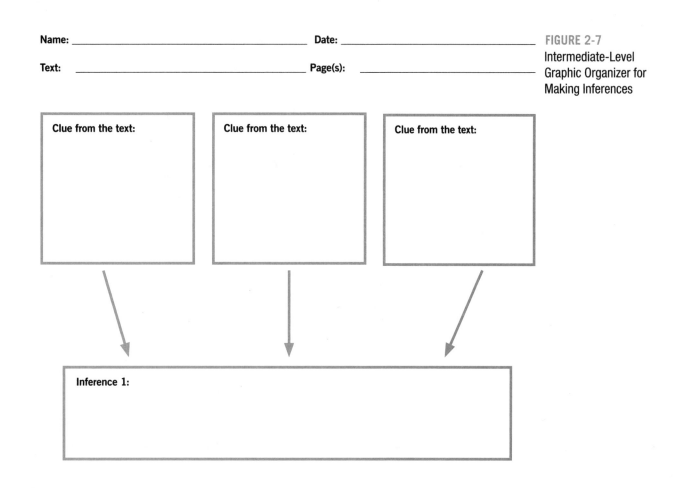

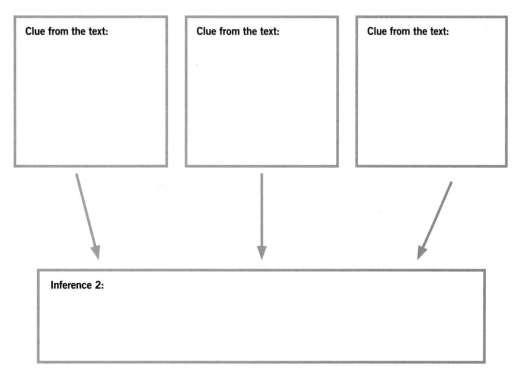

FIGURE 2-8

Advanced-Level Graphic Organizer for Making Inferences

Name: _____   Date: _____

Text: _____   Page(s): _____

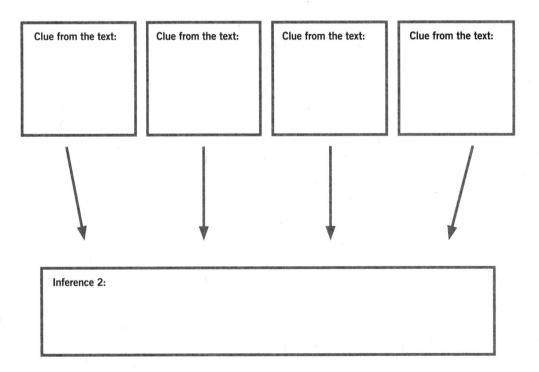

| Clue from the text: | Clue from the text: | Clue from the text: | Clue from the text: |

Inference 1:

| Clue from the text: | Clue from the text: | Clue from the text: | Clue from the text: |

Inference 2:

AT-A-GLANCE CHART OF GRAPHIC ORGANIZERS MATCHED TO ACADEMIC GOALS

We close this chapter with a recap. Research from education and neuroscience has shown why graphic organizers are so "brain-friendly" to middle grades or high school learners (or any learners, for that matter). There are a handful of general tips for selecting and developing graphic organizers in the most effective ways. These tips seem to distill into a simple truth: To use them well, know your students and your teaching purposes.

Now, before you turn to the "how to" chapters, we share a matrix so you have a big-picture view of what lies ahead. In the following chapters, you will find many examples of graphic organizers we have used along with sample lessons or examples, each linked to Common Core State Standards. This matrix shows the graphic organizers by chapter (also see the Appendix for a matrix showing the organizers aligned with the eight academic skills).

Chapter 3: Using Graphic Organizers to Acquire Academic Vocabulary	Frayer Organizer Vocabulary Triangle Concept/Definition Map Word Map
Chapter 4: Graphic Organizers Support Literary Text Reading and Writing Tasks	Freytag's Pyramid
Chapter 5: Graphic Organizers Support Informational Text Reading and Writing Tasks	Text Search and Find Board 4-Square With a Diamond Modified KWL
Chapter 6: Graphic Organizers Support Students' Reading Proficiencies	Note-Card Organizer Tabbed Book Manipulative Somebody-Wanted-But-So Understanding Text Structures (sequential, descriptive, cause/effect, compare and contrast, problem/solution) Rereading Organizer
Chapter 7: Graphic Organizers Boost Questioning and Responding	I-Chart and I-Guide Flip Chart Manipulative Text-Dependent Question/Response Organizer
Chapter 8: Graphic Organizers Foster Understanding and Writing Arguments	Seven-Part Graphic Organizer for Composing an Argument Thinking Map
Chapter 9: Graphic Organizers Support Collaboration	Project Management Organizer

Photo by Thinkstock

USING GRAPHIC ORGANIZERS TO ACQUIRE ACADEMIC VOCABULARY

Teaching students to comprehend and use the language of school, and the various disciplines is certainly a Common Core State Standard (CCSS) shift that is also a goal of every teacher. Graphic organizers offer major support in this knowledge and language acquisition by providing an organizing visual that helps to illustrate academic terminology within a viewed context that supports developing a deep understanding of the term, its meaning, and its contextual family.

FRAYER ORGANIZER

THIS ORGANIZER ADDRESSES THESE STANDARDS

CCSS.ELA-Literacy.CCRA.L.4.

Determine or clarify the meaning of unknown and multiple-meaning words and phrases by using context clues, analyzing meaningful word parts, and consulting general and specialized reference materials, as appropriate.

CCSS.ELA-Literacy.CCRA.L.5.

Demonstrate understanding of figurative language, word relationships, and nuances in word meanings.

CCSS.ELA-Literacy.CCRA.L.6.

Acquire and use accurately a range of general academic and domain-specific words and phrases sufficient for reading, writing, speaking, and listening at the college and career readiness level; demonstrate independence in gathering vocabulary knowledge when encountering an unknown term important to comprehension or expression.

What Is a Frayer Organizer?

The Frayer organizer (Figure 3-1) is intended to be used as an in-class activity that capitalizes on the interactions students have with sources and with each other as they learn concepts, usually represented as a vocabulary term. If the Frayer is simply given to students as homework (IRIS Center, n.d.), the value of the discussion is lost. The Frayer organizer helps students go beyond definitions and look at the attributes of a given concept.

FIGURE 3-1
Frayer Organizer

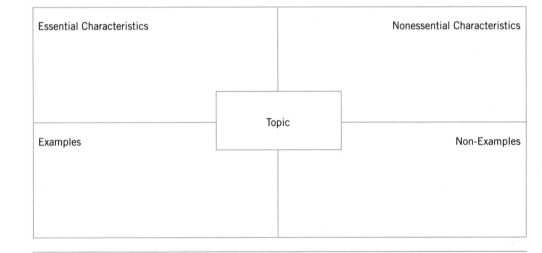

Source: Adapted from the original Frayer Model, created by Dorothy Frayer, University of Wisconsin.

How Do I Use a Frayer Organizer?

- You, the teacher, determine which terms you want your students to explore. The terms should be critical to understanding the reading students will do, the videos they may see, and the writing they will do.

- Next, provide students with accessible definitions of the terms, or students may consult student-friendly resources to find their own appropriate definitions. (Alternatively, you can provide just enough context to help students find a reasonable definition on their own.)

- Students work in pairs or small groups to complete the remainder of the organizer, adding examples, characteristics, and non-examples.

- Circulate as students work, providing support where needed. Sometimes coming up with non-examples can be difficult for students, so be prepared to offer a model of what this means. Tip off students that useful non-examples often share attributes with examples. For example, a peach and a plum share attributes, yet a peach is a non-example of a plum. By contrast, saying that a rock is a non-example of a plum doesn't contribute useful information. So guide students to learn to identify the relevant attributes of the examples and non-examples, then indicate why the non-examples are helpful.

- Let students know when it is okay to adapt information. For example, instead of naming characteristics, students might illustrate the concept or term or find an image of it online. This promotes their independent use of this graphic organizer.

- Consider digital tools as a means for students to share work with parents, other students, and you. Students can refer to each other's digital Frayer organizers to reinforce or adjust their learning if they are shared on a class web page or blog.

INTO THE CLASSROOM

Ninth Grade—Science

CCSS.ELA.Literacy.L.8.4.

Determine or clarify the meaning of unknown and multiple-meaning words or phrases based on grade 8 reading and content, choosing flexibly from a range of strategies.

THIS CLASSROOM EXAMPLE ADDRESSES THESE STANDARDS

CCSS.ELA.Literacy.L.8.5.

Demonstrate understanding of figurative language, word relationships, and nuances in word meanings.

Determining the Need

Eighth-grade science teacher Mr. Mullis was beginning his unit on the hazards caused by agents of diseases that affect living organisms. After determining the core vocabulary students would need to know, Mr. Mullis decided to use the digital Frayer organizer so students could explore these words and begin to build knowledge of the concepts before he presented the first lesson.

Introducing It

Mr. Mullis first listed the vocabulary words on the whiteboard and read them aloud, taking care to pronounce them clearly: *carrier, virus, organism, vector, transmit,* and so on. He deliberately included more accessible terms such as *transmit* that most students may have known from other contexts, because he wanted to make sure that all students had a precise, content-specific understanding, and he knew that some of his English language learners might find even so-called easy words elusive. He asked students to think about the context in which all of these words might be used, thus setting the conceptual framework for the unit. He then asked students to choose one word from the list to focus on, making sure that the words were evenly distributed among the class. Students then looked up their words using an Internet source, classroom dictionary, classroom textbook, or other reference material approved by Mr. Mullis.

Guided Instruction and Independent Practice

Students filled in the first part of the Frayer organizer using the definition they found most apt (this can be done on a paper copy or a digital version). As they did this work, Mr. Mullis offered support as needed. He then asked the class to get into groups based on the vocabulary word they chose. Each group synthesized the information about the word and recorded it on the Frayer organizer. Once the groups were done, Mr. Mullis referred them to the digital Frayer template located on Prezi (see Figures 3-2 and 3-3; it's important to note that some digital tools, complying with U.S. laws, require that students be age 13 or older to have an account). Students put their gathered information into the template, using pictures and text to add information and visual detail. Again, Mr. Mullis moved throughout the classroom, providing support to students. Once all the groups had their organizers complete and saved, Mr. Mullis invited each group to present their vocabulary word to the class. Each group presented as "experts" on their vocabulary word, and in essence peer-taught the important vocabulary for the unit. This experience provided students with opportunities to use and add to this graphic organizer and a chance to showcase their creativity, too. Peer work such as this has a strong research base behind it; here, it created powerful buy-in to the unit and built students' confidence that they could handle the often-rigorous reading that lay ahead.

FIGURE 3-2
Digital Frayer
Template Using Prezi

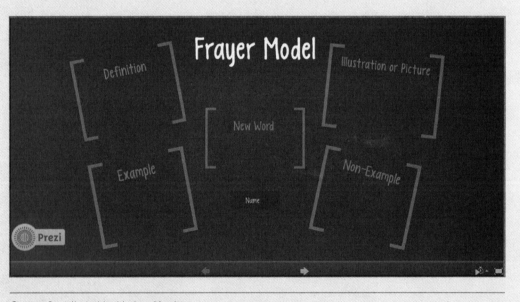

Source: Contributed by Lindsay Merritt.

Reading, Writing, and Discussion Extensions

The Frayer model is designed to accommodate the reality that students' understanding of a term deepens and changes over time. It takes into account the possibility that students will need to explore a term before they begin reading, and will also want to circle back to it during and after reading, to refine their understandings based on new learning. To use it to its fullest potential, provide students with opportunities to discuss the terms they have been assigned to learn so that they may compare what they have included on the organizer with what others have included. Finally, offer discussion and writing tasks that help you evaluate whether students are able to use the terms conversantly in academic speech and in their academic writing.

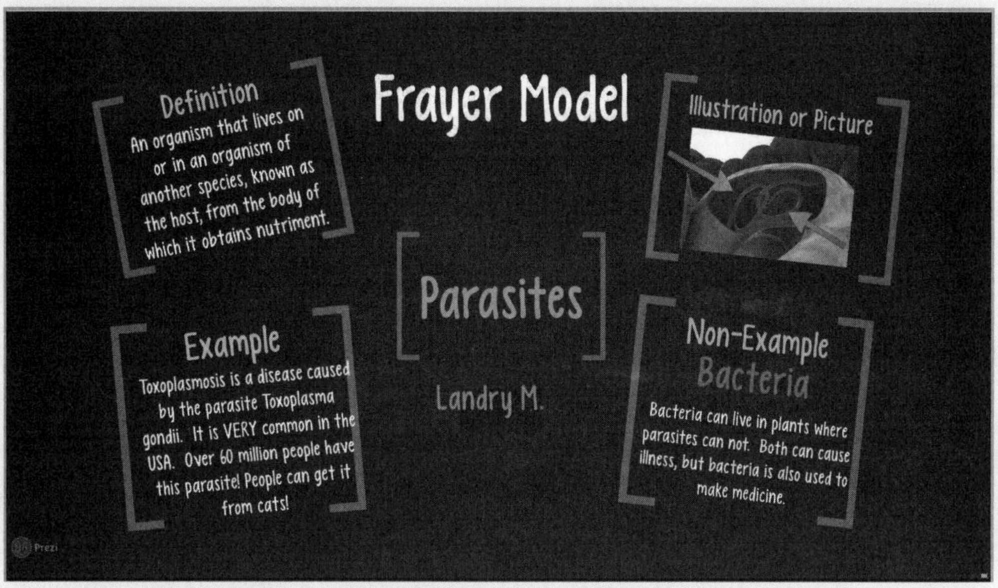

FIGURE 3-3
Digital Frayer
Parasites Example
Using Prezi

Source: Contributed by Lindsay Merritt. Photo is used with permission of Thinkstock.

VOCABULARY TRIANGLE

CCSS.ELA-Literacy.CCRA.R.2.

Determine central ideas or themes of a text and analyze their development; summarize the key supporting details and ideas.

CCSS.ELA-Literacy.CCRA.R.3.

Analyze how and why individuals, events, or ideas develop and interact over the course of a text.

CCSS.ELA-Literacy.CCRA.W.6.

Use technology, including the Internet, to produce and publish writing and to interact and collaborate with others.

CCSS.ELA-Literacy.CCRA.SL.5.

Make strategic use of digital media and visual displays of data to express information and enhance understanding of presentations.

What Is a Vocabulary Triangle?

Vocabulary triangles (Figure 3-4) are used in making connections among any group of words or phrases. They are a simple support that can be used in any discipline. Connections can be made with vocabulary words, characters, concepts, or stories.

How Do I Use a Vocabulary Triangle?

- Draw a triangle. Place (or have students place) words or concepts in each corner of the triangle.
- Encourage students to create sentences connecting the words. These should be written on the edge of each side of the triangle. Consider allowing students to work in pairs to check facts and grammar, and to encourage creativity.

FIGURE 3-4
Vocabulary Triangle

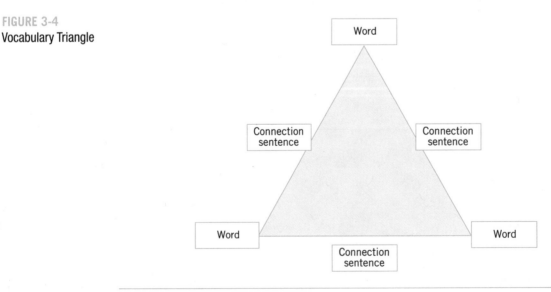

Source: Created by Kyle Kester.

- To challenge students, encourage them to write one sentence in the interior of the triangle using all three words correctly.

One student created the vocabulary triangle in Figure 3-5 in her biology class.

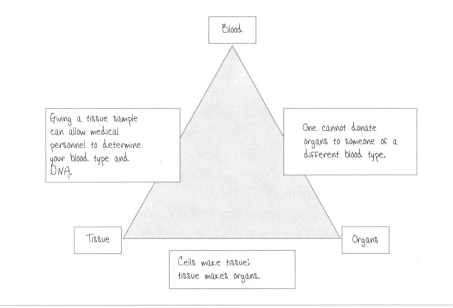

Source: Created by Kyle Kester.

FIGURE 3-5

Student Example of the Vocabulary Triangle for Biology

INTO THE CLASSROOM

Eighth Grade—English

CCSS.ELA-Literacy.CCRA.R.8.2.

Determine a theme or central idea of a text and analyze its development over the course of the text, including its relationship to the characters, setting, and plot; provide an objective summary of the text.

CCSS.ELA-Literacy.CCRA.R.8.3.

Analyze how particular lines of dialogue or incidents in a story or drama propel the action, reveal aspects of a character, or provoke a decision.

CCSS.ELA-Literacy.CCRA.W.8.6.

Use technology, including the Internet, to produce and publish writing and present the relationships between information and ideas efficiently as well as to interact and collaborate with others.

CCSS.ELA-Literacy.SL.8.5.

Integrate multimedia and visual displays into presentations to clarify information, strengthen claims and evidence, and add interest.

THIS CLASSROOM EXAMPLE ADDRESSES THESE STANDARDS

After students finished reading Chapter 1 from *To Kill a Mockingbird* (Lee, 1960), Mr. Vicente realized some of them were confused about a few of the characters in the text. For example, Chapter 1 starts with the main character, Scout, looking back at a situation and seeing herself exactly as she was. Many students were confused by the characters' relationships with one another. Mr. Vicente knew that a vocabulary triangle, designed to show the characters' relationships, would help students understand character development from the onset of the text.

Introducing It

Mr. Vicente asked students to draw a vocabulary triangle like the one he drew on the Promethean board. He wrote three characters' names in each corner of the rectangle: Scout, Jem, and Atticus. Then he presented a think-aloud:

> Let's see. What do I know about Scout? I know that she is the narrator of the text. I know that she is remembering a particular summer [models skimming the pages of the novel to find the detail that confirms this assertion]. But let's see. Right here [to the word *Jem* written on the graphic organizer] I need to know how Scout and Jem are related. I know that she is Jem's sister. I also know from the text that Scout is younger than Jem. I'm going to write a connecting sentence between these two words, these two characters, to show how the characters relate.

Mr. Vicente did the think-aloud as he filled out the organizer. Students recorded this information, absorbing the way he returned to the novel to mine the text for information. This explicit demonstration and think-aloud is key; yes, we want students to do more of the heavy lifting of using graphic organizers, but hearing and seeing the thinking modeled first often leads students to do deeper independent work because the expectations are vivid.

Mr. Vicente's vocabulary triangle example, shown in Figure 3-6, served as a guide for students as they completed their own later in the lesson.

FIGURE 3-6
Mr. Vicente's Vocabulary Triangle Model

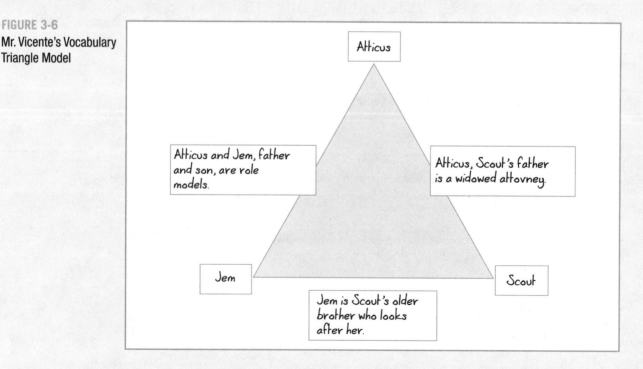

Guided Instruction and Independent Practice

After Mr. Vicente's think-aloud, students worked with partners during guided instruction. Each pair completed the vocabulary triangle graphic organizer with three other characters from the novel: Dill, Rachel Haverford, and Boo Radley. Mr. Vicente circulated, prompting students' thinking with questions such as this: "When did we meet this character, Rachel Haverford? Think about when we first learned about her; doing so might tell you how she relates to the others. Skim the text if you'd like." These types of questions and comments helped support students in understanding the relatedness of the characters from the text. Once pairs completed their organizers, they turned to their tablemates to compare information.

Reading, Writing, and Discussion Extensions

Students in Mr. Vicente's classroom knew that graphic organizers were always a step, often the first step, toward completing a more extended task. This organizer isn't just an activity, but sets expectations for students that as readers, their job is to notice all the ways the narrator and author send signals about characters—how they relate, how they change, what drives them, and so on. The graphic gives them an uncomplicated visual space on which to record and refine sophisticated thinking about text. When you use this type of organizer, consider how you might use it at multiple points in a novel or literature unit. For example, Mr. Vicente's students were asked to create new vocabulary triangle organizers after reading each chapter of *To Kill a Mockingbird*. Doing this work greatly supported students' quest to notice and articulate how the characters were developing. Mr. Vicente asked them to create an avatar, using Voki (http://voki.com) to write from the perspective of the character being studied. Because the students had thought critically about the characters and understood the relationships among multiple characters (thanks to the vocabulary triangles), creating the avatars as a writing extension proved to be a motivating and very doable task.

CONCEPT/DEFINITION MAP

CCSS.ELA-Literacy.CCRA.L.4.

Determine or clarify the meaning of unknown and multiple-meaning words and phrases by using context clues, analyzing meaningful word parts, and consulting general and specialized reference materials, as appropriate.

CCSS.ELA-Literacy.CCRA.L.5.

Demonstrate understanding of figurative language, word relationships, and nuances in word meanings.

What Is a Concept/Definition Map?

Concept/definition maps (Figure 3-7) are typically represented through a bubble-type format. In our version, we created squares that may be easier for writing or typing. The central concept or term appears in the center, and three key questions appear in surrounding bubbles. The questions help students explore and brainstorm what they know and can find out about a term or concept from their own collective experiences and from other sources. The key questions are: What is it? What is it like? What are some examples? A final section of the graphic supports students in synthesizing the information and then using their newly learned language to write their own definitions.

The goal is for students to use the questions as a vehicle to make richer connections to the term or concept (really, terms relate to concepts) and, by doing so, deepen their understanding. Schwartz and Raphael (1985) originally called these organizers *concept*

FIGURE 3-7
Concept/Definition Map

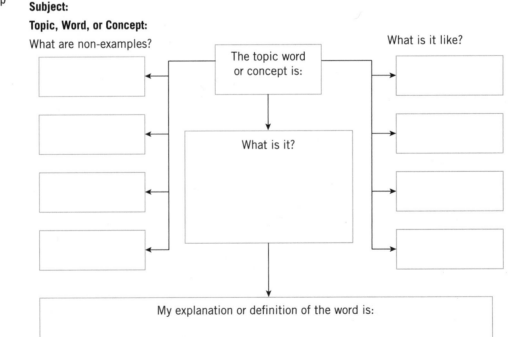

Name: Date:

Subject:

Topic, Word, or Concept:

What are non-examples?   What is it like?

The topic word or concept is:

What is it?

My explanation or definition of the word is:

of definition. They suggested that students who encounter a new term must be able to organize their current knowledge of the word and also determine what additional information other than a dictionary definition might assist their expanding understanding of the meaning.

How Do I Use a Concept/Definition Map?

- You will need chart paper, a software program, and a way to display the map; perhaps with a document camera on a whiteboard. Each student will need a copy of the reproducible or a blank piece of copy paper.
- Choose the topic, concept, or vocabulary term that might be confusing to students or one they may need to more broadly understand.
- Display your version of the chart with the topic in the center surrounded by the three key questions: What is it? What is it like? What are some examples?
- The ensuing discussion can be conducted with the entire class, in small groups, or even individually. Students should draw on their own background knowledge about the topic, but then expand their search by investigating assigned texts and other Internet sources that support their responding to the key questions.
- Students then complete the fourth area of the organizer by writing their own definition or explanation of the topic, word, or concept ("Concept/Definition Maps to Comprehend Curriculum Content," 2011).
- *Variations*: A variation on this idea from Gill (2007) suggests using this organizer approach with a central term and related areas for deep vocabulary explanation to break down the word by word part in a less formal way. Students might divide a word by its component parts, such as syllables, or find other words that incorporate the same root or affix. In Gill's organizer, students use Kidspiration to include both text and images as they explore vocabulary.

Websites That Provide an Opportunity for Concept/Definition Maps

- www.prezi.com: This program allows users to create a graphic organizer using bubbles, shapes, and text, and to navigate through it easily. Pictures, music, and graphics can be added to enhance the organizer.

- www.padlet.com: With this program a teacher or student can post a main idea (vocabulary word) and other students can attach "sticky note" type boxes around the word. This is a great way to collaborate.

A quick note to remember to check the terms of service if students create their own accounts using tools like these. In many cases, the students must be 13 years or older.

CCSS.ELA-Literacy.L.9-10.4.

Determine or clarify the meaning of unknown and multiple-meaning words and phrases based on grades 9-10 reading and content, choosing flexibly from a range of strategies.

CCSS.ELA-Literacy.L.9-10.5.

Demonstrate understanding of figurative language, word relationships, and nuances in word meanings.

Determining the Need

Mrs. Sasser's 10th-grade world history class was engaged in a unit on the governments of ancient civilizations. By the end of the unit, students would be expected to analyze each government, comparing and contrasting them in terms of development, structure, and function within various societies. Mrs. Sasser selected a concept/definition map because it provides a forum to both introduce and assess concept knowledge.

Introducing It

Mrs. Sasser first showed the class an example of a concept/definition map on the white-board, using a term with which students were familiar. She modeled how to fill in each section and did a think-aloud as she demonstrated what makes a sufficiently detailed example versus one that would be considered as not having enough information.

Guided Instruction and Independent Practice

Next she had the class work in 10 different groups, each pair or small group focusing on one of the following words: *theocracy, democracy, oligarchy, tyranny, aristocracy*. She instructed students to complete the "What is it?" portion of the map using their textbook. Once they were done, they moved onto the "What are some examples" section, using supplemental text and Internet sources Mrs. Sasser provided. She encouraged discussion, and when students were done they were to complete the "What is it like?" section independently. Either that same day or the next, students returned to their groups to share what they wrote. Next, Mrs. Sasser had students compare their answers and maps with the other group that explored their same word. Later she gave her students a chance to share their maps with the class and then post their maps on a bulletin board for reference. In doing this activity the class gained a better understanding of the words they would be interacting with throughout the unit.

Reading, Writing, and Discussion Extensions

Once students have developed a reasonable concept of the definition for a given word, they can be expected to use this in their written work and in discussion. Their usage may still be somewhat unsophisticated, but that's okay. The more students use terms representing difficult or challenging concepts, the more likely they will be to become proficient and conversant with the terms. When students use concept/definition maps to increase their knowledge of a word or concept, they are initially drawing on their own experiences, but this is where the learning begins, not ends. As they explore additional sources, they experience new ways of using the term, which promotes an expanded conceptualization of its meaning.

You might adjust this chart so that students can indicate the source(s) of the information they consulted and have a space to explain how the sources expanded their understanding of the word.

At the end of a unit, a great way to demonstrate this new vocabulary knowledge is to have students create a class informational guide using the vocabulary they learned throughout the unit of study. Students can work in pairs or individually to create a page that will be entered into the classroom book. Each student will be considered an "expert" in his or her field, using the newly obtained vocabulary. Students can include a paragraph or page (grade-level-appropriate) demonstrating their understanding of the word according to the information they gained using the concept/definition map. Students can include a picture or diagram to show understanding and any other information that can relate back to the newly learned vocabulary.

Once the pages are assembled, the book can be put in the classroom library for continuous reading throughout the year. The students and you can look back to make connections to future units or reference when learning comparable vocabulary.

WORD MAP

Contributed by Lindsay Merritt

THIS ORGANIZER ADDRESSES THESE STANDARDS

CCSS.ELA-Literacy.CCRA.L.4.

Determine or clarify the meaning of unknown and multiple-meaning words and phrases by using context clues, analyzing meaningful word parts, and consulting general and specialized reference materials, as appropriate.

CCSS.ELA-Literacy.CCRA.L.5.

Demonstrate understanding of figurative language, word relationships, and nuances in word meanings.

CCSS.ELA-Literacy.CCRA.L.6.

Acquire and use accurately a range of general academic and domain-specific words and phrases sufficient for reading, writing, speaking, and listening at the college and career readiness level; demonstrate independence in gathering vocabulary knowledge when encountering an unknown term important to comprehension or expression.

What Is a Word Map?

A word map (Figure 3-8) is a graphic organizer with space for definitions, synonyms, words and sentences in context, and pictures or symbols. Students can complete these for vocabulary that is important in a given lesson individually or as groups. The word map format allows students to reinforce their understanding of the concept represented by the vocabulary by looking at it in a number of different ways. Students' background knowledge is enhanced because they are encouraged to make connections to prior knowledge and experience.

FIGURE 3-8
Word Map

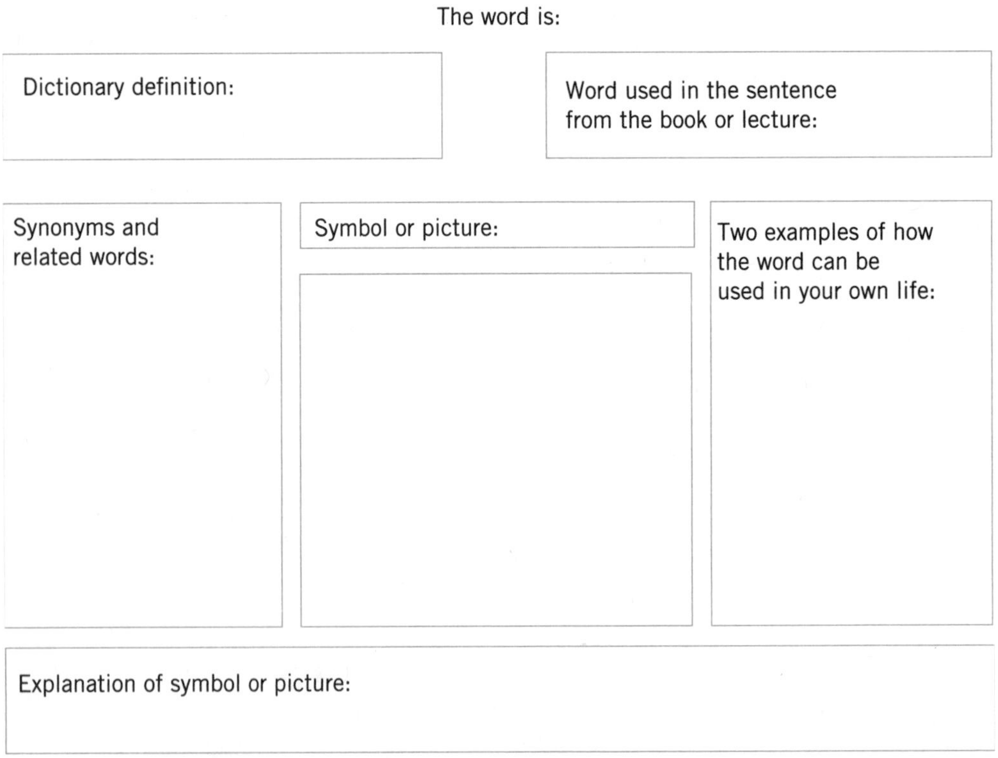
The word is:
Dictionary definition:
Word used in the sentence from the book or lecture:
Synonyms and related words:
Symbol or picture:
Two examples of how the word can be used in your own life:
Explanation of symbol or picture:

How Do I Use a Word Map?

- Choose target terms you want students to learn. These should be tier two words (Beck, McKeown, & Kucan, 2002) that are academic in nature but cut across content areas or tier three words that are specific to a given content area or discipline.

- If a single term is the target, students might work independently. If there are many terms, students may work as a group, dividing up the terms among themselves.

- Students work to complete the map, then share their understanding and examples with other members of the group or class. Through discussion and group presentation, they build on the knowledge gained from completing the graphic organizer.

Word maps can easily be adapted for use with digital resources such as Google Drive, PowerPoint, or Prezi, or they can be used with a SMART Board or chart paper.

INTO THE CLASSROOM — Ninth Grade—World History

CCSS.ELA-Literacy.RI.9-10.4.
Determine the meaning of words and phrases as they are used in a text, including figurative, connotative, and technical meanings; analyze the cumulative impact of specific word choices on meaning and tone (e.g., how the language of a court opinion differs from that of a newspaper).

CCSS.ELA-Literacy.L.9-10.4.
Determine or clarify the meaning of unknown and multiple-meaning words and phrases based on grades 9-10 reading and content, choosing flexibly from a range of strategies.

CCSS.ELA-Literacy.RST.9-10.4.
Determine the meaning of symbols, key terms, and other domain-specific words and phrases as they are used in a specific scientific or technical context relevant to grades 9-10 texts and topics.

THIS CLASSROOM EXAMPLE ADDRESSES THESE STANDARDS

Determining the Need

Coach Ruiz knew the important role that language plays in physical education. Though the focus of the class was on physical activity, she worked to build students' speaking, listening, and reading skills so that students would be able to bring the evolving knowledge base behind physical health into their lives. At the outset of her ninth-grade unit on the benefits of regular physical activity, she selected terms that she expected her class to know well enough to read fluently and use correctly in instructional conversations. For example, *obesity* is a term that is bandied about in the media and elsewhere, and is often understood by students as related to being overweight. Coach Ruiz wanted them to know its precise definition.

Introducing It

Coach Ruiz introduced the word map activity as a homework assignment that students could work on together via social media. She uploaded a blank word map to a cloud storage website (e.g., Google Drive, Box) and linked it on the class web page (a blank version of the word map with fill-in fields is available for download on the Corwin website at **www.corwin.com/miningcomplextext/6-12**). After modeling how to use the word map, she assigned one of the following words to each member of a group: *obesity, osteoarthritis, cardiovascular, diabetes, body mass index (BMI)*. Each team was to log on at home or in the school library after school, save the template with their word and names, and create the word map. She told students it was okay to use definitions or images directly from a website as long as they cited the source and were confident that they could define the term in their own language.

Guided Instruction and Independent Practice

That afternoon and evening, students began to complete the assignment. First, they read a web page, also linked on the class site, about childhood obesity from the Centers for Disease Control and Prevention (www.cdc.gov/healthyyouth/obesity/facts.htm). Next, they explored other websites that they knew to be reliable and identified what they needed to know to create an accurate word map. Students with printers at home printed out their work and brought it to class the next day, as there weren't enough computers in the PE area (see Figure 3-9 for an example). In school the next day, the groups met to discuss the terms using the word map as their guide, getting ready to present their findings to the class. Coach Ruiz moved from group to group, listening and providing support when needed. With one group she had to revisit the selected website because they had some questions about the symptoms of a disease that was presented.

Closure

After the groups taught other groups the words and the concepts they represented, Coach Ruiz asked them to summarize the activity with a partner in the group by using all the words in a brief conversation about obesity and the importance of physical activity. For this part of the lesson, the students were not allowed to use the word map, and instead had to rely on what they learned to fully explain their understandings of the five key terms.

Reading, Writing, and Discussion Extensions

The word map affords students the opportunity to explore an important term before or after reading to further build their knowledge of the word. Through the written aspects of the word map, students work with the term, then illustrate it. Finally, their written and illustrated work becomes the foundation for discussion as each student teaches other members of the group using the term in context. As a result, students become more conversant with the term and may employ it more fluently as they understand the concept underlying the word. Students can use a combination of the vocabulary words to create sentences, paragraphs, or even stories focused on the vocabulary words. Classroom dictionaries can be created using each of the word maps to reference terms during the unit of study. New vocabulary words can be added, and dictionaries can be referenced throughout the year.

FIGURE 3-9

Word Map for the
Word *Obesity*

The word is:

Dictionary definition:
Obesity means having too much body fat. It is different from being overweight, which means weighing too much.

Word used in the sentence from the book or lecture:
Childhood obesity has more than doubled in children and quadrupled in adolescents in the past 30 years.

Related words:
Overweight (not just from fat)
Calories
Diabetes
Heart Disease
Arthritis
Cholesterol

Symbol or picture:

Photo by Emilio Labrado (Creative Commons Attribution License: https://flic.kr/p/6esCV2)

Two examples of how the word can be used in your own life:

I like to eat things that can lead to obesity, so I need to be more careful about what I eat. My uncle died of heart disease and he was very obese. I don't want this to happen to me or to my family or friends.

Explanation of symbol or picture:
This couple shows how obese some Americans are becoming.

Photo by Thinkstock

GRAPHIC ORGANIZERS SUPPORT LITERARY TEXT READING AND WRITING TASKS

Literary texts differ in several ways from informational texts. In addition to being fictional works, they follow a narrative structure that informational texts may not. Readers pay attention to characters and plot development to appreciate the overall theme of the work. In this chapter, we look at a few graphic organizers that are especially well suited to literary text.

FREYTAG'S PYRAMID

CCSS.ELA-Literacy.CCRA.R.2.

Determine central ideas or themes of a text and analyze their development; summarize the key supporting details and ideas.

CCSS.ELA-Literacy.CCRA.R.3.

Analyze how and why individuals, events, or ideas develop and interact over the course of a text.

CCSS.ELA-Literacy.CCRA.R.5.

Analyze the structure of texts, including how specific sentences, paragraphs, and larger portions of the text (e.g., a section, chapter, scene, or stanza) relate to each other and the whole.

What Is a Freytag's Pyramid?

FIGURE 4-1

Freytag's Pyramid

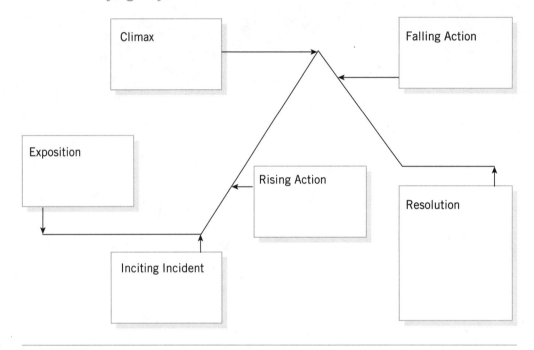

Source: Adapted from Holman and Harmon, 1992.

Freytag's pyramid (Figure 4-1), an organizational diagram first published in 1863, was intended to explain a five-act tragedy. Named after its designer, Gustav Freytag, the diagram has been used to analyze many types of fiction. We have found it makes the task of summarizing short stories and novels considerably easier for students.

How Do I Use a Freytag's Pyramid?

Begin by ensuring that students understand the plot structure of a literary text and that these elements are represented on the Freytag's pyramid graphic organizer. To ensure that students have this understanding, model how to fill in one section of the pyramid; model filling in only those sections you assess that students do not clearly understand. This can be done in one class period or over the course of several days, through a think-aloud as you read a literary text together. If this is a review, you may want to use a familiar class novel or a target text that all students have read and then interactively discuss and model how to complete the graphic organizer. The following descriptions of the section of the pyramid will help as you explicitly share the components of Freytag's pyramid with your students.

- *Exposition:* This section sets the scene for the text. It is when the author introduces the main characters and setting.

- *Inciting Incident:* Also known as the complication, this juncture is when the action begins. Often, but not always, there is a single event that causes the text's main conflict.

- *Rising Action:* This constitutes most of the plot line and is the series of related incidents among characters that the author crafts in such a way as to ratchet up the tension so readers are compelled to read on to discover what will happen.

- *Climax:* This is most often the plot point of greatest tension, where the inciting event and the incidence of the rising action collide or coalesce.

- *Falling Action:* These are the events that occur as a result of the climax. This signifies that the story will end soon.

- *Resolution:* During this segment of the story, the main problem or conflict is solved. The main character is usually the problem solver, but it can also be the part of the story when someone solves it for him or her. A related term is *denouement*, the ending of the story. It is here that any secrets, questions, or mysteries that remain after the resolution are solved by the characters or explained by the author. Sometimes the author chooses not to reveal everything, but leaves the reader or viewer to think about the theme or future possibilities for the characters. The solution is ours.

Once you sense students have a solid understanding of each segment of the pyramid, have them complete the pyramid as they read a short story or novel. Interacting with the pyramid scaffolds their understanding of the structure of the story, and the notes they jot down will help them recall and summarize later. Their notes can be used for additional independent writing projects.

Tips

- You might also ask students to complete the pyramid after reading a story or novel as a way of assessing their understanding.

- We have found that an effective practice is to have students complete a rough draft of the pyramid on their own, then work on chart paper

Stacy Miller, a teacher at Patch American High School, in Stuttgart, Germany, puts graphics right in the graphic organizer. She asks her students to be creative with technology, and she models this for her students. In the image below, notice how the model uses graphics (actually a font that uses graphic images instead of alphabetic text). She and her students create a Freytag's pyramid as a graphic organizer in PowerPoint, use artsy fonts to create the final pyramid, and export to an image file which can be shared on the class web page or wiki. In PowerPoint, go to "Save as type" and choose one of the image formats (we suggest TIFF, JPG, or GIF). If you are familiar with *The Great Gatsby*, you will find this Freytag's pyramid intriguing and creative as we did.

Source: Created by Stacy Miller.

You will find more of these creative and digitally designed organizers in Chapters 6 and 9.

or an interactive website. Completing the online version with a partner invites collaboration, during which they can compare their insights. When students' interpretations differ, encourage them to return to the text to support their ideas. An online version can be found if you navigate to www.readwritethink.org/resources/resource-print.html?id=904, then choose "Plot Diagram" to start the interactive Freytag's pyramid generator.

- We have found that having partner teams compare their work with other partner teams is really beneficial when students are reading a complicated novel or short story. Doing so gives them more time to check to see that they have not missed key elements of the plot. This conversation among students is so valuable because it leads them to deeper understanding of characters and their complexities as well as how peers infer. As you listen to these discussions, encourage them to keep returning to the text to support their stances. Students need to know that rereading, skimming, and raising questions are a natural part of reading. When adolescents see and hear how peers find textual support, look at descriptions within dialogue, mine final paragraphs of chapters, notice recurring images, and so on, it's powerful teaching and learning.

INTO THE CLASSROOM

Sixth Grade—English

THIS CLASSROOM EXAMPLE ADDRESSES THESE STANDARDS

CCSS.ELA-Literacy.R.1.

Read closely to determine what the text says explicitly and to make logical inferences from it; cite specific textual evidence when writing or speaking to support conclusions drawn from the text.

CCSS.ELA-Literacy.RL.6.3.

Describe how a particular story's or drama's plot unfolds in a series of episodes as well as how the characters respond or change as the plot moves toward a resolution.

CCSS.ELA-Literacy.SL.6.1.

Engage effectively in a range of collaborative discussions (one-on-one, in groups, and teacher-led) with diverse partners on grade 6 topics, texts, and issues, building on others' ideas and expressing their own clearly.

CCSS.ELA-Literacy.SL.6.5.

Include multimedia components (e.g., graphics, images, music, sound) and visual displays in presentations to clarify information.

CCSS.ELA-Literacy.6.6.

Adapt speech to a variety of contexts and tasks, demonstrating command of formal English when indicated or appropriate.

Determining the Need

Mr. Chapman's sixth graders have just read *A Wrinkle in Time* (L'Engle, 1962) as an interactive whole-class read-aloud. The book was part of a unit based on the essential question "Are we governed by fate, free will, or greater power?" Mr. Chapman could tell from his students' work with this novel, and with the previous novel they read, that students needed more practice in identifying the rising action, climax, and falling action and grasping how these elements relate. He used Freytag's pyramid as a way of doing some explicit teaching of story elements. He was confident that the graphic organizer would help students get a deeper understanding of this—or any—novel, because it so effectively helps readers know how to continually connect the incidents and various plot points of a narrative.

Introducing It

Mr. Chapman began by asking students to identify their favorite movies. Students pair-shared answers and then the whole class discussed favorite movies and the reasons why each was chosen. As expected, students responded with comments like "It's exciting!" "It's suspenseful!" "I was on the edge of my seat!" and "It had a sad ending!" With this enthusiasm, Mr. Chapman knew his students would be motivated to think of *A Wrinkle in Time* as a movie, using Freytag's pyramid for support. Mr. Chapman asked students to think like movie directors for the period and to identify which parts of the story would need to be captured as a visual in order to show an audience the most important moments.

Mr. Chapman displayed Freytag's pyramid on the Promethean board and passed out a copy to all students. He explained how he was also going to take on the role of a movie director and think aloud parts of this graphic organizer and then the "student directors" were going to have a turn. Mr. Chapman modeled for students how to think about the exposition section of the graphic organizer.

> Let's see, I know that the exposition is where the characters and setting are introduced. This book is about Meg, who is the main character. Yes, Meg Murray and her family live in a small town, which is the setting for the story. The town is in England and Meg attends a boring rural high school. These are a few details that help us visualize the character and the setting.

As Mr. Chapman did the think-aloud about the exposition section of the "movie," students could hear his thinking and see how he recorded notes. Observing Freytag's pyramid, students listened and jotted the notes on their graphic organizer while Mr. Chapman wrote on his graphic organizer, which they could see on the Promethean board. Mr. Chapman and the students interactively discussed the other sections of the graphic organizer.

Guided Instruction and Independent Practice

Once students have an understanding of how to think, talk, and write about different components of the story's plot, they are ready to work together—and independently—to add to their own graphic organizers. Mr. Chapman asked students to work as partners to complete one section at a time. He circulated throughout the room, assessing their understanding of the content by looking at what they'd written on their pyramids and listening to them converse. He prompted with questions, cues, and prompts to support their understanding of the plot features. If he saw that many partners needed the same kind of support, he directed everyone's attention back to the Promethean board for a brief think-aloud. For example, when he observed that many students were confused about a rising action, he said:

> Everyone, let me direct your attention back to the board. Let's take a look at the rising action section of the pyramid. Listen to me as I think about this section. I know that the rising action is the part of the story that builds and gets more exciting for readers. It gets very exciting in Chapter 4. I can visualize this part as a movie director [reads several key sentences from the novel]. It's getting more exciting when the children leave with Mrs. Whatsit. It makes me think about an adventure and the danger they are about to encounter.

This think-aloud spurred students on to skim and reread sections of *A Wrinkle in Time* that would constitute rising action. They teased apart what incidents and passages seemed like rising action and what scenes belonged more squarely in the climax of the narrative. Mr. Chapman dropped hints about the types of places in novels that can shed light on things—internal monologues, descriptive passages, moments of strong emotion, and so on. As students gained confidence and knowledge, they worked in pairs and eventually independently to complete all sections of their graphic organizer by adding details that might be unique to their pyramid.

Students in Mr. Chapman's class were well aware that using graphic organizers is a step toward engaging in a larger task. They knew that using a graphic organizer is like getting to see the novelist's notes, where the basic story structure is laid bare, much like glimpsing an architect's plans for a building. In short, the graphic helped them create something bigger. So when Mr. Chapman asked them to use their graphic organizer to write a movie trailer, they were up to the task. They had to meet with other directors to provide narration and images that captured the essence of the plot and hinted at how it connected to the theme/essential question "Are we governed by fate, free will, or a greater power?"

A completed Freytag's pyramid *as is* provides plenty from which to craft a movie trailer, but with Mr. Chapman's encouragement, some students modified the pyramid to suit their plans. As you can see in Figure 4-2, one group decided how to combine ideas, cut apart their pyramids, and glued the sections onto a big piece of chart paper, creating a pyramid that represented many ideas and multiple perspectives.

Reading, Writing, and Discussion Extensions

The power of a well-written or well-told narrative, especially as fiction, is part of the psyche of every human (see Olson, 1968). Freytag's pyramid gives students opportunities to discuss a story during or after reading. Because of its focus on plot, students can lean on the pyramid from the narrative's first to last page, using it to really get a handle on a novel's "who what when and where," grasp the arc of any story, and ultimately use these organized understandings to mine ever deeper an author's themes and ideas. Learners can rely on the pyramid when they write or create multimodal compositions as well. Additional interactive graphic organizers your students may like can be found on the ReadWriteThink website at www.readwritethink.org/files/resources/interactives/storymap. After your students consider these, invite them to design a graphic they think could be used when reading or writing fiction. Be sure they explain their thinking. We encourage you to take every opportunity to move students toward crafting their personal graphic organizers as they illustrate information that moves them beyond the initial pyramid. This type of activity encourages students to independently illustrate and present insights that they gain when reading and interacting with a text.

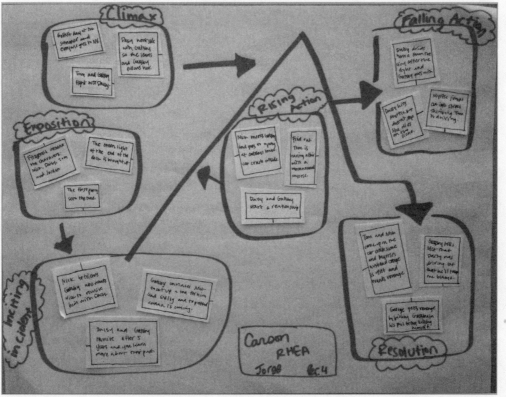

FIGURE 4-2
Student-Created
Freytag's Pyramid

Photo by Thinkstock

GRAPHIC ORGANIZERS SUPPORT INFORMATIONAL TEXT READING AND WRITING TASKS

Informational texts are often referred to in a variety of ways. They may be characterized as nonfiction or as expository text, for example. They may advance a persuasive perspective (a term that is not included in the Common Core State Standards [Common Core State Standards Initiative, 2010b]), develop an argument, or report only what is observed. However one characterizes informational text, graphic organizers help students understand the genre as they read to determine the author's purpose or to develop their own written or multimodal compositions in these forms.

TEXT SEARCH AND FIND BOARD

Contributed by Rebecca Kavel

THIS ORGANIZER ADDRESSES THESE STANDARDS

CCSS.ELA-Literacy.CCRA.R.3.

Analyze how and why individuals, events, or ideas develop and interact over the course of a text.

CCSS.ELA-Literacy.CCRA.R.4.

Interpret words and phrases as they are used in a text, including determining technical, connotative, and figurative meanings, and analyze how specific word choices shape meaning or tone.

CCSS.ELA-Literacy.CCRA.SL.1.

Prepare for and participate effectively in a range of conversations and collaborations with diverse partners, building on others' ideas and expressing their own clearly and persuasively.

What Is a Text Search and Find Board?

FIGURE 5-1

Text Search and Find Board

Title	Main Idea	Key Details	Vocabulary
Include the book title and your name here.	*What's the main idea? Write a complete sentence that tells the main idea.*	*Provide at least three key facts that support your main idea.*	*List and define at least three important vocabulary words from the book.*
Connections	**Chart, Illustration, or Graph**	**Questions**	**Answers**
How does this text remind you of something in your life or another text you have read?	*Create a chart, illustration, or graph to display some of the information you learned from the book.*	*After reading your book, create questions.*	*Choose at least one of your questions and provide an answer with supporting details from the text.*

Source: Created by Rebecca Kavel.

Adapted from Laura Candler's (2012) informational text sharing boards, a text search and find board (Figure 5-1) allows students to determine the main idea, explain events or procedures, and determine the meaning of selected vocabulary. As students create and answer questions using the informational text as their source they are pushed to think more deeply about each word and the relationship among the words. When answering the questions, students cite evidence, offering written interpretation of a text while using relevant evidence to support their points and the main idea.

Comprehension improves when teachers give explicit instruction in the use of comprehension strategies (Duke & Pearson, 2002). When using a text search and find board, students must think about what they read and record their thoughts. The board allows students to engage as active readers by analyzing and organizing important information and identifying key details. The text search and find board can be used with a variety of genres and subject areas but fits particularly well with social studies and science curricula as students articulate their knowledge stating the main idea, providing supporting details, and using higher order thinking skills to craft questions about their reading. Students can, without significant scaffolding, comprehend and evaluate complex texts across a range of disciplines. This graphic organizer allows students to build strong content knowledge needed for successful reading skills using informational text.

How Do I Use a Text Search and Find Board?

- Model how to complete the board.
- Explain to students that they will work independently or with a partner to complete at least three boxes. (You may adjust the number of boxes students must complete in one class period as this may take more than 2 days to complete depending on the length of the text.)
- Review the expectations for each section.
- Give each student a text search and find board to complete, or allow students to use construction paper to create their own by folding the paper in half "hot dog" style or lengthwise and then fold it over three times to create squares and then unfold to have eight boxes.

INTO THE CLASSROOM

Sixth Grade—Social Studies

CCSS.ELA-Literacy.RI.6.3.
Analyze in detail how a key individual, event, or idea is introduced, illustrated, and elaborated in a text (e.g., through examples or anecdotes).

CCSS.ELA-Literacy.RI.6.4.
Determine the meaning of words and phrases as they are used in a text, including figurative, connotative, and technical meanings.

CCSS.ELA-Literacy.SL.6.1.
Engage effectively in a range of collaborative discussions (one-on-one, in groups, and teacher-led) with diverse partners on grade 6 topics, texts, and issues, building on others' ideas and expressing their own clearly.

THIS CLASSROOM EXAMPLE ADDRESSES THESE STANDARDS

Determining the Need
Sixth-grade teacher Mr. Allen launched a unit on systems of social structure within various civilizations. It was his students' first exposure to the topic, so he selected a text search and find board to give students a scaffold as they learned new information.

Introducing It
Mr. Allen modeled how to use the board with the U.S. government as an example, since students were familiar with its structure. Next, he had students work with a partner and

gave each pair a social system: Roman class structure; Indian caste system; and feudal, matrilineal, and patrilineal societies. He also preselected texts and/or websites on the topics and provided these materials to students.

Guided Instruction and Independent Practice

Students worked together to read the texts and then filled out the top line of the text search and find board. Mr. Allen provided support as needed. Next, each student worked alone to fill in the second row, again using his or her text, prior experiences, and previous readings. Mr. Allen then asked them to team up with their partner again to discuss what they each included in their chart. He advised them to really dig in and discuss and debate each other's choices and understandings.

Closure

Mr. Allen had the class form new groups, with one person from each system represented. They spent the remainder of the class period sharing their text and findings in the new group. In doing this Mr. Allen gave students the opportunity to become the "experts" on their system while continuing to collaborate.

Reading, Writing, and Discussion Extensions

As students read the assigned or self-selected text, they engage with specific purposes in mind that include thinking about and expressing new questions that arise from the reading. Based on what students learn from their reading, they might also create a written or multimodal product that supports learning even more, and sharing through presentation or discussion with classmates, parents, or the world via the Internet. Consider in what ways their thinking might have similarities with the I-chart and I-guide (see Chapter 7).

Title	Main Idea	Key Details	Vocabulary
Include the book title and your name here. Remember to write neatly and include the date.	What's the main idea? Write a complete sentence that tells the main idea. Remember that the main idea is only one sentence long. You will have the opportunity to provide a summary at the end.	Provide at least three key facts that support your main idea. Use the text to find answers. Be sure to use the charts and illustrations the author provides.	List and define at least three important vocabulary words from the book. Choose words that are unfamiliar. If it is applicable, please include a small sketch.
Connections	**Chart, Illustration, or Graph**	**Questions**	**Answers**
How does this text remind you of something in your life or another text you have read? Remember to think about the news, TV shows, books, and experiences.	Create a chart, illustration, or graph to display some of the information you learned from the book. You may use the back of this paper for this activity.	After reading your book, create four questions. (Note to teacher: Based on the level of your students, you may want to require them to use higher-level thinking stems such as Marzano's or Bloom's questioning.)	Choose at least two of your questions and provide answers with supporting details from the text. If you are working with a partner, you may trade questions for this portion of the lesson.

Source: Created by Rebecca Kavel, adapted from Laura Candler's (2012) Informational Text Sharing Board.

FIGURE 5-2

Directions for Using a Text Search and Find Board

Title	Main Idea	Key Details	Vocabulary
Astronomy and Space Completed by: (student name)	*This selected text provides examples of how astronomers find out about the universe and special equipment they use.*	*Astronomers use optical telescopes, radio telescopes, space stations, and space probes to learn about the universe. Space is too dark and far away to just use a telescope so astronomers need a lot of special equipment.*	*Asteroid: large chunks of rock or rock and metal formed with the Solar System about 5,000 million years ago. Optical telescope: uses light to magnify objects to look into deep space. Space probe: tools with cameras sent to investigate deep space and transmit findings back to Earth.*
Connections	**Chart, Illustration, or Graph**	**Questions**	**Answers**
This book reminds me of the museum I went to in Washington, DC, with my family. We got to sit in a real rocket.	*Saturn*	*1. What would happen if astronomers did not have access to technology? 2. What is the cause and effect of meteoroids falling into Earth's atmosphere? 3. What is the biggest telescope astronomers use? 4. What are the differences in size between the Sun and the Earth?*	*1. Astronomers would not be able to see any details without technology. 2. When meteoroids fall into Earth's atmosphere they burn up and make a bright streak across the sky. When they fall they are called meteors. 3. The largest radio telescope is the Arecibo dish in Puerto Rico. It is 305m wide. See pages 9 and 10. 4. The diameter of the Sun is about 1,390,000 kilometers. The diameter of the Earth is 12,742 kilometers or about 109 times smaller than the Sun.*

FIGURE 5-3

Student Example of a Text Search and Find Board for an Astronomy Text

4-SQUARE WITH A DIAMOND

THIS ORGANIZER ADDRESSES THIS STANDARD

CCSS.ELA-Literacy.CCRA.W.2.

Write informative/explanatory texts to examine and convey complex ideas and information clearly and accurately through the effective selection, organization, and analysis of content.

What Is 4-Square With a Diamond?

A 4-square with a diamond organizer (Figure 5-4) is a modification of Gould and Gould's (1999) four squares writing graphic organizer that was designed to support students writing a five-paragraph essay (a writing model we don't recommend in most cases), and Zollman's (2009) four-corners-and-a-diamond mathematics graphics organizer designed for problem solving. As students interact with this graphic, they engage in an analysis of what they know and also what they need to know as related to the information being presented. Each iteration of the graphic builds on the work of Ogle's (1986) KWL model that supports students in crafting a visual and spatial representation through their analysis of what they know and also what they are questioning about a text topic or a problem to be solved. By answering questions on the organizer, readers are led into textual and self-analysis of their understanding of the topic. Students might also use the organizer to show and explain steps in a process. The rubric shown in Figure 5-5 supports an evaluation of knowledge, approaches or strategies used, and the explanation of the learning (Zollman, 2009).

For example, in science, this graphic organizer could be used during hands-on investigations. Students could be presented with the investigation/lab procedures and as they

FIGURE 5-4
4-Square With a Diamond

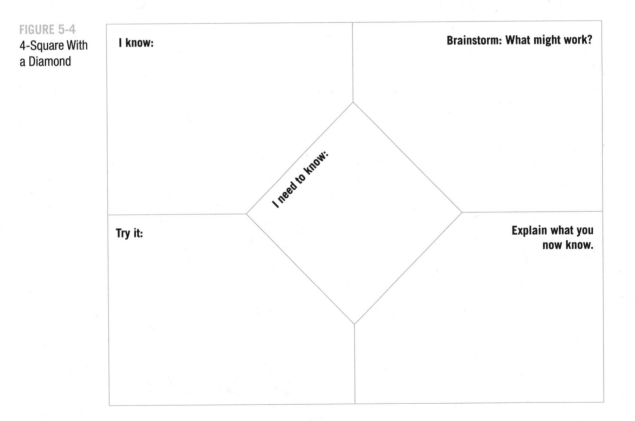

| I know: | Brainstorm: What might work? |

I need to know:

| Try it: | Explain what you now know. |

FIGURE 5-5

Rubric for 4-Square
With a Diamond

Score	Knowledge	Strategy	Explanation
4	All of the work was correct.	Student created a plan and followed through with the plan.	Student's explanation was detailed and included all information.
3	Most of the work was correct.	Student's plan was incomplete but a plan was chosen and used.	Student's explanation included most of the information.
2	Some of the work was correct.	Student's plan and process did not match.	Student's explanation lacked detail.
1	Little of the work was correct.	Student's plan was largely incomplete.	Student's explanation had major gaps.
0	Student did not attempt.	Student did not plan.	Student did not explain.

worked through the steps, the 4-square could serve as a record of their progress and under-standing. In this way, they use the organizer as a framework for listening as directions are given. This organizer could also support the inquiry model as students must decide on the possible processes and record results of each attempt.

How Do I Use a 4-Square With a Diamond?

- Choose a compelling situation or problem that relates to your instructional purpose.
- Model how you would think through the problem.
- Think aloud as you pose and resolve questions as you complete the graphic organizer. As you do so, interactively discuss the process with your students.
- Invite students to identify how this graphic is supportive of their investigation.
- Give the 4-square organizer and new problem to students and have them work through it on their own. Circulate and provide support.

INTO THE CLASSROOM

Sixth Grade—Science

CCSS.ELA-Literacy.RI.6.1.

Cite textual evidence to support analysis of what the text says explicitly as well as inferences drawn from the text.

CCSS.ELA-Literacy.SL.6.1.

Engage effectively in a range of collaborative discussions (one-on-one, in groups, and teacher-led) with diverse partners on grade 6 topics, texts, and issues, building on others' ideas and expressing their own clearly.

CCSS.ELA-Literacy.SL.6.2.

Interpret information presented in diverse media and formats (e.g., visually, quantitatively, orally) and explain how it contributes to a topic, text, or issue under study.

THIS CLASSROOM EXAMPLE ADDRESSES THESE STANDARDS

THIS CLASSROOM
EXAMPLE ADDRESSES
THESE STANDARDS

CCSS.ELA-Literacy.W.6.2.

Write informative/explanatory texts to examine a topic and convey ideas, concepts, and information through the selection, organization, and analysis of relevant content.

CCSS.ELA-Literacy.W.6.2.a.

Introduce a topic; organize ideas, concepts, and information, using strategies such as definition, classification, comparison/contrast, and cause/effect; include formatting (e.g., headings), graphics (e.g., charts, tables), and multimedia when useful to aiding comprehension.

Determining the Need

Ms. Mestman showed students how to use the 4-square with a diamond graphic organizer at the outset of a study of rocks and minerals. Her students had some prior knowledge; her purpose was to expand their understanding of the characteristics of rocks and minerals. This graphic organizer works well with the task of applying prior knowledge to new knowledge.

Introducing It

The students worked in teams. They were to assume the role of geologists who test rocks and minerals to identify and describe a specimen's color, luster, hardness, texture, streak, and gravity, and to record their findings. Later, they would write an informational article about their findings.

Ms. Mestman used a piece of rose quartz to model how to use the graphic organizer. To keep her demonstration brief, she focused only on luster.

> Let's see, as I look at this rock, I know I need to identify the luster of this rock. I will write *luster* in this center diamond. Next, let me think about what I already know about luster. I will write in this upper left-hand box that luster has to do with light. I also know words like *shiny*, *glassy*, and *resinous* have to do with luster, so I will also write those words in this box because those are ways to describe the luster of a rock.

Her students watched, listened, and jotted down notes on their own graphic organizers to help them remember how to gather information. This demonstration provided students with some of the language and thinking behind this scientific investigation.

Guided Instruction and Independent Practice

Students worked in teams of three to each complete two 4-square with a diamond graphic organizers, which together described all six characteristics of their rock or mineral specimen (Figure 5-6). This gave them an opportunity to work as an investigative geologist who is part of a larger team. Ms. Mestman guided her student geologists with questions, cues, and prompts to help them arrive at an understanding of the characteristics of the different rocks and minerals: "It looks like you are stuck on texture as a characteristic. Remember to pay attention to the grain size as you determine the texture. The magnifying glass will help you observe it."

To make this process more collaborative and hold individual students accountable, each of the geologists on a team completed their two graphic organizers describing two characteristics of their rock. As students worked, Ms. Mestman did a quick visual check to ensure that all students were completing their graphic organizers accurately (and provided feedback if she saw they were not). After teams completed six graphic organizers that detailed the characteristics of their rock or mineral, they worked together to complete a manipulative guide like the one shown in Figure 5-7 that synthesized all they now knew about the characteristics of their

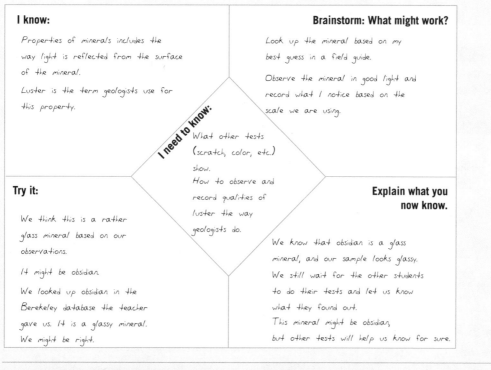

FIGURE 5-6
Students Create a
Four-Square With a
Diamond for Geology

I know:

Properties of minerals includes the way light is reflected from the surface of the mineral.

Luster is the term geologists use for this property.

I need to know: What other tests (scratch, color, etc.) show.

How to observe and record qualities of luster the way geologists do.

Brainstorm: What might work?

Look up the mineral based on my best guess in a field guide.

Observe the mineral in good light and record what I notice based on the scale we are using.

Try it:

We think this is a rather glass mineral based on our observations.

It might be obsidian.

We looked up obsidian in the Berekeley database the teacher gave us. It is a glassy mineral. We might be right.

Explain what you now know.

We know that obsidian is a glass mineral, and our sample looks glassy. We still wait for the other students to do their tests and let us know what they found out.

This mineral might be obsidian, but other tests will help us know for sure.

Source: Created by Jennifer Harahus.

rock or mineral. (Please see Chapters 6 and 7 to learn more about tabbed book manipulatives and flip chart organizers.) Notice all the different handwriting, which shows multiple students worked to complete this graphic organizer. This manipulative guide would then be presented to other teams of student geologists.

Reading, Writing, and Discussion Extensions

After geologist teams completed their manipulative guides, which synthesized information about their rock or mineral, they orally shared and compared their work through discussion with other teams. For another lesson you may again want to invite them to consider that, when working as a team of geologists, each must play a significant part in investigation and analysis of a specimen. Each time they work as a team, encourage them to discuss: What did each student contribute to the investigation? What did each student add to his or her 4-square with a diamond organizers after discussion? This graphic organizer is useful when instructional tasks require students to apply background knowledge, define the problem, identify what they may not know, and then create a presentation of the information.

FIGURE 5-7
Student Groups Create a Tabbed Book Manipulative

MODIFIED KWL

CCSS.ELA-Literacy.CCRA.R.2.

Determine central ideas or themes of a text and analyze their development; summarize the key supporting details and ideas.

CCSS.ELA-Literacy.CCRA.R.3.

Analyze how and why individuals, events, or ideas develop and interact over the course of a text.

CCSS.ELA-Literacy.CCRA.R.10.

Read and comprehend complex literary and informational texts independently and proficiently.

What Is a Modified KWL?

FIGURE 5-8
KWL

K What do we know about the KWL instructional strategy?	W What do we want to know about the KWL instructional strategy?	L What did we learn about the KWL instructional strategy?
Categories:		

One of the most widely recognized instructional routines is KWL (know, want to know, learn; Ogle, 1986). There are more than a dozen published variations on the elegant theme captured in this approach. A challenge teachers face with this approach is that what students want to know is somewhat uninformed because they simply lack sophisticated knowledge of the topic that could lead toward increasingly deep connections to the content. Adapting the approach to feature disciplinary texts may help. You may have noticed a section at the bottom of the KWL chart in Figure 5-8 for "Categories." This part is often left off, but it should not be. After brainstorming in column one what they already know about the topic, students are asked to categorize the information they have brainstormed. Doing so is what Ogle (1986, p. 566) calls "content structuring" and helps students create cognitive maps of the material they already know.

One adaptation of KWL is intended to support students as they propose questions about problems they encounter in mathematics. In KWC (Hyde, 2006), students identify in the first column "What do you know for sure?" In the second column, they identify "What are you trying to find out?" In the third column, they decide, "Are there special conditions [the C] or precise words to address?" A space underneath asks students to show how they solve the problem using pictures, numbers, and words (see Figure 5-9).

What do you know for sure?	What are you trying to find out?	Are there special conditions or precise words to address?
Solution:		

FIGURE 5-9
Using What I Know to Solve a Problem

Example: Social Studies

In middle and high school, learners have both the cognitive capacity and the experience to read critically—that is, to reckon with the author of a document (in elementary school this vantage point on a text isn't as fruitful). With understanding literary works, this inquiry may play out as students consider the life of a novelist, his or her social/cultural background, the era in which he or she lived or lives, or the era depicted in the text in order to speculate on how an author's point of view might influence a text. Similarly, critical to understanding history is the capacity to handle dissonance or noise (Vansledright, 2012) between and among accounts of events that constitute the historical record. Like historians, students must ask: Who are the actors and their purposes for creating an account? Teachers and students often use a KWL to support this work, for it helps learners tease apart and keep track of current understandings, what various texts assert, and where there is agreement and disagreement about some aspect of the topic.

It's not difficult to gather texts that provide strikingly different takes on historical events and figures. Source documents, readily available via the Internet, provide differing views and accounts of social phenomena. By dividing the columns into rows for each document examined (and one document might be a textbook), the familiar pattern of know–want/need to know–learned becomes a scaffold to assist students as they begin their thinking work with multiple documents (see Figure 5-10).

	What I know about the document before reading:	What I need to learn as I read:	What I learned about this document and its author:
Document A			
Document B			
Document C			
Synthesis and conclusions:			

FIGURE 5-10
KWL Adapted for Analysis of Multiple Historical Accounts

Example: Science

Scientists often work back and forth between alphabetic texts and the graphs, charts, and other images that accompany and expand on alphabetic texts (Shanahan & Shanahan, 2008). To help students make sense of these discipline-specific texts and comprehension moves, you can modify a KWL. Doing so is especially helpful to English language learners and any students who struggle with reading. In this example, students work with a single text; their teacher added a column to highlight the role of graphics in the text (see Figure 5-11).

FIGURE 5-11
KWL for Science
Texts With Graphics

Text and page or chapter numbers:			
What I know about this topic:	What I need to know about it:	What I learned from the written text:	What I learned from the graphics or data:
Categories:		Synthesis of text and graphics/data:	

How Do I Use a Modified KWL?

- Decide what the features of the text might be that are particular to the discipline.
- Adapt the KWL chart to emphasize those text features.
- Choose texts that challenge readers but don't overwhelm them. Often, having texts on a topic at several levels of difficulty is helpful.
- Make copies of the KWL chart for each student, or share it digitally, or help students construct their own.
- Ask students to read the text and use the KWL chart to guide their thinking.
- In small groups, or with the whole class, use the students' individually created and modified KWL charts to discuss the standards-based concept that is characterized in the text.

INTO THE CLASSROOM

Seventh Grade—Science

THIS CLASSROOM EXAMPLE ADDRESSES THESE STANDARDS

CCSS.ELA-Literacy.RI.7.8.
Trace and evaluate the argument and specific claims in a text, assessing whether the reasoning is sound and the evidence is relevant and sufficient to support the claims.

CCSS.ELA-Literacy.RI.7.9.
Analyze how two or more authors writing about the same topic shape their presentations of key information by emphasizing different evidence or advancing different interpretations of facts.

CCSS.ELA-Literacy.RST.6–8.7.
Integrate quantitative or technical information expressed in words in a text with a version of that information expressed visually (e.g., in a flowchart, diagram, model, graph, or table).

"How do scientists know what the inside of the Earth looks like if they can't dig deep enough to see it?" wondered Alfonso aloud. Mr. Begay knew this was the perfect question to lead his science class to an understanding of density, a principle that permits scientists to create models of things that are difficult to observe directly, such as the inside of a planet. Students logged onto the class web page using their tablet computers and downloaded their own copies of the science KWL shown in Figure 5-11. Then they clicked the link to the Utah Education Network's *Sci-Ber* text and reviewed the rules for labs they found on the homepage (http://www.uen.org/core/science/sciber/sciber7/rules.shtml).

Introducing It

Students brainstormed in small groups what they knew about density from previous science reading and experiments. Next, they looked at the science objectives for the lesson and the navigation bar of the *Sci-Ber* text to decide what they might need to learn about the concept.

Guided Instruction and Independent Practice

After working together to think through the first two columns, with Mr. Begay's support and modeling, students began reading the text, carrying out the experiments, and discussed what they learned.

Closure

Students still had some questions after completing the reading and experiments. Mr. Begay anticipated this; as you can see in Figure 5-12, he added a section for questions on the organizer. Students worked on a short synthesis of what they learned.

FIGURE 5-12
Modified KWL for Science

How does density affect the Earth?			
What I know about this topic:	**What I need to know about it:**	**What I learned from the written text and experiments:**	**What I learned from the graphics or data:**
• Density has something to do with how heavy something is. • It could be a way to figure out how much the Earth weighs. • X-rays work because bones are more dense than other parts of the body.	• How do scientists use density to make a model of the inside of the Earth? • How do scientists figure out the density of the inside of the Earth if they cannot go there?	• There is a formula for calculating density: density = mass/volume. • If the mass of one object is greater than another, the object will sink. The reverse is also true. • I learned how to calculate density. • More dense objects settle toward the bottom or center of an object that is spinning. • Earthquake waves help scientists figure out the density of different layers.	• The pictures on the page about Earth's structure helped me see how size and mass work together to calculate density. • The interactive visuals that included labels when I hover over words helped me visualize what I would never be able to see with my own eyes.
Questions: I'm still not sure how earthquake waves help scientists calculate the density of the interior of earth. Are mass and weight the same thing?		**Synthesis of text and graphics/data:** The size and the mass of an object determine its density. More dense items work their way toward the bottom while less dense items stay toward the top. Layers of the earth are created this way.	

KWL is predicated on the idea that engaged learners want to know more about the world and the texts they encounter there. What other graphic organizers in this book, and elsewhere, encourage students to engage with text in a way that leads them to want to know more than they currently do? Why do you think so?

When students recognize that they know some things, but they need or want to know more, they tend to want to read to find out what they do not know. They tend toward writing and other expressive communications to share what they have learned, and they want to talk about the ideas they have found and the new questions that have presented themselves as they investigate their learning.

Photo by Thinkstock

GRAPHIC ORGANIZERS SUPPORT STUDENTS' READING PROFICIENCIES

As teachers and students grapple with the staircase of text complexity (Common Core State Standards Initiative, 2010a; Wolsey, Grisham, & Heibert, 2012), the demand that students work with increasingly complex texts means that teachers must show students how to work with texts that often challenge them. Graphic organizers, thoughtfully used, can assist students to make sense of texts that may seem difficult, at first.

NOTE-CARD ORGANIZER

Contributed by Debbie Abilock

THIS ORGANIZER ADDRESSES THESE STANDARDS

CCSS.ELA-Literacy.CCRA.R.1.

Read closely to determine what the text says explicitly and to make logical inferences from it; cite specific textual evidence when writing or speaking to support conclusions drawn from the text.

CCSS.ELA-Literacy.CCRA.R.7.

Integrate and evaluate content presented in diverse media and formats, including visually and quantitatively, as well as in words.

CCSS.ELA-Literacy.WHST.6–8.8.

Gather relevant information from multiple print and digital sources, using search terms effectively; assess the credibility and accuracy of each source; and quote or paraphrase the data and conclusions of others while avoiding plagiarism and following a standard format for citation.

What Is a Note-Card Organizer?

In every discipline there are threshold concepts—ideas that are central to mastery of a subject which, once understood, transform how one understands and thinks within a discipline (Meyer & Land, 2003). One such concept is that writing from one's research is a form of inquiry, an evolving conversation with one's sources that builds toward a synthesis differentiated by purpose and subject. Whether students are analyzing a literary theme, scientific hypothesis, or historical argument, they are better able to comprehend an author's words, reinterpret them in their own voice, arrive at insights, and present their learning when they use a structured note-taking and graphic organization process.

Though there are many possibilities and tools (see Wolsey & Grisham, 2012), we use NoodleTools[1] as an example that shows how graphic organization helps students make sense of the complex texts they encounter when they do research. It provides an integrated, real-time platform both for students' inquiry and for teachers or teams who are monitoring students' progress and offering direct feedback on their evolving work. NoodleTools offers several benefits:

- The author's words are clearly separated from a student's interpretation, analysis, and original ideas.
- Software interventions add "friction," that is, opportunities for deliberative thinking, as well as just-in-time help where problems and misconceptions are likely to arise (Kuhlthau, 2003).
- Feedback from multiple teachers is embedded directly into a student's work.
- Notes and a copy of the digital source are permanently attached to each citation in the bibliography (see Figure 6-1).

Reading

A three-part note card (Figure 6-2) contains a relevant quote which is annotated with highlighting and color coding to assist with close reading and comprehension. To develop voice, deepen analysis, and proactively address plagiarism or "patchwriting" (Howard, 2001a), note cards maintain the visual connection between the author's words and the student's interpretation and original thinking in "My Ideas."

---

1. Debbie Abilock, a former school administrator and school librarian, co-founded and directs the education vision of NoodleTools, Inc., an online platform for teaching academic research.

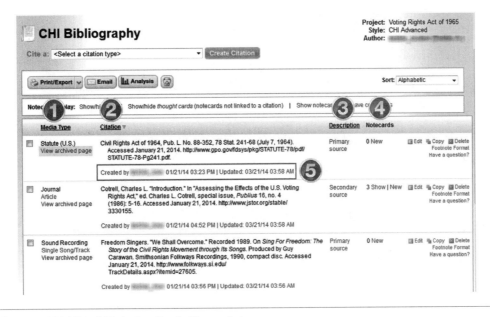

FIGURE 6-1

A working bibliography showing (1) the type of source with a link (highlighted) to the archived copy of the web page or PDF, (2) the citation, (3) classification as primary or secondary source, (4) number of note cards created, and (5) when and by whom the citation was created, which is important for individual accountability in teams.

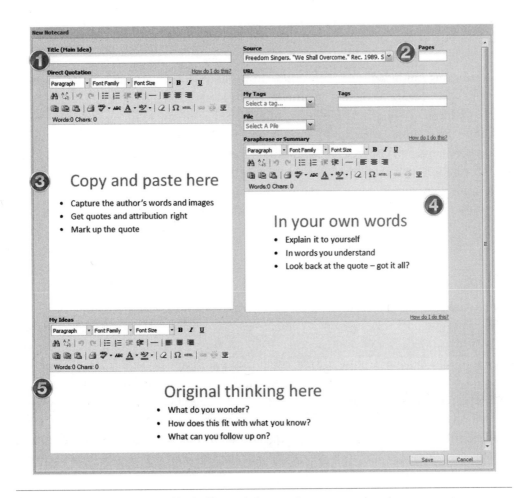

FIGURE 6-2

A note card organizes a student's thinking about extracted information through structured responses: (1) main idea; (2) citation; (3) author's words; (4) student's summary, paraphrase, or bullet-point notes, and (5) response.

FIGURE 6-3

Annotation can scaffold
close reading for
comprehension and
analysis.

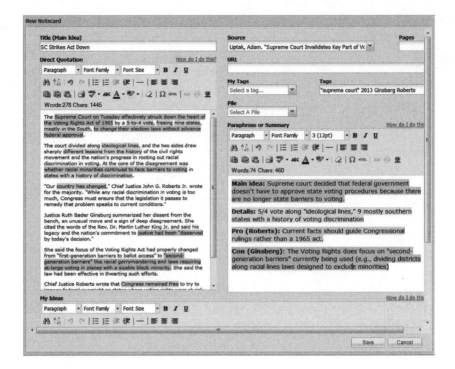

Source: ©2014 NoodleTools, Inc. Used with permission.

Note cards can be annotated for different reasons: to read closely in order to iden-tify the main idea and details, a process that assists deeper comprehension (Figure 6-2); to locate claims, evidence, or counterclaims for an argument (Figure 6-3); to gauge the strength of an author's endorsement, bias, or point of view by identifying evaluative language (Figure 6-4); to evaluate the strength of the author's endorsement of information or a referenced source (Figure 6-5); to analyze the data or evidence in a visual (e.g., photograph, chart) for its implications (Figure 6-6); or to build voice by responding to a quote from a literary work in advance of consulting secondary criticism (Figure 6-7).

Writing

While students may be able to define plagiarism and cite sources, they can rarely articulate or demonstrate how they insert and combine ideas from multiple sources in preparation for synthesis (McGregor & Streitenberger, 1998; McGregor & Williamson, 2011). The vir-tual note-card tabletop (Figure 6-8), a visual metaphor for a student's desk or floor, is a concrete manifestation of how to experimentally compare and integrate multiple sources of information. Students shift to metacognitive thinking as they decide when and why to tag notes with colors, key words, and visual cues; determine which notes belong together in piles (subtopics); or organize their information in the nodes of a graphic organizer (text structures). Word tags are labels for concepts or themes; icon tags tell the teacher that a

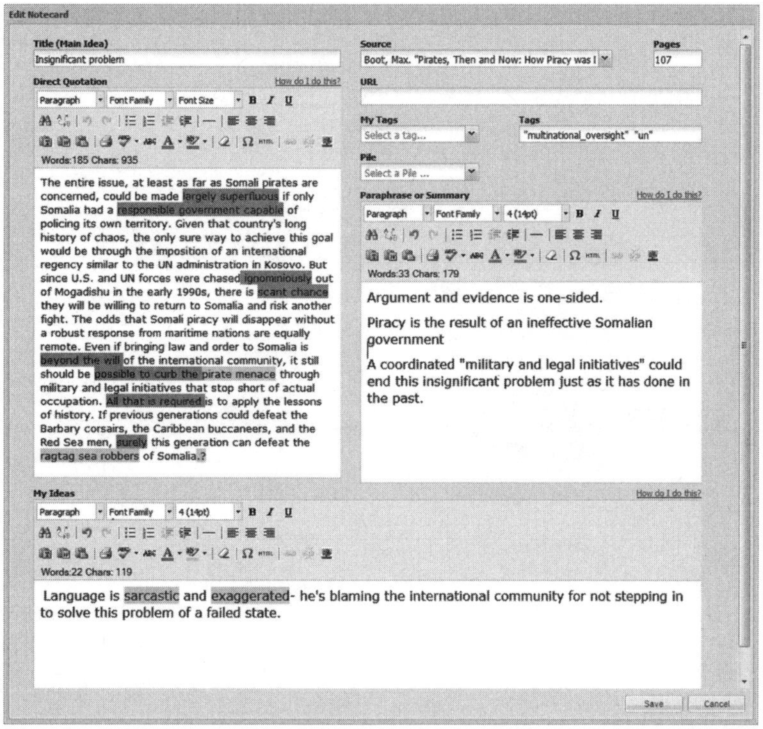

FIGURE 6-4

Annotation can scaffold the identification of tone and bias.

FIGURE 6-5

Annotation can scaffold evaluation of the strength of the author's endorsement of information or a referenced source.

FIGURE 6-6

Annotation can scaffold
visual analysis.

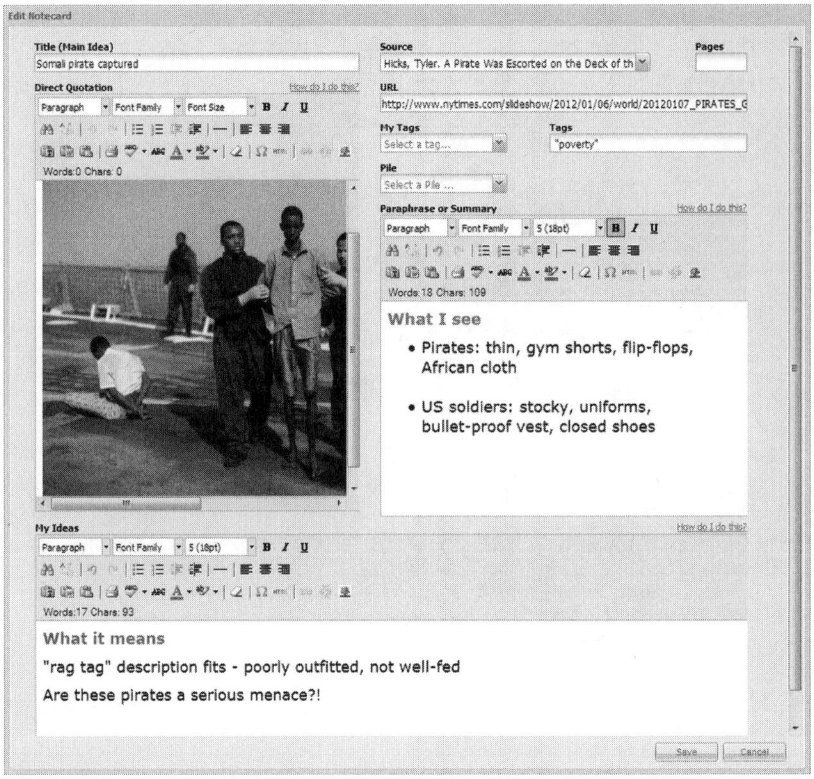

Source: ©2014 NoodleTools, Inc. Used with permission.

FIGURE 6-7

A view of a note card in
the Works Cited list
shows (1) a link to the
source followed by
(2) an analysis of a
quote from a novel.

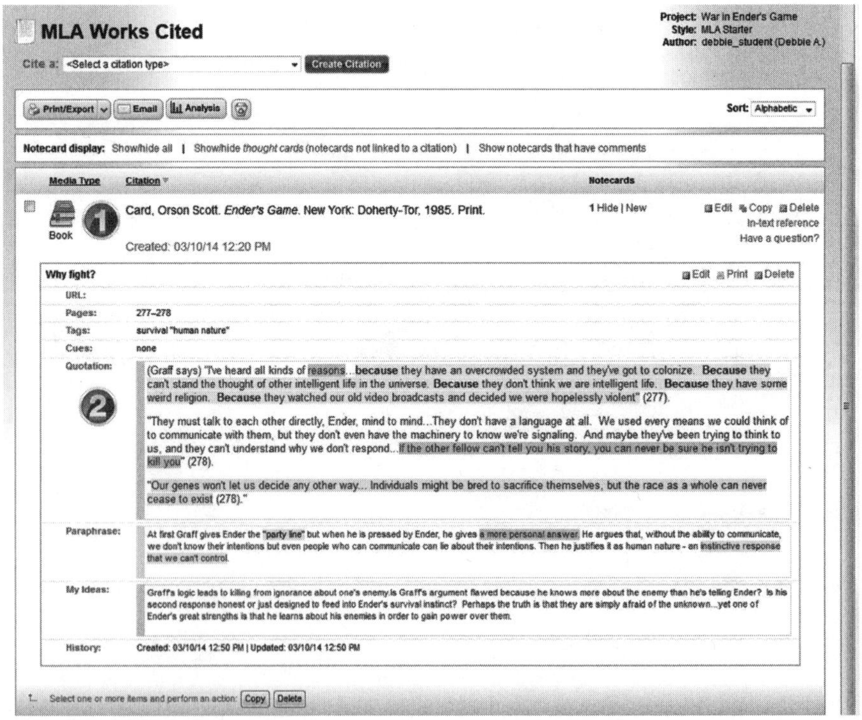

Source: ©2014 NoodleTools, Inc. Used with permission.

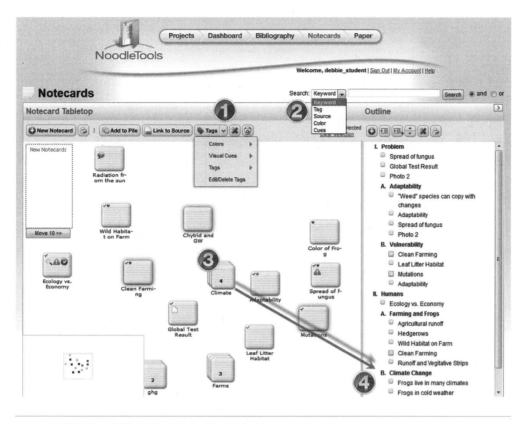

Source: ©2014 NoodleTools, Inc. Used with permission.

FIGURE 6-8

Note cards can be (1) tagged with colors, visual cues, and key words; (2) searched by tags and compared; (3) piled by subtopics; and (4) moved into an outline or graphic organizer.

note is incomplete or a self-selected example of one's best work, or that the student needs help; and colored-dot tags represent individually created attributes (e.g., green or red for pro or con arguments; blue or yellow for strong or weak evidence) that will prove useful when sifting and sorting evidence. Since students' metacomprehension accuracy improves through tagging and piling, teachers should permit students to delay key word labeling until their knowledge of the subject improves (Thiede, Dunlosky, Griffin, & Wiley, 2005).

Credibility (e.g., believable, expert, objective, reliable, trustworthy) varies by discipline, purpose, and audience; it is a result of a series of contextualized judgment calls (Hilligoss & Rieh, 2008). As students create citations in NoodleTools, embedded information-literacy modules suggest differentiated ways to evaluate sources by type, in contrast to static checklists which epitomize a formulaic approach to evaluation (Kimmel, 2005; Meola, 2004). Gathering and sifting notes evokes nuanced judgments as students compare the strength of their sources in relation to their subject and the purpose of their inquiry. Aligned with this, teachers' formative feedback on note cards and citations, drawn from a comment bank (or created on the fly), offers concrete strategies for improvement (Figure 6-9).

As students move from analysis toward synthesis, they map ideas to one or more graphic organizers (e.g., claims and evidence, cause/effect, compare and contrast, problem/solution) that match the structure of their information and their rhetorical purpose. Recognizing that their writing is a conversation among their sources from which they will gain authority from their readers (Gaipa, 2004), students craft their outline as a "function diagram" (Abilock, 2014)—a visual synthesis of this dialogue (Figure 6-10). The student's version should be specific to the topic, sources, and purpose of the product.

Quotation:	A Salinas Valley grower who requested anonymity because of contract negotiations with processors called the current situation "extremely touchy, with the people who put their names on produce bags having the most to lose. One association with a pathogen and they can lose their brand."
Paraphrase:	When E coli contamination caused sales to fall quickly - a grower might decide to sacrifice habitat renewal efforts to reestablish trust with the company he sells to and stay in business.
My Ideas:	When people got sick, nobody bought any spinach - even brands that weren't named. All farmers might give up habitat renewal efforts because they fear the loss of trust!
History:	Created by: damon_student (Damon Abilock) on 05/28/12 08:50 PM	Updated: 08/07/13 01:00 PM

Notecard Comments

New Your quote is important : This quote highlights the importance of addressing economic issues related to frog decline
Mr. Abilock (03/11/14 10:36 AM PST)
Delete Comment

New Tags are missing or too general : Tags are labels for people, places, organizations, and ideas you may want to group together and think about later.

Tags are smaller concepts than the main idea in your title and may become a subtopic later. You can search on tags to find new patterns, themes or connection.

Use our SOAPSTone (Speaker, Occasion, Audience, Purpose, Subject, Tone) to decide what tags you might apply.

If you cannot add tags, add the visual cue "Need help" and we can look at it together.
Mr. Abilock (03/11/14 10:36 AM PST)
Delete Comment

Source: ©2014 NoodleTools, Inc. Used with permission.

B   B

Compare and contrast to settle a dispute

C   C

Describe and piggyback   D

A   A

Outline the sequence and pick a fight

A

Weighing and weaving a conversation

Source: ©2014 NoodleTools, Inc. Used with permission.

How Do I Use a Note-Card Organizer?

• Draw and explain a model of "weighing and weaving a conversation" specific to the rhetorical style (history position paper, book review, newspaper article, etc.) students will use. Explain that their function diagram will map the way they use their sources and their own ideas.

- Ask students to read through the sources they have gathered about their topic to build background knowledge, to identify common knowledge, to notice how subject experts communicate, and to provisionally identify their most important source.

- Tell students that before they take any notes they should create a working bibliography for the first round of sources. If they decide not to use some of them, they can be moved into a "Works Consulted" list. Conversely, they should expect to add sources later, when they identify gaps or generate new questions.

- Explain that creating citations can help them pre-evaluate a source's usefulness and credibility. For example, as they fill out the citation form for a source, when they locate the publisher, they should ask themselves why that organization is distributing this information. Similarly, when they locate the publication date, they should ask themselves if currency is important for their topic. In NoodleTools a "List Analysis" assembles information on such criteria for an entire bibliography and prompts for self-evaluation.

- After students complete this preliminary reading, require them to take notes on their most important source first. While this may appear counterintuitive, it means they will grapple with central ideas immediately, experiencing research as inquiry rather than as a stockpiling of facts. Instruct students to read through the source once again, copying and pasting relevant chunks of text into individual note cards.

- Since annotating and summarizing a quote requires critical thinking and tenacity (and will be worthy of your time and feedback), assign this process selectively for only the most important sources. Explain that while a key source is rich and valuable, it is usually challenging to understand at first. This rationale for close reading and annotation makes sense to students, and your acknowledgment of their likely effort will motivate them to persevere.

- Most often students will summarize the author's main ideas, which involves understanding the text, including its structure and purpose; combining and generalizing, which leads to identifying key ideas and details; and explaining it in their own words. Distribute "How to Summarize a Note-Card Quote in Your Own Words" (www.noodletools.com/debbie/ethical) and, using a chunk of text they are likely to encounter, think aloud as you annotate it for a particular purpose. Encourage students to choose (and even modify) annotation strategies to match the structure of the quoted text and their purpose.

- Explain "My Ideas" as a parking place for questions or ideas that bubble up, inferences, concerns or problems, and reminders about things to do. This is the place to develop their voice and ownership of ideas that will result in original thinking.

- After students have completed the note cards for this first source, introduce the process of organizing (i.e., piling related notes together in preparation for an outline and graphic organizer). Paper note cards can be grouped into subtopics much as digital note cards are piled on the note-card tabletop.

- Ask students to open one of their piles and look for nouns, data, or concepts which are not necessarily stated in the text but stand out because of the grouping. The digital word tags (key words) they add now can be searched in combination with others later to present a different way of grouping ideas or suggest a new thread to investigate. Acknowledge that this process involves sophisticated thinking, so remind them to add a "need help" icon to a note card when they'd like your advice.

- Finally, reintroduce the function diagram (Figure 6-10) as their roadmap for writing. Unlike "patchwriting," in which hunks of undigested material from one author after another are inserted into paragraph after paragraph, their goal is to weave the voices of several authors with their own into "They say . . . , I say . . ." conversations (Graff & Birkenstein, 2010) within each paragraph. As a visual self-check, they will mark each author's contribution in a different color in their rough draft, which should look like a multi-hued weaving, not a patchwork quilt.

From weighing source credibility through citations to reading closely in order to understand, organize, and develop their own ideas, students grapple with how to express their rich inquiry and insights in their own voice. When you evaluate a student's work, use the annotations, tags, labels, piles, and organizers as "trail markers," culled evidence of how the student has navigated a path toward synthesis. By giving formative feedback on a limited number of note cards taken from a source just beyond a student's independent level of reading, you have put your efforts at the heart of synthesis.

INTO THE CLASSROOM — 11th Grade—History

THIS CLASSROOM EXAMPLE ADDRESSES THESE STANDARDS

CCSS.ELA-Literacy.RH.11–12.7.
Integrate and evaluate multiple sources of information presented in diverse formats and media (e.g., visually, quantitatively, as well as in words) in order to address a question or solve a problem.

CCSS.ELA-Literacy.RI.11–12.1.
Cite strong and thorough textual evidence to support analysis of what the text says explicitly as well as inferences drawn from the text, including determining where the text leaves matters uncertain.

CCSS.ELA-Literacy.RI.11–12.7.
Integrate and evaluate multiple sources of information presented in different media or formats (e.g., visually, quantitatively) as well as in words in order to address a question or solve a problem.

CCSS.ELA-Literacy.W.11–12.1.
Write arguments to support claims in an analysis of substantive topics or texts, using valid reasoning and relevant and sufficient evidence.

CCSS.ELA-Literacy.W.11–12.6.
Use technology, including the Internet, to produce, publish, and update individual or shared writing products in response to ongoing feedback, including new arguments or information.

CCSS.ELA-Literacy.W.11–12.7–9.
Research to build and present knowledge.

Determining the Need

Mrs. Sano's 11th-grade history classes participated in the National History Contest (www.nhd.org) along with more than half a million students each year. She and Mr. Cardoza, the school librarian, collaboratively mentored individuals and teams in choosing a question of significance, conducting extensive primary and secondary research, extracting notes from multiple sources, analyzing and comparing their sources, and drawing conclusions about the importance of their topic in history.

Introducing It

Mr. Cardoza helped students find and evaluate sources and provided feedback on the required *Chicago Manual of Style* citations, often used by historians. Mrs. Sano focused on historical thinking and reasoning and commented on students' note cards and organization.

Guided Instruction and Independent Practice

In multidisciplinary projects such as capstone or senior projects, or International Baccalaureate extended essays, teachers ask students to tag note cards *math, science, English,* or *history* so that members of the collaborating team can find and give feedback on the appropriate subset of note cards. Next, students use the online resources in their school's digital library (look ahead to Figure 8-3 on page 135 for examples of online resources for student research). They use the note-card digital organizer to gather their thoughts and work toward a synthesis of their research. Each student team selects a format for presenting their work from the NHD website and finishes their entries. As students work in groups, teachers have many opportunities to assess their developing understandings. When it appears that an individual or small groups of students are not comprehending a particular dimension of the task or information within the text, additional guided instruction in the form of reteaching, prompting, and questioning can provide the immediate intervention needed to support continued learning.

Closure

NHD students present their original papers, exhibits, performances, or documentaries accompanied by a Works Cited list at a series of local, state, and national competitions in the spring, where they are evaluated by professional historians and educators.

TABBED BOOK MANIPULATIVE

CCSS.ELA-Literacy.CCRA.R.1.

Read closely to determine what the text says explicitly and to make logical inferences from it; cite specific textual evidence when writing or speaking to support conclusions drawn from the text.

CCSS.ELA-Literacy.CCRA.R.5.

Analyze the structure of texts, including how specific sentences, paragraphs, and larger portions of the text (e.g., a section, chapter, scene, or stanza) relate to each other and the whole.

CCSS.ELA-Literacy.CCRA.W.4.

Produce clear and coherent writing in which the development, organization, and style are appropriate to task, purpose, and audience.

What Is a Tabbed Book Manipulative?

FIGURE 6-11

Example of a Tabbed Book Manipulative

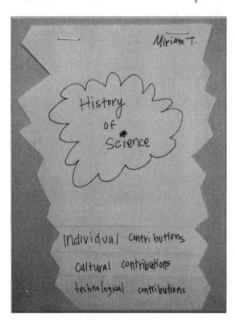

The manipulative strategy guide is both a manipulative guide and a graphic organizer (Wood, Lapp, Flood, & Taylor, 2008). This type of foldable or manipulative guide is described as a "3D, student made, interactive graphic organizer" (Zike, n.d., p. 1). A tabbed book is a version of a foldable guide that can be used to create any sort of book (see Figure 6-11). It can be used to create books or used as a graphic organizer to display information. It is easy to manipulate because of the tabbed edges.

Example: Science

Tenth-grade curriculum often calls for students to study the history of science as a human endeavor. Students could use a tabbed book to demonstrate their understanding of this information. On the first tab, students could summarize how individuals contribute to scientific knowledge. On the second tab, students could explain how culture contributes to scientific knowledge. And on the third tab students could explain how technology contributes to scientific knowledge. In this example, there are three big ideas, but teachers (and students!) can easily adjust the number of tabs from this manipulative guide as needed by removing or adding pages.

How Do My Students Create a Tabbed Book?

1. Collect several pieces of 8½ × 11 paper. We have noticed that students seem to like colored copy paper for activities such as this.
2. Fold the stack in half lengthwise.
3. Staple together to form a book.
4. Starting with the front of the book, cut overlapping pieces so a tab is left on each page.
5. Add labels to address the instructional purpose.

CCSS.ELA-Literacy.RI.9–10.2.

Determine a central idea of a text and analyze its development over the course of the text, including how it emerges and is shaped and refined by specific details; provide an objective summary of the text.

CCSS.ELA-Literacy.SL.9–10.1.c.

Propel conversations by posing and responding to questions that relate the current discussion to broader themes or larger ideas; actively incorporate others into the discussion; and clarify, verify, or challenge ideas and conclusions.

CCSS.ELA-Literacy.SL.9–10.4.

Present information, findings, and supporting evidence clearly, concisely, and logically such that listeners can follow the line of reasoning and the organization, development, substance, and style are appropriate to purpose, audience, and task.

CCSS.ELA-Literacy.SL.9–10.5.

Make strategic use of digital media (e.g., textual, graphical, audio, visual, and interactive elements) in presentations to enhance understanding of findings, reasoning, and evidence and to add interest.

CCSS.ELA-Literacy.SL.9–10.6.

Adapt speech to a variety of contexts and tasks, demonstrating command of formal English when indicated or appropriate.

THIS CLASSROOM EXAMPLE ADDRESSES THESE STANDARDS

Determining the Need

Mrs. Hollander, a 10th-grade world history teacher, wanted her students to summarize a complex article on democratic ideals. While planning the lesson, she noticed that the article put forth five big ideas: the rule of law, limited government, due process of law, individual liberty, and consent of the governed. Mrs. Hollander selected a tabbed book graphic organizer to help students understand relationships among the main points of the text and to give them a place to record notes that would later be used for a discussion and extended writing assignment.

Introducing It

Using several pieces of paper and a stapler, Mrs. Hollander modeled for students how to make the tabbed book manipulative guide. She explained that because she wanted them to take away five big ideas from the reading, three pieces of paper were needed. Once the manipulative guide was made, Mrs. Hollander modeled how she would think aloud about the main ideas from the reading and summarize the information from the first section. She emphasized the importance of writing notes about what the text says, what it means, and why the information matters:

> Okay, I've just read this first chunk of text and I am trying to figure out what this text is saying about the rule of law. The text is saying that the government shall be

carried out according to established laws. I'm wondering, who is bound by these laws? Let me keep reading so I can pull this information out of the text and add it to my tabbed book.

Mrs. Hollander modeled her thinking about how to summarize important information and also showed students how to use the tabbed book for note-taking.

Guided Instruction and Independent Practice

After modeling with the first section of the text, Mrs. Hollander released the responsibility to her students. She asked them to work with a partner to summarize the next section of the text, reminding them to pay careful attention to what the text said and meant and why this information mattered. While students worked, Mrs. Hollander circulated, prompting, raising questions, and offering clarifications when needed.

For example, when she heard Antonio and Diana, two English-only speakers, expressing confusion about exactly what the "due process of law" meant she pointed to an earlier section of the text that explained that the Fifth Amendment's reference to "due process" was one of many promises of protection offered to citizens. As these students reread this section Diana said, "Oh, I see. This means the government can't interfere with your rights to life, liberty, and property." Antonio added, "Yeah, without following rules, like giving you a lawyer." As they continued their discussion, Mrs. Hollander moved to other partners, offering supports as needed.

Once she was confident that her students understood the process of using this graphic organizer, Mrs. Hollander encouraged them to continue working together as partners to finish their reading and note-making. Each tab was designed for a different section of text (see Figure 6-12) and students became thoughtful readers and critical thinkers because they slowed their reading down, attending to main ideas and summarizing along the way. Their conversations with their partners also supported their use of both academic language and the content language related to the topic.

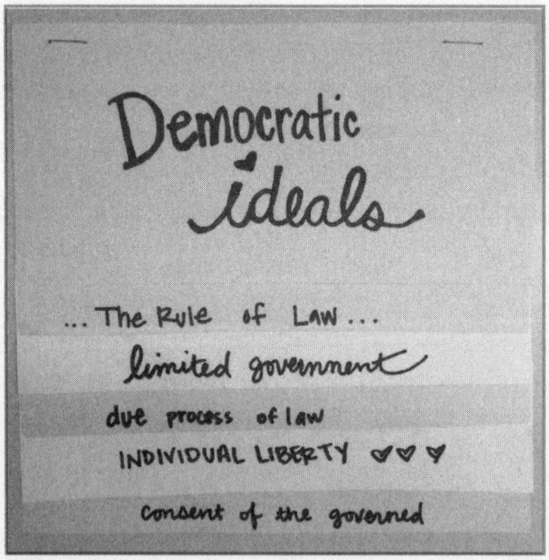

FIGURE 6-12
Students use a tabbed book to build on their thinking about the text in social studies.

Closure

Once partners created and completed their tabbed books, they worked with a different set of partners to share information. As these new groups collaborated, students added and modified information as their knowledge about the democratic ideals grew.

Reading, Writing, and Discussion Extensions

Tabbed books are an excellent note-making tool during reading and as a guide during related writing experiences. Build in peer work so that the organizers provide a basis for discussion, too. This type of organizer can easily be used in other content areas. Once students understand the process of using this graphic organizer, they can easily create variations of it as they read across the disciplines.

SOMEBODY-WANTED-BUT-SO

Contributed by Brian Williams

CCSS.ELA-Literacy.CCRA.R.2.

Determine central ideas or themes of a text and analyze their development; summarize the key supporting details and ideas.

CCSS.ELA-Literacy.CCRA.SL.4.

Present information, findings, and supporting evidence such that listeners can follow the line of reasoning and the organization, development, and style are appropriate to task, purpose, and audience.

THIS ORGANIZER ADDRESSES THESE STANDARDS

Somebody (Characters)	
Wanted (Plot motivation)	
But (Conflict)	
So (Resolution)	

FIGURE 6-13
Somebody-Wanted-But-So

What Is a Somebody-Wanted-But-So Graphic Organizer?

The somebody-wanted-but-so (Macon, Bewell, & Vogt, 1991) graphic organizer (Figure 6-13) is a template that invites students to summarize a lengthy piece of literature in one or two sentences. The words *somebody, wanted, but,* and *so* guide students to zero in on the central plot elements that drive a fiction or nonfiction narrative. *Somebody* prompts students to name the protagonist (and other main characters), *wanted* prompts them to identify the want or need that compels the character(s), *but* reminds students that in any good story there is an obstacle or some kind of conflict impeding the character from having his or her need met. (In many works of literature, the conflict can be an internal one, such as a character struggling to trust others after a parent abandons the family.) *So* signals to students that the tension and conflict rises to a high point but then resolves. Somebody-wanted-but-so helps students describe the basic chronological development of the story, which in a sense gives them the clear-headedness to mine the text for deeper meanings.

Students often use this organizer to help them look at the quest of the protagonist, but it can also be a helpful frame for them to think about another character who may advance the *but*—a character who may want something counter to what the main character wants, creating the story's dramatic tension. In this light, the template is a terrific tool to use in studying nonfiction texts, because often in history, famous figures are going up against—or inspiring—other famous figures, from rival military generals, to scientists pursuing the same cure, to rival sports heroes. And in every content area, even when it's not full-tilt rivalry, there are interesting affinities that somebody-wanted-but-so can help unearth. For example, in art history, the association of painters Edgar Degas and Mary Cassatt could be explored, or a painter like Thomas Eakins, who *wanted* recognition *but* was at first rebuffed by established norms *so* never received the renown he deserved in his own lifetime. In science, Tesla versus Edison is the most well known, but other illuminating rivalries abound (see below for more content area ideas).

How Do I Use a Somebody-Wanted-But-So Graphic Organizer?

- Review the literary terms *characters, plot motivation, conflict,* and *resolution.*
- Read aloud a short story to students or have them read in groups or independently.
- On large paper or on the board, model your thinking while filling out the somebody-wanted-but-so graphic organizer.
- Model converting the completed graphic organizer into a one- or two-sentence summary.
- On another day, give students a new short story and template.
- Allow students to complete a new template in pairs.
- Review answers to the new template.
- Instruct students to read the lesson's main text, and allow them to complete the graphic organizer independently.

In other content areas, whenever there is a narrative involved, the organizer can play a role in supporting students' understanding of what they read. Let's look at math and social studies.

Example: Math

Word problems in story format are a type of text that often befuddles students. By using the somebody-wanted-but-so template, students can break down a word problem in a manner that is comprehensible to them (see Figure 6-14).

FIGURE 6-14
Somebody-Wanted-But-So Math Example

Somebody (Characters)	John
Wanted (Plot motivation)	$20 to attend the upcoming theatrical performance
But (Conflict)	He did not have any money.
So (Resolution)	He cut 2 lawns at $10 each, totaling the needed $20 to attend the show.

Summary Sentence

John **wanted** $20 to attend the upcoming theatrical performance, **but** he did not have any money, **so** he cut 2 lawns at $10 each, totaling the needed $20 to attend the show.

Example: History

History is the story of us. All of us. Life is narrative—one big somebody-wanted-but-so journey. And let's face it, you don't wind up famous and in the history books unless you beat out some incredible *but*. So it makes sense that this graphic organizer lends itself so well to studying historical figures and events. To summarize a historical event through the eyes of *somebody*, students may use this template to get at the essence of the event. For example, students who have just read a text about Abraham Lincoln and the problems associated with putting an end to slavery might construct an organizer like the one in Figure 6-15.

Somebody (Characters)	Abraham Lincoln
Wanted (Plot motivation)	To end slavery
But (Conflict)	He knew that ending slavery was limited by the Constitution.
So (Resolution)	He created and signed the Emancipation Proclamation to free slaves in 10 states not under Union control.

FIGURE 6-15
Somebody-Wanted-But-So History Example

Summary Sentence

Abraham Lincoln **wanted** to end slavery, **but** he knew that ending slavery was limited by the Constitution, **so** he created and signed the Emancipation Proclamation to free slaves in 10 states not under Union control.

INTO THE CLASSROOM — Ninth Grade—Literature

CCSS.ELA-Literacy.RL.9–10.2.
Determine a theme or central idea of a text and analyze in detail its development over the course of the text, including how it emerges and is shaped and refined by specific details; provide an objective summary of the text.

CCSS.ELA-Literacy.SL.9–10.4.
Present information, findings, and supporting evidence clearly, concisely, and logically such that listeners can follow the line of reasoning and the organization, development, substance, and style are appropriate to purpose, audience, and task.

THIS CLASSROOM EXAMPLE ADDRESSES THESE STANDARDS

Determining the Need

Mrs. Merritt's ninth-grade literature class was reading the novel *Miss Peregrine's Home for Peculiar Children*, by Ransom Riggs (2011), as part of their examination of character development. Mrs. Merritt wanted her students to focus on Jacob's development throughout the novel and to journal his progression into the dynamic character he becomes. Since this was their initial experience with honing in on how characters evolve, she decided to provide explicit introductory instruction.

Guided Instruction and Independent Practice

Mrs. Merritt began by discussing how to apply the somebody-wanted-but-so strategy to the first three chapters. She explained that they would be looking at Jacob as their somebody and then focus on the plot, the conflict, and the solution to the conflict. She modeled how she used the organizer with Chapter 1 and invited students to comment and raise questions. Next, she provided time for students to read the first three chapters independently, using the organizer to jot down notes as they read. As they did so, Mrs. Merritt observed their work and provided additional instruction as needed.

The next day, Mrs. Merritt asked students to complete the organizer using evidence from the chapters. Once they finished, she put them in pairs to discuss their summary sentence/conclusions about the first three chapters. Students' take on Jacob differed throughout the process, and Mrs. Merritt encouraged discussion about what accounted for these different, sometimes conflicting points of view. Was it because the author created a realistically complex character? Provided several points of view on Jacob? Were the students' divergent conclusions reflective of the fact that Jacob changed in the course of three chapters?

Mrs. Merritt called the class together for everyone to share their summary sentence of the first three chapters. Together they drafted a class summary sentence (see Figure 6-16). The class came away from this experience with an easy guide for looking into the character dynamics of the main character. As they continued to read the novel, they had a keen awareness of the importance of noticing what propelled Jacob to think and behave as he did. Mrs. Merritt planned to have students use the organizer in subsequent chapters as well.

Reading, Writing, and Discussion Extensions

After reading, students might compare their somebody-wanted-but-so summaries with others to note similarities or differences. Often, in writing, students must summarize narrative sources, and this organizer helps students think through the summary process in a succinct way.

FIGURE 6-16

Somebody-Wanted-But-So Literature Example

Somebody (Characters)	Jacob
Wanted (Plot motivation)	To find his place as a 16-year-old in his family, his school, and his job which he hates
But (Conflict)	His senile grandfather calls him claiming he sees monsters. Jacob discovers his grandfather dead and sees monsters fleeing.
So (Resolution)	Jacob has nightmares and sees a doctor who tells him he should take a trip with his family to recover.
Summary	
Jacob, a 16-year-old outsider, witnesses his grandfather's death by monster-like creatures. He begins to have nightmares and sees a specialist who recommends a trip with his family. Jacob is scared and confused.	

Source: Contributed by Brian Williams.

UNDERSTANDING TEXT STRUCTURES: FIVE TEXT TYPES

THESE ORGANIZERS ADDRESS THESE STANDARDS

CCSS.ELA-Literacy.CCRA.R.5.

Analyze the structure of texts, including how specific sentences, paragraphs, and larger portions of the text (e.g., a section, chapter, scene, or stanza) relate to each other and the whole.

CCSS.ELA-Literacy.CCRA.R.8.

Delineate and evaluate the argument and specific claims in a text, including the validity of the reasoning as well as the relevance and sufficiency of the evidence.

In Figure 6-17, notice the progression from Grades 7 through 12 for anchor standards R.5 and R.8:

7th Grade	CCSS.ELA-Literacy.RI.7.2. Determine two or more central ideas in a text and analyze their development over the course of the text; provide an objective summary of the text.
	CCSS.ELA-Literacy.RI.7.5. Analyze the structure an author uses to organize a text, including how the major sections contribute to the whole and to the development of the ideas.
	CCSS.ELA-Literacy.RI.7.7. Compare and contrast a text to an audio, video, or multimedia version of the text, analyzing each medium's portrayal of the subject (e.g., how the delivery of a speech affects the impact of the words).
	CCSS.ELA-Literacy.W.7.2.a. Introduce a topic clearly, previewing what is to follow; organize ideas, concepts, and information, using strategies such as definition, classification, comparison/contrast, and cause/effect; include formatting (e.g., headings), graphics (e.g., charts, tables), and multimedia when useful to aiding comprehension.
	CCSS.ELA-Literacy.W.7.4. Produce clear and coherent writing in which the development, organization, and style are appropriate to task, purpose, and audience. (Grade-specific expectations for writing types are defined in standards 1–3 above.)
8th Grade	CCSS.ELA-Literacy.RI.8.2. Determine a central idea of a text and analyze its development over the course of the text, including its relationship to supporting ideas; provide an objective summary of the text.
	CCSS.ELA-Literacy.W.8.2.a. Introduce a topic clearly, previewing what is to follow; organize ideas, concepts, and information into broader categories; include formatting (e.g., headings), graphics (e.g., charts, tables), and multimedia when useful to aiding comprehension.
	CCSS.ELA-Literacy.W.8.4. Produce clear and coherent writing in which the development, organization, and style are appropriate to task, purpose, and audience.
9th–10th Grade	CCSS.ELA-Literacy.RI.9-10.2. Determine a central idea of a text and analyze its development over the course of the text, including how it emerges and is shaped and refined by specific details; provide an objective summary of the text.
	CCSS.ELA-Literacy.RI.9-10.3. Analyze how the author unfolds an analysis or series of ideas or events, including the order in which the points are made, how they are introduced and developed, and the connections that are drawn between them.
	CCSS.ELA-Literacy.W.9-10.2.a. Introduce a topic; organize complex ideas, concepts, and information to make important connections and distinctions; include formatting (e.g., headings), graphics (e.g., figures, tables), and multimedia when useful to aiding comprehension.
	CCSS.ELA-Literacy.W.9-10.4. Produce clear and coherent writing in which the development, organization, and style are appropriate to task, purpose, and audience.

FIGURE 6-17

Understanding Text Structures and the Common Core State Standards

(Continued)

FIGURE 6-17
(Continued)

11th–12th Grade	CCSS.ELA-Literacy.RI.11-12.2. Determine two or more central ideas of a text and analyze their development over the course of the text, including how they interact and build on one another to provide a complex analysis; provide an objective summary of the text.
	CCSS.ELA-Literacy.RI.11-12.3. Analyze a complex set of ideas or sequence of events and explain how specific individuals, ideas, or events interact and develop over the course of the text.
	CCSS.ELA-Literacy.W.11-12.2. Write informative/explanatory texts to examine and convey complex ideas, concepts, and information clearly and accurately through the effective selection, organization, and analysis of content.
	CCSS.ELA-Literacy.W.11-12.4. Produce clear and coherent writing in which the development, organization, and style are appropriate to task, purpose, and audience.

In the elementary grades, students thoroughly learn the top-level text structures found in this chapter. If you are interested in seeing some examples, visit **www.corwin.com/miningcomplextext/6-12** to find a chart showing the progression from first through fifth grades in the Common Core (Common Core State Standards Initiative, 2010b). However, new, more complex texts require students in the middle grades and in high school to continue attending to these and examining the nuances as they work with and create more complex texts. Of course, these ideas translate nicely to the written and multimodal compositions students will create as well. In Figure 6-17, note the progression of skills from Grade 7 through Grade 12 in these selected reading and writing standards. You will also see some consistency from grade level to grade level even as students are expected to read and write increasingly complex texts. Later in this chapter, we will show you some examples that ask students to apply the cognitive skills these text structures imply across texts and experiences.

Sequential, Descriptive, Cause/Effect, Compare and Contrast, Problem/Solution

FIGURE 6-18 Sequential

FIGURE 6-19 Descriptive

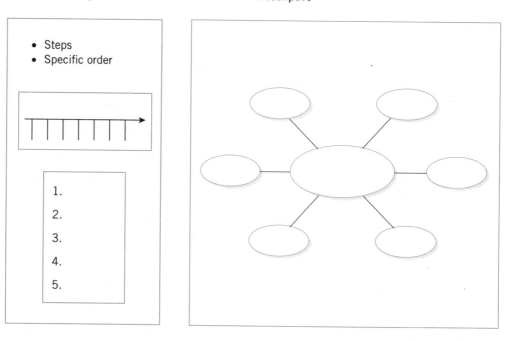

FIGURE 6-20 Cause/Effect

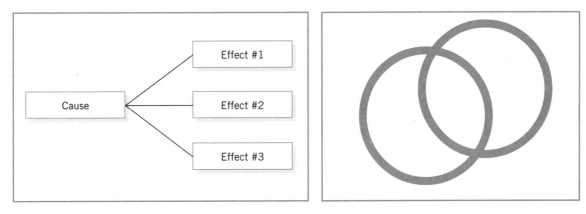

FIGURE 6-21 Compare and Contrast

What Are Text Structures?

Students sometimes struggle with top-level structures that authors use to organize their texts. Five commonly recognized text structures are sequential, descriptive, cause/effect, compare-contrast, and problem/solution (see Figures 6-18 to 6-22) (Akhondi, Malayeri, & Samad, 2011). Earlier work (Meyer, Brandt, & Bluth, 1980) suggested similar categories: stories, description, antecendent [sic]/consequent, problem/solution, and comparison (argumentative text; p. 98). Meyer et al. (1980) found that signaling could also help students identify the structure of the text; for example, when descriptive top-level structures tended to signal this pattern by using terms throughout the text simi-

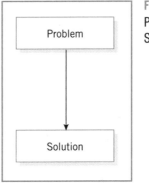

FIGURE 6-22
Problem/
Solution

lar *for example* and *such as.* Top-level patterns that rely on the sequential mode may use terms such as *first, second, third, next,* and *after that.* When they are able to recognize the top-level pattern, often when a signal indicates what the top level may be, effective readers are more able to relate concepts to that structure and attend more completely to the ideas rather than simply noting facts they encounter in a linear manner as they read.

Why are these patterns called top-level structures? Well, because few writers stick to just one pattern. Though a piece may be written as problem/solution in general, it also might include compare and contrast, descriptive, and narration, for example. Graphic organizers can help students see the top-level domains. And for complex texts, graphic organizers are flexible enough to help students attend to signal words and notice additional text structures beyond the top level. A text may begin with a problem/solution as the top-level structure, but it also may include descriptive and compare-and-contrast elements, for example. Also, once students are familiar with graphic organizers for different purposes, teachers can encourage students to construct their own graphic organizers and choose the types that best fit with their purposes for writing.

As writers, students may not set out with the purpose of writing a descriptive essay, but when they encounter a task that calls for description, they will be able to identify the pattern they need and use a graphic organizer to help them plan. The student-created graphic organizers that are based on these top-level structures are powerful planning tools.

Sequential

Much knowledge is organized in a sequential manner, with one event or element following another. Later in this book, we explore other common text and knowledge production patterns, but knowledge presented sequentially is worth a bit of extra time. Processes, such as how waves form or move or how archaeologists excavate a site, can be intricate. Timelines can give students a sense of historical events or some types of processes and how the elements relate to each other. Graphic organizers make it possible for students to comprehend complex processes or events through any of the language and visual arts: Reading, writing, speaking, listening, visualization. Sequential organizers might include processes (think flow chart) or sequences of events (think timeline). Moreover, they have the potential to cut across standards. For that reason, this section does not list any anchor standards, but the following lessons will.

Processing is a term we encounter often when we press a submit button on a web page. But what are processes? In some ways, they differ from products, the things that result from a process. For example, we authors have a process we have evolved over the years that resulted in this book. Waves at sea are evidence of a natural process. Food is preserved following established processes. And your favorite online retailer uses specific processes to ensure that your products arrive at your door in a timely way. Mathematicians use processes or procedures, known as algorithms, for solving certain types of problems (e.g., Ives, 2007; Ives & Hoy, 2003), and your computer processes information according to a very specific, but complicated process. Some processes are straightforward while others are more complicated. Whatever the process is, if it is new or unfamiliar to students, graphic organizers can help them understand it.

Timelines are sequential organizers that permit students to understand how events unfold over time. A variety of timeline formats help students think about how events occur over fixed or regular intervals (a second, a year, a decade, and so on). Gallavan and Kottler (2010) show how timelines can help students understand patterns and positions over time. In their example, students compare the life of King Henry VIII with other events in Europe and then further compare his life with current times. Henry VIII, for instance, was born in 1491, just one year before Columbus sailed for what we now think of as the Western Hemisphere. By putting his life in the context of an event students know well (Columbus's first voyage), they can make connections and notice patterns.

When students recognize how texts are organized, the cognitive load required to determine that pattern is reduced, allowing them to focus more on what they can gather from the text and its structure. Graphic organizers can be an important tool that may help students notice that texts do, in fact, have a structure. And the more quickly they understand that structure, the more they increase the possibility of understanding what they are reading, including and going beyond that text structure (Akhondi et al., 2011).

Descriptive

"Can you describe that pizza?" he asked. "Sure," I replied, "that pizza was fantastic and the most delicious I've ever ordered. It was off the hook." As an endorsement, if you know me and what I like in pizza, this might suffice as a general description. To us, description seems to demand a bit more in academic contexts, however. Description asks readers to allow themselves to be transported outside themselves to realms about which they know little. Description permits us, when we read, to believe we are riding with Eleanor of Aquitaine on the second crusade. Description gives us a license to be, for a time, a professional tennis player (see Wallace, 1997) as we read about the sport. Description leads us to sense how the bread in the oven might taste just from the words alone.

Ray Bradbury, like many good authors, had a sense of description that brought his readers into the story. In *Something Wicked This Way Comes*, Bradbury (1962) does far more than say his two protagonists ran to the library. Come along with Will and Jim in Bradbury's words on their way to the local library:

> Like all boys, they never walked anywhere, but named a goal and lit for it, scissors and elbows. Nobody wanted to win. It was in their friendship they just wanted to run forever, shadow and shadow. Their hands slapped library door handles together, their chests broke track tapes together, their tennis shoes beat parallel pony tracks over lawns, trimmed bushes, squirreled trees, no one losing, both winning, thus saving friendship for another time of loss. (p. 10)

As you read Bradbury's words, you can see Will and Jim running after a question they believe they will find behind the library doors, and you feel their friendship that will carry them to the end of the story many pages later. By the time you finish the paragraph above, you probably find yourself hooked, as a reader, wanting to follow the story and the mystery in the novel. Description captures in words what our senses know intuitively. It leads readers to worlds and experiences, fictional and real, beyond their own experiences, igniting senses and emotions more specific than general.

Aristotle cautioned speakers (and we can apply the concepts to written work as well) to call things by their own special names and to avoid ambiguity (*Rhetoric*, book 3, part 5). That pizza we mentioned? If the reader or listener cannot tell the difference between the combination pizza at Two Pizza Guys restaurant and the one at The Village Pizza Palace from the written description, there is little value in reading or hearing about it in the first place. What is it that makes you want that Village Pizza over the one from the Pizza Guys anyway? Graphic organizers can help the teacher who wants students to understand the role of description in works of exposition and fiction, write more effectively in either genre, speak to an audience convincingly, or understand the inner workings of the atom.

As with many things, when learners are novices with the content, processes, or culture of academic life, it is possible to overthink or tease out the parts such that the original is no longer recognizable. Graphic organizers have the power to make the parts visible, the thinking evident, the context broken into categories, but this is also a point of caution. If we pull too many threads in the beautiful tapestry, we have nothing more than a pile of colorful thread. Judicious use of graphic organizers to pry the lid from the

FIGURE 6-23
Visual Representations
of Words and Ideas
Online

WordSift: http://wordsift.com

Visual Thesaurus: www.visualthesaurus.com

Wordflex (for iPad): http://wordflex.com

box of description is a means toward thoughtful reading, interesting writing, and engaging speech. Some of our favorite digital tools, which represent ideas and terms visually, are in Figure 6-23.

Effective description often includes some of these features, but not all of them simultaneously:

- implication on the part of the author (and the capacity for inference on the part of the reader)
- judicious use of descriptive words
- possible connection between the known and unknown
- variation and nuance of a topic that is new, underdeveloped, or specialized
- specificity relative to the concept or topic

Description lends itself well to the cluster or bubble format of graphic organizers (Olson, 1996). Clusters allow the user to expand infinitely, to work within a framework that is tightly defined, or to explore potential new connections.

Cause/Effect

Cause/effect patterns are sometimes straightforward. If we put a match next to a wadded-up newspaper, the effect is likely to be a small fire. In other instances, the cause/effect pattern is more complicated. In many ways, cause/effect text patterns are similar to the sequential and process patterns we explored earlier. Cause/effect patterns are typically thought of in terms of events. One event directly leads to and causes another. In some cases, a set of causes may lead to a single event, one cause may lead to a multiplicity of events, one event may conditionally cause another, and so on. You can infer that cause/effect text patterns are rarely as simple as they may first appear.

In addition, it is possible to mistake correlation for cause. If crime rates rise during the summer months, and ice cream sales rise during the summer, it would be incorrect to assume that ice cream consumption causes crime or vice versa. We might look for an underlying cause, however. As you can see, the opportunities to teach students to be careful thinkers about cause and effect are ample. These opportunities include explorations of science topics, historical events, political discussions, and problem/solution.

Herringbone or fishbone diagrams are useful tools for looking at cause and effect with multiple contributing variables. Refer to Figure 2-5 (page 26) for one example, though these can be quite a bit more complex.

Compare and Contrast

Compare and contrast is a common direction given to students. "Compare and contrast the articles in the *New York Times* with the *San Francisco Chronicle* on the recent visit of the President to the drought-stricken west." "Compare and contrast the models of the atom we have discussed this week." And on it goes. But just what does it mean to compare and contrast? The role of analogy is important here. As Gick and Holyoak (1983) remind us, "The analogist notes correspondences between the known problem and a new unsolved one, and on that basis derives an analogous potential solution. More generally, the function of an analogy is to derive a new solution, hypothesis, or prediction" (p. 5). An important key to comparison is that it is all about noting similarity between things. Contrast is all about noting the differences. Overarching all is that the task is not an end unto itself. We could compare and contrast the proverbial apples and oranges, but unless we can identify a purpose for doing so and the attributes that are worth studying, the exercise might be futile.

In compare-and-contrast tasks, students must look at two or more different things, be they concepts, objects, texts, and so on. Then the task becomes one of noting what is common among the items to be compared and what is relevant to the purpose of comparison in the first place. Next, the items to be compared must be contrasted to note what is different about them. The process of determining relevant similarities and distinguishing features comes down to what attributes are important. Teachers may ask students to compare and contrast the characters of Harry Potter and Hermione Granger from the Harry Potter series of books by J. K. Rowling. They may notice that Harry is a boy and Hermione is a girl. Harry has a scar on his forehead and Hermione does not. However, these features may only be superficial to the task of compare and contrast since these are obvious and do not encourage deeper examination of the characters or the text in which they appear. For a useful interactive tool for thinking about compare-and-contrast structures, go to www.readwritethink.org/files/resources/interactives/compcontrast/.

Venn diagrams are popular and useful graphic organizers for compare-and-contrast tasks. They are organizational devices with two or more overlapping circles for charting similarities (comparisons) and differences (contrasts) between characters in a story, ideas explained in an essay or lecture, two opposing points of view, and so on. Students may work individually, with partners, or in groups to examine a text or compose one using the Venn diagram format. The word *Venn* is capitalized because it is named after a famous mathematician who, among other interests, specialized in set theory; some of his work showing how the Venn diagram is used may be found online for free. Students label the diagram with the names of the two entities under analysis. They are shown how to list the elements particular to each entity in the outer parts of the circles. Within the overlap of the circles, they place the information common to both entities. This information may be recorded in note form or in sentences and may include illustrations. Venn diagram generators can be found online at www.readwritethink.org/files/resources/interactives/venn_diagrams and www.venngen.com. Learn how PowerPoint can be used to create Venn diagrams at http://office.microsoft.com/en-us/templates/venn-diagram-examples-TC101875471.aspx.

Stacy Miller, whom you met in Chapter 4 in the sidebar on page 53, uses PowerPoint as a digital medium for creating Venn diagrams. She provides the template, and students create the diagram based on their reading. Figure 6-24 displays a Venn diagram filled out for the novel *The Outsiders* (Hinton, 1967). The creative fonts and "chalkboard" background add to the fun of learning through compare and contrast. Adding some art to the activity makes this digital graphic organizer more appealing.

Stacy also advises the yearbook club at her school. She uses Venn diagrams to help students look critically at a number of tasks yearbook photographers and editors must consider. For example, she wanted students to think about the yearbook portraits they will use and the more informal Instagram-like selfies they may make. She asked them to

FIGURE 6-24
Venn Diagram for
S. E. Hinton's *The
Outsiders*

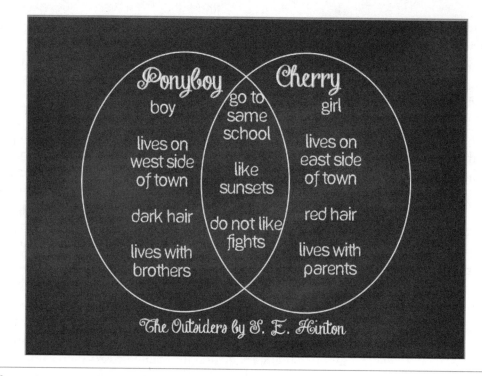

FIGURE 6-24
Venn Diagram for
S. E. Hinton's *The
Outsiders*

Source: Created by Stacy Miller.

read from the yearbook information sheets the publisher sends about portraiture and to compare that to their experiences with selfies. She created the template in PowerPoint, then the students went to work. You can see the template and one student response in Figures 6-25 and 6-26.

FIGURE 6-25
Pictures of Teenagers,
Venn Diagram
Template

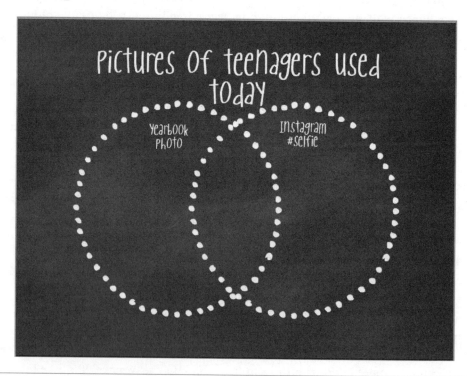

Source: Created by Stacy Miller.

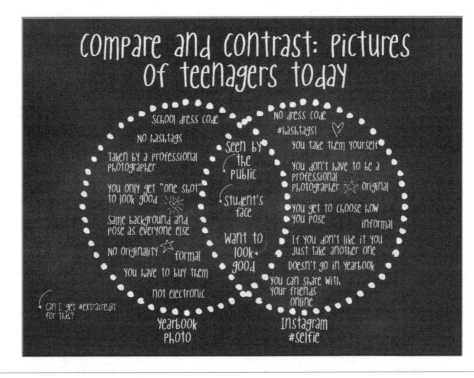

FIGURE 6-26
Pictures of Teenagers,
Student Example

Source: Created by Stacy Miller.

Venn diagrams definitely have their uses, but sometimes they may not encourage students to look deeply at a text or other information source. Looking back at Figure 6-24, the items compared are all accurate, but few of them really explore anything more than the surface-level identifying features of the characters, Ponyboy and Cherry. Who they are as characters still lies buried and invisible to the reader and to those with whom the Venn diagram is shared. What can a teacher do about that? It is all about the attributes that are really important; the values they share, their experiences living in different parts of a Midwestern city, and possibly what makes them approach those values and experiences in different ways. The attributes of the comparison are critical if compare and contrast is to be a worthwhile exercise.

Using the principle that compare-and-contrast graphic organizers can assist students to hone in on the attributes that are particularly relevant to the learning targets at hand, we constructed the compare-and-contrast attribute chart in Figure 6-27. Others are available online, and you can find our downloadable version (go to www .corwin.com/miningcomplextext/6-12). On this organizer, students are asked to compare and contrast two or more things (e.g., ideas, characters in a novel, things in the physical world) using a framework of relevant attributes. In some cases, students might brainstorm a list of important attributes based on their own experiences or on prior learning in class. Sometimes the framework will be determined by content-specific conventions. For example, characters in a novel might be compared one with another based on their personal strengths and challenges, their interactions with others, moral uprightness, or other personality traits that might be important considerations as determined by the teacher or a framework from previous learning in class. In

FIGURE 6-27

Compare-and-Contrast
Attribute Chart

Name: Date:

Subject:

Topic or Concept:

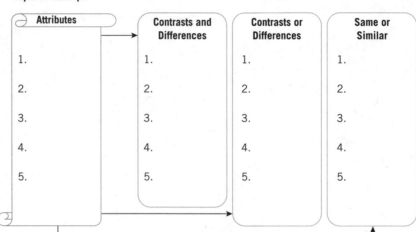

Attributes	Contrasts and Differences	Contrasts or Differences	Same or Similar
1.	1.	1.	1.
2.	2.	2.	2.
3.	3.	3.	3.
4.	4.	4.	4.
5.	5.	5.	5.

science, it sometimes surprises students that the image of the atom they hold in their heads has evolved over time and that the most current thinking may not be reflected in their mental models.

Earlier, we pointed out that there is a great deal of overlap between these text structures. We leave this topic with a connection question: How might compare-and-contrast attribute charts help students be more proficient with description?

Problem/Solution

What is the problem anyway? When working with problem/solution text structures, determining if there is a problem and the exact nature of the problem is the first step. In this way, the pattern aligns closely with inquiry modes of learning and the inquiry organizers found elsewhere in this book when students are the authors or makers of a product. When students read, they sometimes encounter a text that clearly identifies the problem and suggests one or more solutions. Often, however, the problem may be implied and the solutions not identified as such. Students must grapple with the text to identify the pattern. A graphic organizer for problem/solution may help guide the reader to determine if there is a problem discussed in the text, what that problem is, and what the solutions may be (Figure 6-28).

Example: English Language Arts

Gerald McDermott's (1972) classic, *Anansi the Spider: A Tale From the Ashanti,* is a perfect picture book to explore problem/solution text patterns. In the folk tale, Anansi runs into a bit of trouble, and his six sons rescue him using their particular gifts and talents. Later, Anansi must decide which of his sons will receive the globe of light as a prize; the solution follows the traditional creation myth pattern, with Anansi acting the typical trickster archetype. Using the problem/solution organizer, students can track the problems the sons face in rescuing Anansi, and the final problem Anansi faces as he seeks to reward six sons with just one prize.

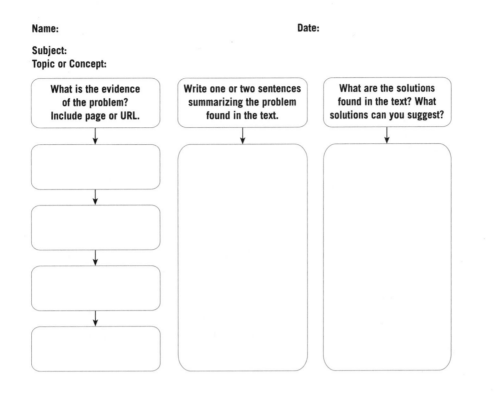

Name: Date:

Subject:

Topic or Concept:

FIGURE 6-28
Problem/Solution
Graphic Organizer

What is the evidence of the problem? Include page or URL.

Write one or two sentences summarizing the problem found in the text.

What are the solutions found in the text? What solutions can you suggest?

CCSS Anchor Standards

CCSS.ELA-Literacy.CCRA.R.2.

Determine central ideas or themes of a text and analyze their development; summarize the key supporting details and ideas.

CCSS.ELA-Literacy.CCRA.R.5.

Analyze the structure of texts, including how specific sentences, paragraphs, and larger portions of the text (e.g., a section, chapter, scene, or stanza) relate to each other and the whole.

How Do I Use Top-Level Text Structures as Graphic Organizers?

- Determine the top-level text structure, or ask students to draw on their prior experience with text to determine what the top-level structure is for a given piece.
- Use the graphic organizer that is appropriate to the top-level structure as a means of guiding student reading.
- After students read and complete the graphic organizer, they may work in small groups to compare the information and perhaps adjust any aspects of the organizer based on their discussion.
- With teacher guidance or on their own, students should discuss or note how the organization of the text helps them learn what the text may be trying to convey.
- Use these organizers to help students respond to and construct text-dependent questions.

CCSS.ELA-Literacy.RI.11–12.2.

Determine two or more central ideas of a text and analyze their development over the course of the text, including how they interact and build on one another to provide a complex analysis; provide an objective summary of the text.

CCSS.ELA-Literacy.RI.11–12.5.

Analyze and evaluate the effectiveness of the structure an author uses in his or her exposition or argument, including whether the structure makes points clear, convincing, and engaging.

CCSS.ELA-Literacy.RI.11–12.6.

Determine an author's point of view or purpose in a text in which the rhetoric is particularly effective, analyzing how style and content contribute to the power, persuasiveness or beauty of the text.

CCSS.ELA-Literacy.RI.11–12.10.

By the end of grade 11, read and comprehend literary nonfiction in the grades 11-CCR text complexity band proficiently, with scaffolding as needed at the high end of the range.

Determining the Need

Damien entered Mr. Scott's 11th-grade history class, and he was furious about a newspaper article in the *Los Angeles Times* that seemed to say that the U.S. Supreme Court had just ruled against affirmative action. Damien's outrage happened to dovetail with the schoolwide essential question "What is fair?" and the current unit they were doing on major social problems and domestic issues (see California Department of Education, 2000, standard 11.11). Mr. Scott saw an opportunity to use this as a teachable moment about how to analyze issues in the news.

Introducing It

Mr. Scott photocopied the *Los Angeles Times* article and an editorial in that same newspaper and immediately went online to gather other editorials about the Supreme Court decision. He noticed that editorials often are organized using a problem/solution structure. They state the problem, analyze it, and either praise or criticize the solution. Indeed, the editorial in the *Los Angeles Times* that day ("Affirmative Action Banned? It's Not That Simple," 2014) followed a problem/solution pattern. The article began by explaining the problem the Supreme Court was attempting to correct. Next, it examined the specific points of the decision and pointed out parts of the decision with which the editors agreed and disagreed. Finally, the article suggested a solution for advocates of affirmative action to take in the wake of the court's decision. Mr. Scott had the makings of a rich, timely lesson. He decided to use just the *Los Angeles Times* editorial as the lesson's reading.

Guided Instruction and Independent Practice

Mr. Scott handed a copy of the editorial to each student. He reminded them that they had been reading news stories, using textual evidence to craft an argument, and responding to the essential question "What is fair?"

He said that now they were going to try writing an editorial of their own. They would read and draft over the next several days and present their final editorials to a mock editorial board for consideration. "First, let's read this editorial on the Supreme Court decision on affirmative action," he said. "Let's look at it with an eye toward how the authors structured it."

Students read the article and annotated in the margins. They came back together to compare notes. Then they brainstormed topics that their editorials might address and discussed which topics most lent themselves to a problem/solution top-level structure. They would use the problem/solution organizer (see Figure 6-28) and the note-card organizer to keep track of all they had read and all they needed to read (and anyone they wanted to interview for this assignment).

Mr. Scott adapted the organizer so the headings were geared to writing rather than analysis of a text. The students got to work, gathering evidence to first understand the problem fully, then analyze or propose a solution to it.

Closure

Once the students wrote their editorials, the class elected an editorial board whose job was to vote on the editorials most worthy of being hosted on the class website. They also took their editorials to the student newspaper, and some were selected for publication there. A few students decided to reposition their articles as letters to the editor of a local newspaper.

Reading, Writing, and Discussion Extensions

The text structures discussed in this chapter are useful for students who are still learning to recognize the patterns and the information those patterns convey when students read. However, these structures are also useful for students as they think about their own written and multimodal compositions. Ask students to go beyond the top-level structure and consider how description fits into a composition that is basically a cause/effect exploration, for example. These structures are useful as students organize a composition in written or multimodal formats (see Sundeen, 2007). Lorenz, Green, and Brown (2009) found that average readers in primary grades benefited from the use of graphic organizers to give structure to their written work. Often, top-level text structures are a starting point for informing what students know and can do with a given text, but the organizers that represent those structures often pair well with other organizers. For example, problem/solution organizers may be an effective preliminary tool that can lead to inquiry organizers such as the I-chart and I-guide (see Chapter 7).

REREADING ORGANIZER

Contributed by Missy Provost

THIS ORGANIZER ADDRESSES THESE STANDARDS

CCSS.ELA-Literacy.CCRA.R.1.

Read closely to determine what the text says explicitly and to make logical inferences from it; cite specific textual evidence when writing or speaking to support conclusions drawn from the text.

CCSS.ELA-Literacy.CCRA.R.4.

Interpret words and phrases as they are used in a text, including determining technical, connotative, and figurative meanings, and analyze how specific word choices shape meaning or tone.

CCSS.ELA-Literacy.CCRA.R.10.

Read and comprehend complex literary and informational texts independently and proficiently.

What Is a Rereading Organizer?

The rereading graphic organizer (see Figure 6-29) supports students as they reread texts. It reinforces the idea that rereading is an integral part of reading and deeply understanding a text. The organizer helps students reread with a specific purpose in mind and helps them understand that proficient readers sometimes reread sentences, sections, even pages several times with different agendas in mind. It might be to appreciate sensory details and language, to better understand a section that they flew over too quickly on "auto pilot" (which is something that good readers do as well), to look closely at character conflict, to try to infer theme from details and nuances they may have missed, or to look for clues about how the plot will unfold. The purposes are many.

How Do I Use a Rereading Organizer?

- Make sure students understand why they will be rereading the text.
- After students read the text the first time looking for the gist and general ideas, hand out the graphic organizer or have students download it from the class web page.
- Explain to students that they will be rereading the text, or a portion of it, to increase their comprehension and notice details and nuances, and they will use the organizer to help them respond to the text.
- Show students that the organizer is foldable along the center line, so they can focus on one section at a time.
- You may ask students to work in groups to explain what they learned from the second reading that they did not notice or fully understand after the first reading.
- Students may be given the organizer as a way to respond to their independent reading, but make sure it isn't used so often that it becomes something that impedes motivation to read.
- You can use the organizer as a formative assessment early in the school year, midway, and at the end of the year.

FIGURE 6-29
Example of a Rereading Organizer

Name: _____   Date: _____   Reread Book: _____

List five MAJOR things that happened in your independent reading book this week.

1.

2.

3.

4.

5.

Term 1: Reread Book Analysis;
TESTING Words

Explain one thing that you noticed during your reread that you did NOT notice the first time you read the book. Write a full paragraph with as many specific details as possible.

Describe the protagonist (main character) in your book.

Illustrate a scene from your reading this week. Include a caption that tells what is happening.

Term 1: Reread Book Analysis;
TESTING Words

THIS CLASSROOM EXAMPLE ADDRESSES THESE STANDARDS

CCSS.ELA-Literacy.RL.7.1.

Cite several pieces of textual evidence to support analysis of what the text says explicitly as well as inferences drawn from the text.

CCSS.ELA-Literacy.RL.7.4.

Determine the meaning of words and phrases as they are used in a text, including figurative and connotative meanings; analyze the impact of rhymes and other repetitions of sounds (e.g., alliteration) on a specific verse or stanza of a poem or section of a story or drama.

CCSS.ELA-Literacy.RL.7.10.

By the end of the year, read and comprehend literature, including stories, dramas, and poems, in the grades 6-8 text complexity band proficiently, with scaffolding as needed at the high end of the range.

Determining the Need

Mrs. Provost used Bloom's taxonomy (Anderson & Krathwohl, 2001) throughout the year and even displayed it on a pillar in her classroom (see Figures 6-30 and 6-31). In this way, her students became familiar with the words and the thinking tasks associated with them.

FIGURE 6-30
Bloom's Taxonomy Column

Source: Contributed by Melissa Provost.

Mrs. Provost used the rereading graphic organizer with her students often, as it helped them analyze their reading. She wanted them to recognize that rereading is something effective readers do to make sense of challenging texts and that there is more they could gain and bring to the text (see Rosenblatt, 1995) through a second or even a third reading.

Her students often used the organizer as they reread text from assigned readings (or read-alouds) and from their independent reading material. Students knew to look at the layout of the graphic organizer for hints about how to respond in each section; open space invited them to take notes in a style of their own choice, lines called for a well-developed written response, and compare and contrast signaled them to draw a Venn diagram or the like.

Midway through the year, Mrs. Provost asked students to

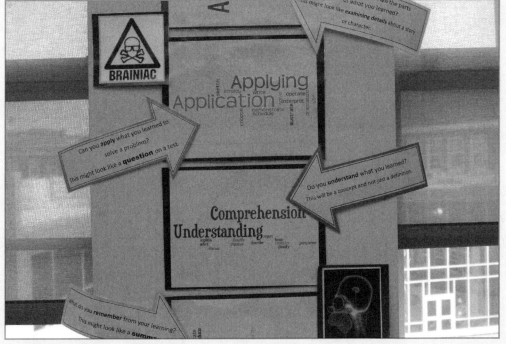

FIGURE 6-31
Bloom's Taxonomy
Column Close-Up

Source: Contributed by Melissa Provost.

reread a text that had challenged them early in the school year and to fill out the organizer. She had given them this same task early in the school year to assess their comprehension and ability to write a well-supported paragraph, so now she was checking to see how much they had progressed in being able to construct a paragraph and make sense of complex text.

Introducing It

At the beginning of the week, Mrs. Provost gave a copy of the organizer to each student or had them access it digitally. She explained to students that they should choose a text that they had read earlier. The text should be one they felt was a challenge and that they would benefit from rereading, and they needed to get it approved by her. She said that although this was an assessment, they could work on it at home over the course of the week.

Guided Instruction and Independent Practice

Apart from the assessment, Mrs. Provost's students used the organizer to guide their independent reading and thinking about texts. They turned it in to her in the morning to review (see Figure 6-32 for an example). You can also use the organizer with assigned texts that are complex and present a comprehension challenge.

Closure

After assessing her students' responses on the organizer, Mrs. Provost handed the organizers back to students. She asked them to look at them in relation to the Bloom's wall (see Figures 6-30 and 6-31): "Look at your responses, and think about what level of critical thinking each task on the organizer represents." She engaged them in a discussion about

FIGURE 6-32

Matt's Rereading Organizer

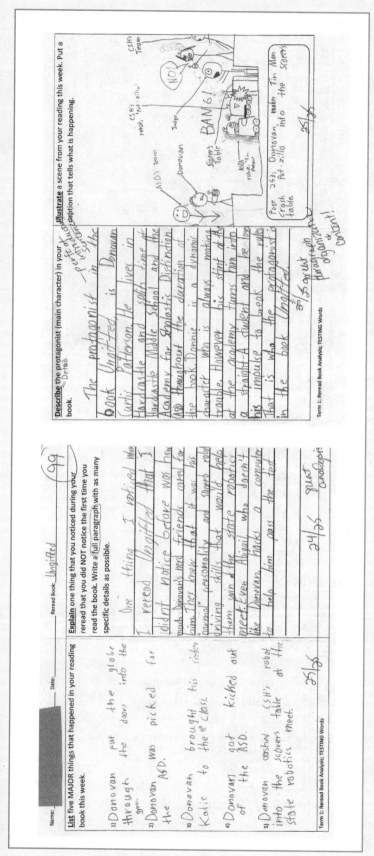

Name: _____ Date: _____

List five MAJOR things that happened in your reading book this week.

1) Donovan put the globe through the gym doors into the

2) Donovan was picked for the ASD.

3) Donovan brought his sister Katie to the 8th class.

4) Donovan got kicked out of the ASD.

5) Donovan washed CSH's robot into the scorers table at the state robotics meet.

25/26

Term 1: Reread Book Analysis; TESTING Words

Reread Book: Ungifted   99

Explain one thing that you noticed during your reread that you did NOT notice the first time you read the book. Write a full paragraph with as many specific details as possible.

One thing I noticed when I reread Ungifted that I didn't notice before was how much Donovan's nerd friends cared for him. They knew that it was his "normal" personality and superb robotics driving skills that would help them win at the state robotics meet. Even Abigail who doesn't like Donovan, hacks a computer to help him pass the test

24/25   quest analysis

Describe the protagonist (main character) in your book.

The protagonist is Donovan Curtis Patterson. He lives in the book Ungifted in the Hardcastle Middle School and the Hardcastle Academy for Scholastic Distinction (ASD) throughout the duration of the book Donnie is a dynamic character who is always getting into trouble. However his stint at the Academy turns him into a straight A student and we lose his impulse to break the rules. That is who the protagonist is in the book Ungifted

35/35 quest

25/26

Term 1: Reread Book Analysis; TESTING Words

which task requires more thinking, more effort. She found this metacognitive discussion really helped her seventh graders realize that reading and thinking about text is an active, problem-solving endeavor. She wanted them to leave her class realizing that, yes, reading can be tough, texts can be challenging, but it's stimulating work—and work that even the most accomplished thinkers and readers have to power through.

Finally, Mrs. Provost was interested in finding out what her students thought of the value of rereading. In the course of the conversation, here are several statements that resonated with her:

"Rereading lets us pick it apart more and notice new things."

"The second time we can read between the lines more."

"The first read we get the main idea, the second time we already know the story so we can focus more on the smaller details."

"The first time we just want to get to the end, but when we reread we learn more about the characters and author's style."

"Yeah, we can comprehend the characters' emotions more . . ."

". . . and pick up on foreshadowing."

"I just like it for enjoyment."

Reading, Writing, and Discussion Extensions

Mrs. Provost used this graphic organizer early in the year to get a baseline on the skill set of her new seventh graders. From this, she could determine a great many things: Are they reading and following written directions, listening to and following oral instructions (annotating directions, folding organizer to chunk the task), and comprehending independent reading across various levels of thinking? In addition, she used the organizer to assess students' ability to write an organized paragraph and their ability to sketch a picture of what they "saw" in their reading.

GRAPHIC ORGANIZERS BOOST QUESTIONING AND RESPONDING

Inherent in the Common Core State Standards (Common Core State Standards Initiative, 2010b) is the notion that students are inquirers. Part of their identities as individuals resides in the possibility that they want to know more about the world they inhabit and the world they want to change in positive ways. Several Common Core standards ask that students look closely at the texts they read, the media they view, the compositions they create, and then ask questions about those texts. The graphic organizers in this chapter support their doing so.

I-CHART AND I-GUIDE

CCSS.ELA-Literacy.CCRA.R.7.

Integrate and evaluate content presented in diverse media and formats, including visually and quantitatively, as well as in words.

CCSS.ELA-Literacy.CCRA.R.8.

Delineate and evaluate the argument and specific claims in a text, including the validity of the reasoning as well as the relevance and sufficiency of the evidence.

CCSS.ELA-Literacy.CCRA.R.9.

Analyze how two or more texts address similar themes or topics in order to build knowledge or to compare the approaches the authors take.

What Are I-Charts and I-Guides?

Inquiry. It is one of those words that means many different things depending on the context, whom you ask, and when you ask just what *inquiry* means. We argue that inquiry can be, and often is, the soul of learning; when there are intriguing questions and a multiplicity of sources, students might be engaged and want to learn. In this section, we examine two organizers that usefully guide students to think about how inquiry extends learning tasks into the interesting, the useful, and the captivating. The first is the I-chart (I stands for inquiry; Hoffman, 1992) and the second is the I-guide adapted by Wood, Lapp, Flood, and Taylor (2008). As readers, you might recognize that there are parallels with the KWL format (Ogle, 1986) examined earlier in this book as well. If so, you are on the road to inquiry, the road that shows how ideas connect one with the other and sometimes where there are disconnects, too. Working with the many sources available in digital and more traditional environments is a hallmark of learning for millennial generation students. How those sources are evaluated as to their trustworthiness and how they fit, or don't fit, together is paramount for learners in today's schools as they work with multiple sources (Wood, 1998), make connections among sources, and compare concepts and texts.

To take an inquiry stance, in academic worlds, is to wonder. It is to notice that we know and can learn a great many things, but we typically end up with new questions, challenges to long-held assumptions, and creative or innovative solutions to vexing problems. The I-chart and I-guide build on this very notion. How else can we ask the tough questions of our lives except by inquiring, wondering, and questioning?

With the I-chart (Figure 7-1), students identify a topic, often in negotiation against learning goals, with the teacher and each other (Hoffman, 1992). They place their learning from various sources in relation to the questions and subquestions they generate as they investigate texts. The I-guide (Figure 7-2), seen at the beginning of this example, builds on this approach by asking students to develop a reading plan, identifying the major themes from their reading, and then synthesize the texts with which they interact (Wood et al., 2008).

How Do I Use an I-Chart or I-Guide?

- First, choose to use either the I-guide or I-chart format. The I-guide favors overarching themes and questions, while the I-chart concentrates student attention on specific subquestions.

FIGURE 7-1
I-Chart

What We Know						
	Topic	**Question**	**Question**	**Question**	**Other Interesting Facts and Figures**	**New Questions**
Sources						
Synthesis						

FIGURE 7-2
I-Guide

What We Know					
	Topic or Question	**Major Subtopics or Themes**		**Summary of Each Text**	**Importance or Relevance of the Information**
Sources					
Synthesis					

- Determine what resources students will use. Be sure your students have the research skills and reading capacities to fully comprehend the selected materials.
- Model the use of the chart or guide using a familiar topic.
- Allow students to use the chart or guide to work on and shape their research. Be sure to encourage students to redesign the charts or create alternatives when needed.
- Identify a final product that will provide students with opportunities to demonstrate the processes they used in the inquiry and their newfound understandings.

The I-chart and I-guide formats provide a visual format students might use to guide their inquiry and provide a sense of purpose for their readings.

INTO THE CLASSROOM — 11th Grade—U.S. History

THIS CLASSROOM EXAMPLE ADDRESSES THIS STANDARD

CCSS.ELA-LITERACY.RI.11-12.7.

Integrate and evaluate multiple sources of information presented in different media or formats (e.g., visually, quantitatively) as well as in words in order to address a question or solve a problem.

Determining the Need

Mrs. Osgard's 11th graders were studying the 1920s in their U.S. history class. Specifically, they were learning about the changing lifestyles of many Americans due to the cultural, technological, and economic advancements of that decade. Students were particularly interested in studying more about the technological advances, wondering how these advancements compared to technological advances today. After reading an article titled "The Impact of Technology on 1920s Life," they wanted to know more. The I-guide gave them the opportunity to use that source and explore others as they looked for the major themes related to their question: Were the 1920s "roaring" or "boring"? Students were able to use what they knew about argumentative writing when answering this question.

Introducing It

In order for students to have a thorough understanding of technological advancements in the 1920s, Mrs. Osgard and the students knew that reading from multiple sources was necessary. Mrs. Osgard began by modeling how to complete an I-guide after the entire class read "The Impact of Technology on 1920s Life." She did a think-aloud and recorded her thoughts on the graphic organizer while students watched, listened, and also recorded notes on their own organizer. Mrs. Osgard listed a few reliable websites students might refer to in order to learn more about their topic but encouraged them to search on their own for additional information when completing their graphic organizer.

Guided Instruction and Independent Practice

Students worked in pairs searching the Internet, reading, and discussing, and they each completed their own individual I-guide. Mrs. Osgard gathered small groups of students to a table to provide more explicit instruction for those who needed it. For example, a few students needed additional support identifying subthemes and topics from the reading. To provide this support, Mrs. Osgard had students reread and identify the specifics regarding the advancement of the automobile and travel. Once she was confident that they could read for detail, she had them return to their paired tasks. While students worked in pairs, they negotiated meaning, modified their graphic organizers, shared ideas, and collaborated for deeper understanding.

Once pairs of students had completed their I-guides, they joined another pair to create a "paired squared" group. This group of four students was now charged with taking information from their four graphic organizers to begin to construct their response to the essential question. One student's I-guide is shown in Figure 7-3. Notes in different colored pencil are the additional ideas this student obtained from peers in his paired group. By asking students to write in different colored pencils or pens, Mrs. Osgard held them accountable for the work they completed not only individually but in pairs and groups as well.

At the end of the period, Mrs. Osgard was able to quickly check her students' graphic organizers to see how much they accomplished in the period and how much time would need to be devoted for this work in subsequent days. Some students were motivated by the topic and process and asked if they could work on their graphic organizers outside of class. In order to provide closure to this day's lesson and quickly check for understanding, Mrs. Osgard asked students to write down the most important or interesting thing they read from an article and the most important or interesting thing they learned from their

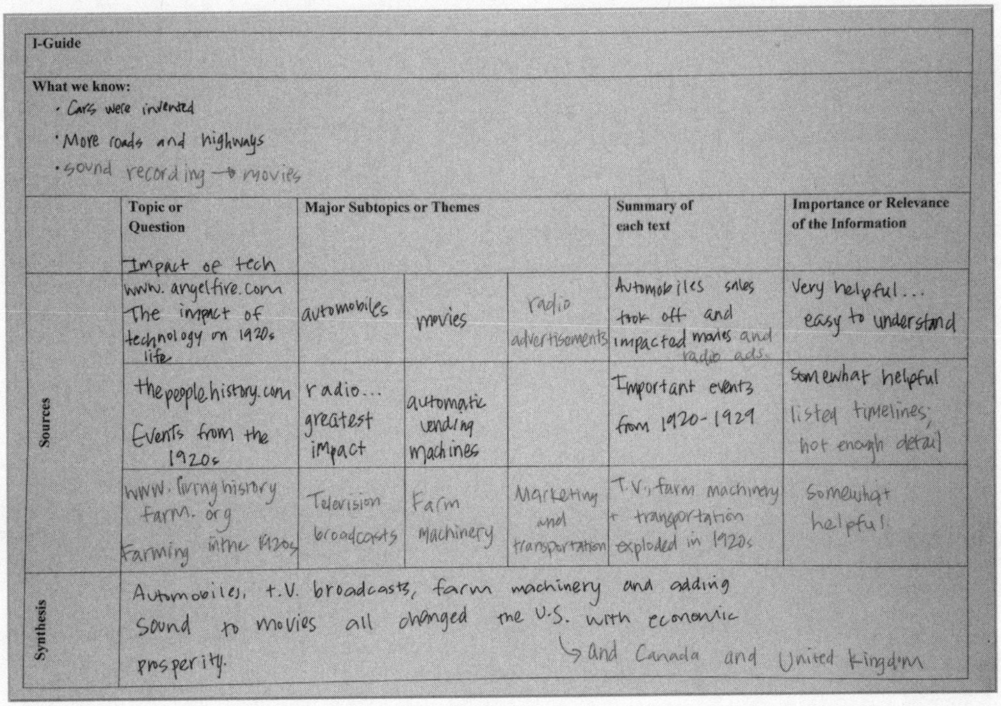

I-Guide

What we know:
- Cars were invented
- More roads and highways
- sound recording → movies

	Topic or Question	Major Subtopics or Themes			Summary of each text	Importance or Relevance of the Information
	Impact of tech					
Sources	www.angelfire.com The impact of technology on 1920s life	automobiles	movies	radio advertisements	Automobiles sales took off and impacted movies and radio ads.	Very helpful... easy to understand
	thepeoplehistory.com Events from the 1920s	radio... greatest impact	automatic vending machines		Important events from 1920-1929	Somewhat helpful listed timelines; not enough detail
	www.livinghistoryfarm.org Farming in the 1920s	Television broadcasts	Farm Machinery	Marketing and transportation	T.V., farm machinery + transportation exploded in 1920s	Somewhat helpful.
Synthesis	Automobiles, t.V. broadcasts, farm machinery and adding sound to movies all changed the U.S. with economic prosperity. ↳ and Canada and United Kingdom					

FIGURE 7-3
I-Guide Created by a Team of Students

peers. This "exit slip" information was collected as students were dismissed from class. Students were used to wrapping up lessons this way and quickly wrote ideas on a small piece of paper. This practice holds students accountable for individual and group work and helps teachers as they formatively assess students to identify areas that need to be addressed in future instruction.

Reading, Writing, and Discussion Extensions

Inquiry is often thought of as a process that generally results in some kind of product, such as a report, presentation, or model. Consider the many ways I-charts and I-guides might contribute to comprehension processes as students read to learn and provide evidence of that learning in written work or in discussion. How might you use I-charts and I-guides in your classroom?

FLIP CHART MANIPULATIVE

CCSS.ELA-Literacy.CCRA.R.1.

Read closely to determine what the text says explicitly and to make logical inferences from it; cite specific textual evidence when writing or speaking to support conclusions drawn from the text.

CCSS.ELA-Literacy.CCRA.R.5.

Analyze the structure of texts, including how specific sentences, paragraphs, and larger portions of the text (e.g., a section, chapter, scene, or stanza) relate to each other and the whole.

CCSS.ELA-Literacy.CCRA.W.4.

Produce clear and coherent writing in which the development, organization, and style are appropriate to task, purpose, and audience.

THIS ORGANIZER ADDRESSES THESE STANDARDS

What Is a Flip Chart Manipulative?

A flip chart (Figure 7-4), a type of manipulative strategy guide (Wood et al., 2008), is a powerful way for students to organize information about a story or ideas related to a topic. It is similar to the tabbed book manipulative guide we explored earlier in this book. This manipulative is an outgrowth of those shared by Dinah Zike that can be found at www.dinah.com. Flip charts are easy to make, and each page can display information that contributes to analysis of a whole—understanding a story, solving a problem, completing a research project, displaying information about different books that allow for comparisons across texts. Once students know how to create and use a flip chart manipulative, the possibilities are endless.

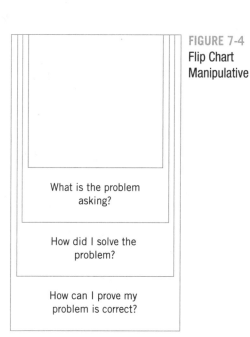

FIGURE 7-4
Flip Chart Manipulative

What is the problem asking?

How did I solve the problem?

How can I prove my problem is correct?

How Do I Use a Flip Chart Manipulative?

- Stack three to five sheets of paper on top of one another with a half-inch overlap. (If you would like to make a larger flip chart, simply add more pages.)
- Fold in the middle.
- Staple the top just below the fold.
- Direct students to write labels that correspond with the major components of the text.

Teacher Danielle Knight, a high school special education teacher in New Jersey, uses flip books (another term for flip chart) with graphic organizers and other resources embedded on each page. See the following page for her description of a flip book for *The Old Man and the Sea* (Hemingway, 1952).

Contributed by Danielle Knight

Study guides. A necessity? Yes, they are. But they are not an active guide to reading. Actually, a study guide is a passive guide to reading. So what can a secondary teacher do to create a more active student-centered experience while reading literature? Today's inclusive classroom has students at all levels. All skills are represented. Differentiation is the key to our instructional success. A flip book is a fresh approach to the run-of-the-mill study guide. In this flip book, the visual organization to guide reading is evident on the tabs.

Inside the flip book, graphic organizers, other visuals, and guiding questions can be found for each section of the book.

All the sections are visible, easily accessible, and engaging! You will see your students refer to their completed pages while engaged in additional classroom activities. One strategy I like to implement is bringing the flip book PDF file up on the SMART Board as students fill it in and take turns going to the board. Secondary students experience some frustration in a flipped classroom due to "not knowing what to do next." With a flip book your students will "own" their learning experience and take pride in the outcome.

The flip book, assembled.   Graphic organizer inside the flip book.

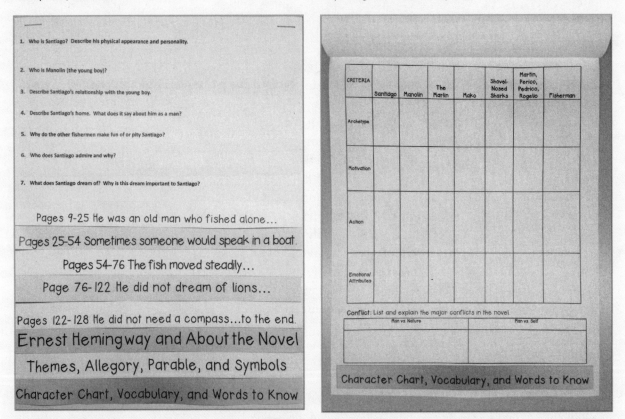

Source: Photographs reproduced with permission of Danielle Knight, high school special education ELA teacher, New Jersey, http://www.teacherspayteachers.com/Store/Danielle-Knight

CCSS.ELA-Literacy.RI.9-10.1.

Cite strong and thorough textual evidence to support analysis of what the text says explicitly as well as inferences drawn from the text.

CCSS.ELA-Literacy.RI.9-10.2.

Determine a central idea of a text and analyze its development over the course of the text, including how it emerges and is shaped and refined by specific details; provide an objective summary of the text.

CCSS.ELA-Literacy.SL.9-10.1.

Initiate and participate effectively in a range of collaborative discussions (one-on-one, in groups, and teacher-led) with diverse partners on grades 9–10 topics, texts, and issues, building on others' ideas and expressing their own clearly and persuasively.

THIS CLASSROOM EXAMPLE ADDRESSES THESE STANDARDS

Determining the Need

Ninth-grade mathematics teacher Ms. Jackson continually encouraged her students to think critically about mathematical word problems and be able to articulate their thinking when solving problems. She found that flip charts were a way that students could support this critical analysis. As shown in Figure 7-4, students can create a flip chart that is written as a friendly version of the eight mathematical practices addressed in the Common Core State Standards for Mathematical Practice:

CCSS.Math.Practice.MP.1.

Make sense of problems and persevere in solving them.

CCSS.Math.Practice.MP.1.

Reason abstractly and quantitatively.

CCSS.Math.Practice.MP.3.

Construct viable arguments and critique the reasoning of others.

CCSS.Math.Practice.MP.4.

Model with mathematics.

CCSS.Math.Practice.MP.5.

Use appropriate tools strategically.

CCSS.Math.Practice.MP.6.

Attend to precision.

CCSS.Math.Practice.MP.7.

Look for and make use of structure.

CCSS.Math.Practice.MP.8.

Look for and express regularity in repeated reasoning.

Being able to have this reference provided students with the scaffolds they needed to analyze a problem and also reflect on the area(s) of the problem that caused them difficulty.

Introducing It

Ms. Jackson introduced the flip chart manipulative graphic organizer to her ninth-grade students through explicit modeling. She began by labeling her first tab and asking herself, "What is this problem asking?" She continued to think aloud through this one problem. On the first page she wrote key words that identify the question. She also modeled how to draw or write what the problem was asking. On the second tab, she modeled how to draw examples and different ways to solve a problem. On the third tab she wrote, and said aloud while writing, "How can I prove my solution is correct?" On the inside of this tab, she illustrated other ways of solving problems, such as objects, drawings, diagrams, and actions.

Guided Instruction and Independent Practice

Once Ms. Jackson had finished modeling a problem, she assigned a next problem and invited students to work with a partner to analyze it using their flip chart graphic organizers. When she observed that a few students were having trouble solving two-step equations, she refocused them as a whole class to discuss this. Once she was secure that they understood how to solve a two-step equation, she asked them to solve an additional problem.

Closure

When she was confident her students understood how to use the chart to support problem solving, Ms. Jackson encouraged partners to write a problem to be shared with an additional partner team. Her goal was to have them solve problems and also become skilled at using the flip chart for problem analysis.

Reading, Writing, and Discussion Extensions

In this mathematics class students read the problems and used their flip charts to support their analysis. The flip chart served as a visual that provided a means to organize information they gathered from demonstrations and from the textbook. This can happen in all disciplines. Flip charts can become a visual aid as students compare thoughts and ideas about a myriad of topics and within partner, small-group, and larger-class configurations. Using this manipulative helps them understand how scientists organize their work, how historians make sense of many documents, or how readers understand and talk about the fiction they read.

TEXT-DEPENDENT QUESTION/RESPONSE ORGANIZER

CCSS.ELA-Literacy.CCRA.R.1.

Read closely to determine what the text says explicitly and to make logical inferences from it; cite specific textual evidence when writing or speaking to support conclusions drawn from the text.

CCSS.ELA-Literacy.CCRA.R.3.

Analyze how and why individuals, events, or ideas develop and interact over the course of a text.

CCSS.ELA-Literacy.CCRA.R.10.

Read and comprehend complex literary and informational texts independently and proficiently.

CCSS.ELA-Literacy.CCRA.W.7.

Conduct short as well as more sustained research projects based on focused questions, demonstrating understanding of the subject under investigation.

THIS CLASSROOM EXAMPLE ADDRESSES THESE STANDARDS

What Is a Text-Dependent Question/Response Organizer?

Name: **Date:**

Subject:

| Circle one:
• This is my first reading
• Second reading
• Third or more readings | The text-dependent question is: |

After reading the text again, I found this evidence to support my answer (with page or section numbers):

And now my response to the question is:

FIGURE 7-5

Text-Dependent Question/Response Organizer

To achieve Common Core State Standards and other rigorous goals for learning, students must attend fully to the words of a text. As students read, they need thinking strategies that support their working through texts. Close reading and text-dependent questions work together to help students

- understand the author's ideas,
- consider how the author's and/or narrator's style and voice enhances or contributes to the narrative and/or the ideas,
- try to determine the nuances of the words the author has chosen,
- consider how the plot and structure convey meaning,
- get at an author's use of myriad literary devices,
- arrive at conclusions about the text's most important points,
- speculate on the author's own point of view apart from, or akin to, the narrator's and character's perspective.

Though what students know and bring to the page is critically essential, what students can make of the words, sentences, and larger blocks of text they encounter is obviously of great importance as well.

Some text-dependent questions can be quite literal, but when these are posed along with higher-level questions, a learner's comprehension of a text is elevated. Also, when students reread to answer a literal-level question, or are asked to notice a specific detail and identify what the text says, in the process of rereading, their understanding deepens. It's not as though a student dives into a text like a pelican grabbing a fish and going quickly back up—the student infers and analyzes what the text says *and* what it means. Our colleagues Doug Fisher and Nancy Frey (2012b) present a continuum of text-dependent questions that include attention to general understandings, key details, vocabulary, text structure, and author's purpose at the lower end of the continuum. While the top level of their graphic calls attention to text-dependent questions that help students make inferences, intertextual connections, and attend to the construction of opinions and arguments, this is not intended as a hierarchical model. The question to be asked depends on the lesson purpose and the students' knowledge. Notice that whereas other organizers in this book focus on five of the six levels of this continuum, this graphic organizer zeroes in on text-dependent questions that help build student capacity to make and work with inferences.

Questions seem so natural to teachers and students that it sometimes appears that there is no need to plan them, but that may not be the case. If students are to learn to make useful inferences as they read, teachers must avoid asking too many literal-level questions at the expense of those that require higher-level thinking, such as those required in making an inference (see Daines, 1986; Fisher & Frey, 2012b). With careful planning, teachers can ask text-dependent questions that scaffold student thinking with complex texts. We think it is important to note that questions are not always deployed just to assess what students know and can do; very often, questions can guide students to the intended cognitive skill as they make inferences along the way.

Another useful protocol is the question–answer relationship strategy that highlights four types of questions students might generate or to which they might be asked to respond: right there, think and search, author and me, and on my own (Raphael, 1984, 1986). The purpose of identifying the question type is that this information guides students to know what they are to do in order to gain deeper and deeper insights about the information in the text. When responding to the first two question types, students rely on information directly in the text at the literal and textually implicit level. When addressing the third and fourth question types, students relate what they know from background or prior knowledge and match that to what they are actually reading in the text. Questions that call for students to make textually implicit assumptions or inferences in order to determine an appropriate response from two or more parts of the text are textually implicit and termed "think and search," or sometimes "figure it out." Questions that ask students to draw on their background or prior knowledge and join that with what they have read are known as "author and me" questions.

The real kicker is that to understand the question and respond to it, students must have read the text and be able to use evidence from the text in order to respond. Using evidence from the text is the foundation of close reading strategies and the text-dependent questions that promote the capacity to make increasingly sophisticated inferences with complex texts in various disciplines.

Authors imply, and readers infer. Thus, what authors say, hint at, or believe their audiences already know is very important when students are asked to actively look for and construct inferences based on what the text actually states.

Look at the text-dependent question/response organizer (Figure 7-5). Notice that even though inferences are constructed by a reader at almost every level (e.g., word level, sentence level), this organizer focuses on inferring across larger blocks of text—at the paragraph, chapter, and whole-text levels. In many close reading schemes (see Fisher, Frey, & Lapp, 2012), students read a text multiple times with a different, scaffolded focus during each reading. Often, the use of text-dependent questions appears after students have read a text two or more times. Thus, students are familiar with the content, and they are now working actively to make inferences.

Text-dependent question/response organizers help to make the process of inferring visible to students who struggle with this task. Just a quick editorial note here: We prefer the more precise term *inferring* to the made-up term *inferencing*. In the close reading process, students read the text under consideration multiple times, and with the support of a graphic organizer they can look at the nuances of the inferences they are able to make from a combination of details from the text and from their own background knowledge.

How Do I Use a Text-Dependent Question/Response Organizer?

- Text-dependent questions focus students' attention on particular aspects of a text, and in this case, inferences are at the foreground. In close reading, students have already read the text at hand at least one time, sometimes more. The inferential question they are asked helps them think about the specifics of the meaning the text actually conveys and how they are gathering information to deepen their knowledge of what the text means.
- Ask a text-dependent question that requires inferences to be made.
- Ask students to respond to the question. They read again to be able to do so.
- To support their analysis, students return to the text to find specific evidence from multiple points in the text that help them build a chain of indicators that support the inference or cause them to adjust the inference they originally made. They often make annotations that will help them later identify exactly what section of the text supported their being able to do so.
- Students discuss their responses to the text-dependent question with partners or in groups, and then they compare their responses with other groups. This type of collaboration supports their understandings of the text.

THIS CLASSROOM
EXAMPLE ADDRESSES
THESE STANDARDS

CCSS.ELA-Literacy.RI.11-12.1.

Cite strong and thorough textual evidence to support analysis of what the text says explicitly as well as inferences drawn from the text, including determining where the text leaves matters uncertain.

CCSS.ELA-Literacy.RI.11-12.3.

Analyze a complex set of ideas or sequence of events and explain how specific individuals, ideas, or events interact and develop over the course of the text.

CCSS.ELA-Literacy.RI-11-12.10.

By the end of grade 12, read and comprehend literary nonfiction at the high end of the grades 11-CCR text complexity band independently and proficiently.

CCSS.ELA-Literacy.WHST.11-12.7.

Conduct short as well as more sustained research projects to answer a question (including a self-generated question) or solve a problem; narrow or broaden the inquiry when appropriate; synthesize multiple sources on the subject, demonstrating understanding of the subject under investigation.

Determining the Need

Struggling with a text, Ms. Perez came to conclude, is not always a bad thing. Tough texts sometimes mean that students are challenged, but on the bright side, when students persevere, it teaches them that they are capable. It has the potential to build their reading stamina.

Some of Ms. Perez's students just needed the appropriate scaffolding to be successful with making inferences, particularly the textually implicit type that requires students to connect ideas across a piece of text as they read. She knew her students were capable of struggling through the text and that such a struggle often resulted in high-quality learning.

Introducing It

To begin, Ms. Perez explained to the students that authors often don't explicitly tell the reader everything they are to think. Instead they use language to offer clues and descriptions that help the reader infer what they are implying or suggesting. Ms. Perez then shared the text-dependent question/response organizer. After explaining the format of the organizer, she handed out copies of Learned Hand's (1944) "I Am an American Day Address" and asked students to read it to get an understanding of what the text says. After they finished reading she invited them to partner talk as a way to share their insights.

Guided Instruction and Independent Practice

As the students read, annotated, and completed their graphic organizers, Ms. Perez circulated among them, making notes about their interpretations. She formulated her next questions based on the students' responses. Although she had prepared questions, she altered them based on the students' responses. She knew the information gained from observing the students would inform the work she would do later with smaller groups as they continued to study the concept of liberty via other written texts, paintings, and poetry.

She then asked, "What does Hand's word choice in the first section tell us about the event?" Again students read, annotated the text, engaged in partner talk, added to their organizers, and then shared their thinking. Ms. Perez posed two additional questions that caused students to reread the text to find information that involved their making additional inferences. Following each reading, students discussed their thinking and the specific evidence prompting it. They used their organizers during each reading to note their insights (see Figure 7-6).

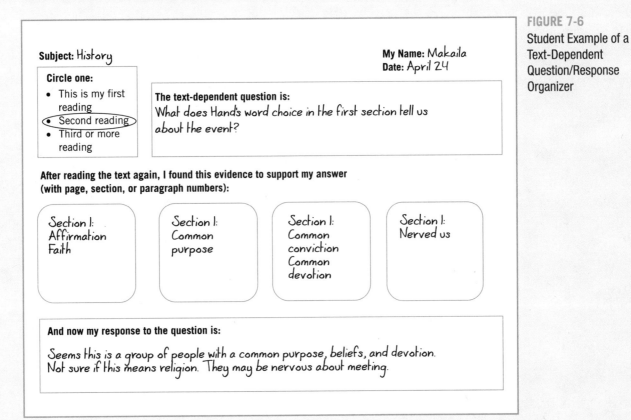

FIGURE 7-6

Student Example of a Text-Dependent Question/Response Organizer

Closure

Most of the students were able to share their inferences based on evidence from the text. Ms. Perez realized that students inferred the main theme of Hand's speech: Freedom and liberty must reside in each person's heart. As she listened to their thinking, she was confident that they had learned how to use the text to support inference making.

To conclude she encouraged students to again reread the text and add any more information from their collaborative conversations and organizers. It is through these rich conversations about the text information that students' initial thinking was enhanced. Her last question was "After reading this text, what do you believe motivated immigrants to come to America? Please support your interpretation with information from the text."

Reading, Writing, and Discussion Extensions

Ms. Perez challenged students to use the Internet to find another medium that presented the same or an alternate perspective about liberty. She also asked them to describe how their thoughts about liberty had changed from interacting with these sources. She had in mind standard CCSS.ELA-Literacy.CCRA.W.8, "Gather relevant information from multiple print and digital sources, assess the credibility and accuracy of each source, and integrate the information while avoiding plagiarism," when she asked them to create a visual that shared their perspectives of liberty and to note the sources that had influenced their thinking. She encouraged them to use information from the graphic organizer to help them synthesize and share their thinking.

Photo by Thinkstock

GRAPHIC ORGANIZERS FOSTER UNDERSTANDING AND WRITING ARGUMENTS

A new goal for young writers in middle and high school is that they form and compose arguments based on the sources they read and can consult in other ways. This chapter examines how the Common Core State Standards expect students to move from their own observations to consultation of sources as they work with more formal argumentation structures that go beyond the opinion structures they learned in elementary grades.

SEVEN-PART GRAPHIC ORGANIZER FOR COMPOSING AN ARGUMENT

THIS ORGANIZER ADDRESSES THESE STANDARDS

CCSS.ELA.Literacy.CCWA.W.1.

Write arguments to support claims in an analysis of substantive topics or texts using valid reasoning and relevant and sufficient evidence.

CCSS.ELA-Literacy.CCRA.W.4.

Produce clear and coherent writing in which the development, organization, and style are appropriate to task, purpose, and audience.

CCSS.ELA-Literacy.CCRA.R.1.

Read closely to determine what the text says explicitly and to make logical inferences from it; cite specific textual evidence when writing or speaking to support conclusions drawn from the text.

What Is a Seven-Part Graphic Organizer for Composing an Argument?

FIGURE 8-1

Seven-Part Graphic Organizer for Composing an Argument

Writing an Argumentative Essay	
Question: Should schools be allowed to have video cameras in classrooms?	
Part 1: Take a Position	
State your position. My current position is:	State what you think might be positions that conflict with yours. I think the position of others might be:
Part 2: Support Your Position	
These points support my position. (Identify at least three. Use multiple sources and types of sources.) • • •	These are the sources that support my position. • • •
Part 3: Present Counter-Perspectives	
Counter-perspectives are positions or views that differ from yours. (Include at least two counter-perspectives.) • •	I found support for these counter-perspectives in these resources. (Match each counter-perspective with its resource.) • •
Part 4: Write Your Thesis Statement	
This is the part of your essay where you explain to readers what your essay is going to talk about. This is your thesis. Your thesis is the statement that shares your position. It should be the one you identified as your position in Part 1.	
Part 5: Craft Your Hook	
Now add a hook that gets the attention of your readers and makes them want to read your essay. Your hook should connect to your thesis statement.	

Part 6: Reflect on the Issue, Your Position, and Possible Other Positions
Think again about the issue you are addressing. Now refer back to Parts 1 and 3 to summarize your position and also the counter-perspectives. Once you've finished, it's time to write your argumentative essay.

Part 7: Writing Your Essay

Now it's time to write your essay. You can use the ideas you compiled in Parts 1–6 of this organizer to write your essay.

Paragraph 1—Introduction

Your first paragraph should begin with the hook you wrote in Part 5. Next, connect your hook to the initial question. Now look at Part 6, and use this summary of information to show all sides of the issue identified in the question. Finally, add your thesis statement from Part 4.

Body Paragraphs (2–4)

The supports you identified in Part 2 should now be added as the next paragraphs in your essay. Each support for your position should be shared as a paragraph that also includes its documentation. After discussing all of your supports, add at least one position that does not agree with yours. Remember to also add the support for this counter-perspective. This counter-perspective should also be a paragraph.

Conclusion

Now write a concluding paragraph. This paragraph should restate your main points and then end with another sentence that is as strong as your hook. Quotes work well in conclusions because they inspire your readers to keep thinking about the issue identified in the question.

The happy challenge teachers face is that they can help their students form supported opinions and argue well-grounded positions that are based on background knowledge, experience, observation, and new knowledge gained from other textual and visual sources. Graphic organizers support students in compiling the information they need to take a position and craft an argument. Gallagher (2011) proposes the four-square argument, a means of assisting students to look at the opposing sides of an argument—not just to counter the opposing side, but to inform their own opinions and arguments as well. In the graphic organizer in Figure 8-1, we adapted and modified Gallagher's four-square argument chart a bit to help students compile and write an argument. This seven-part organizer includes parts to support students taking positions, noting counter-positions, and crafting an argument.

How Do I Use a Seven-Part Graphic Organizer for Composing an Argument?

- Ask students to take a position on a topic that is relevant to the curriculum and content being studied.

- Remind students that they may need to change their positions once they have considered the topic from other points of view.

- As students consult various sources, they should include their notes on the organizer. Remind them to consider how their opinions coincide with those of others, differ from those of others, and change as they investigate an issue.

- Next, model for students how to use the seven-part organizer to create an argument shared verbally, in writing, or through multimodal formats.

CCSS.ELA-Literacy.RI.7.6.

Determine an author's point of view or purpose in a text and analyze how the author distinguishes his or her position from that of others.

CCSS.ELA-Literacy.RI.7.8.

Trace and evaluate the argument and specific claims in a text, assessing whether the reasoning is sound and the evidence is relevant and sufficient to support the claims.

CCSS.ELA-Literacy.RI.7.9.

Analyze how two or more authors writing about the same topic shape their presentations of key information by emphasizing different evidence or advancing different interpretations of facts.

CCSS.ELA-Literacy.W.7.1.

Write arguments to support claims with clear reasons and relevant evidence.

CCSS.ELA-Literacy.SL.7.4.

Present claims and findings, emphasizing salient points in a focused, coherent manner with pertinent descriptions, facts, details, and examples; use appropriate eye contact, adequate volume, and clear pronunciation.

Determining the Need

Mr. Kavanaugh was tired of assigning the same old argumentative essay topics about less homework, longer lunch breaks, dress code rules, and the like. He knew it was time to reach beyond the school walls and give students input on the topics. So using the seven-part organizer as a guide, he asked his students to identify real problems in the community. Here's what his students came up with: lack of a bike lane on major roads, the fact that the community center hours did not extend into the evening when students often really needed them, and the desire for a community garden at the school to replace a barren, unused lot on the school grounds. Next, students used the organizer to generate questions.

Introducing It

Mr. Kavanaugh knew that general Internet inquiries can lead to time-wasting tangents into information that isn't germane to the topic at hand (Wolsey, Lapp, & Fisher, 2012). So he did a preliminary web search on the topics that interested his students, and then he posted the search results to the class web page, sorted by topic. Students could use those resources if they wished and could also conduct searches using kid-friendly search engines for more information. A useful search site for students is www.kidfriendlysearch.com/Kid_Friendly.htm.

Next, Mr. Kavanaugh asked students to select a topic and change the topic into a question they could research and eventually develop an informed opinion of, arguing from a pro or con perspective. He walked his students through how to use the seven-part graphic organizer for composing an argument (Figure 8-1). He wrote on the board, "Should schools be allowed to have video cameras in classrooms?" He did a think-aloud and invited student comments as he filled out Part 1, pointing out to students that he was asserting his position and noting a few positions that he thought might be counter to his. He identified initial sources and explained that he would need to confirm these before he wrote his argument. He continued to explain the additional parts of the graphic organizer as he filled them in. For Part 5, he said,

> There are many possible hooks that can be used to make readers want to read further in your essay. Some possibilities include a rhetorical question, which is a question that the reader isn't expecting you to answer. For example, since this essay is about whether cameras should be in the classroom, a rhetorical question might be *How comfortable would you feel being filmed every second of the day?* Your hook could also be an exaggeration—*The consequences of being viewed are endless.* It could be a surprising fact—*Today there are 10 videos cameras being installed at your school.* Other terrific hooks might be an anecdote about what happened to a student who was filmed by a classroom camera. You could even incorporate a quote into the anecdote. Take time to think about your hook. Remember, your hook should be motivating enough to make readers continue reading your essay.

Then Mr. Kavanaugh invited students to complete Part 1 of the organizer: "My current position is . . . ." Once their positions are noted he asks them to predict and fill out the square for, "What I think the position of others might be." He reminds students that they should also record their sources of information.

Guided Instruction and Independent Practice

Mr. Kavanaugh asked students to begin researching the topic of their question on the Internet. He reminded them to consult other sources in the school library and to consider whether there were people in their community to interview. As students compiled their resources, Mr. Kavanaugh asked them to address Part 3 of the organizer by thinking about and completing the following sentences frames.

The response of others to my argument could be _____.

My response to the arguments of others could be _____.

As they worked, Mr. Kavanaugh observed their actions and their work. One student explained that he was so surprised to learn that anyone would argue against his position that there could be no positive reasons for recycling toilet water. Mr. Kavanaugh asked him to share this insight with the class and then reminded everyone that this was why it was important to keep an open mind about new ideas, even when you have a well-documented position. As the students composed their responses to the counter-opinions and proposed solutions or reactions based on what they were learning, Mr. Kavanaugh invited them to continue completing the graphic. Throughout the process, they tracked their sources of information and noted how their own opinions changed as they engaged in the public sphere with those whose opinions differed from their own.

Closure

Once students formed their positions, read to find support for those opinions, and also read to determine the opinions of others, they were ready to move to Part 7 of the organizer to construct an argument that they could present to the city council, or as a podcast, or as a letter to the editor, or argue before the school board or other appropriate board of directors.

Reading, Writing, and Discussion Extensions

Throughout the process of forming an opinion, consulting other sources to confirm or disconfirm evidence or counter-opinions, students engage with texts and people who help them think about the positions they hold and how these positions can evolve over time. In the example from Mr. Kavanaugh's classroom, students used the seven-part graphic organizer to research an issue and write an argument. Using this graphic organizer supported students in considering multiple sources of information and perspectives. This organizer could easily be used to craft an argument that addresses civic issues in social studies, environmental issues in science, and economic issues in mathematics.

THINKING MAP

THIS ORGANIZER ADDRESSES THESE STANDARDS

CCSS.ELA-Literacy.CCRA.R.6.

Assess how point of view or purpose shapes the content and style of a text.

CCSS.ELA-Literacy.CCRA.R.8.

Delineate and evaluate the argument and specific claims in a text, including the validity of the reasoning as well as the relevance and sufficiency of the evidence.

CCSS.ELA-Literacy.CCRA.R.10.

Read and comprehend complex literary and informational texts independently and proficiently.

CCSS.ELA-Literacy.CCRA.W.1.

Write arguments to support claims in an analysis of substantive topics or texts using valid reasoning and relevant and sufficient evidence.

CCSS.ELA-Literacy.CCRA.W.8.

Gather relevant information from multiple print and digital sources, assess the credibility and accuracy of each source, and integrate the information while avoiding plagiarism.

CCSS.ELA-Literacy.CCRA.W.9.

Draw evidence from literary or informational texts to support analysis, reflection, and research.

What Is a Thinking Map?

A thinking map is a way for students to assess their own background knowledge relative to a given inquiry or classroom task (see Figure 8-2). As students work with sources to compose their thinking and the multimodal or written products that accompany that thinking, they often find that they don't have the needed background knowledge. The thinking map is a means of guiding students through that process when they recognize they may need to develop their background knowledge through further reading and exploration of other sources.

FIGURE 8-2
Thinking Map

Thinking Map: What Do I Know?

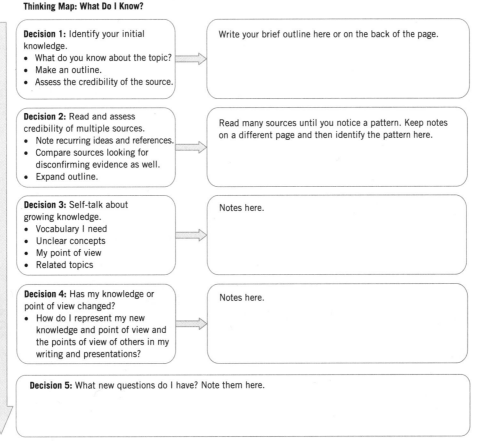

Decision 1: Identify your initial knowledge.
- What do you know about the topic?
- Make an outline.
- Assess the credibility of the source.

Write your brief outline here or on the back of the page.

Decision 2: Read and assess credibility of multiple sources.
- Note recurring ideas and references.
- Compare sources looking for disconfirming evidence as well.
- Expand outline.

Read many sources until you notice a pattern. Keep notes on a different page and then identify the pattern here.

Decision 3: Self-talk about growing knowledge.
- Vocabulary I need
- Unclear concepts
- My point of view
- Related topics

Notes here.

Decision 4: Has my knowledge or point of view changed?
- How do I represent my new knowledge and point of view and the points of view of others in my writing and presentations?

Notes here.

Decision 5: What new questions do I have? Note them here.

How Do I Use a Thinking Map?

Model the process for students using the following decision points. The graphic organizer associated with the thinking map process will help students, step by step, to notice what they still need to learn and how to find that information.

Decision 1: Identify the topic.
- Ask yourself what you know about this topic.
- Make an outline of what you know. If you feel you don't have enough knowledge to assess the credibility of a site, stop and fill your knowledge bank. Ask yourself if the information in the source is true. If you cannot readily confirm the facts in the source, ask yourself if you would be able to find this information elsewhere. If the answer is yes, then you need to do more research.

Decision 2: Investigate and read many sources from various places.
- Determine the credibility and reliability of the source.
- Determine the sources with disconfirming or opposing points of view.

- Expand your outline. Summarize key points of each source. Identify positions which may conflict.

Decision 3: Talk to yourself throughout evaluating your growing knowledge.
- What vocabulary do you need to develop?
- What concepts are not clear to you?
- What is your point of view? How does this differ from the point of view of others (especially for persuasive/argumentative pieces)?
- What other fields or domains are related to your topic?

Decision 4: How has your knowledge or point of view changed?
- How do you represent your new knowledge, your point of view, and the points of view of others in your writing and presentations?

Decision 5: What new questions do you have?

INTO THE CLASSROOM

10th Grade—Health and English

THIS CLASSROOM
EXAMPLE MEETS
ADDRESSES
STANDARDS

CCSS.ELA-Literacy.RI.9–10.7.

Analyze various accounts of a subject told in different mediums (e.g., a person's life story in both print and multimedia), determining which details are emphasized in each account.

CCSS.ELA-Literacy.RI.9–10.1.

Cite strong and thorough textual evidence to support analysis of what the text says explicitly as well as inferences drawn from the text.

CCSS.ELA-Literacy.W.9–10.1.d.

Establish and maintain a formal style and objective tone while attending to the norms and conventions of the discipline in which they are writing.

CCSS.ELA-Literacy.RST.9–10.1.

Cite specific textual evidence to support analysis of science and technical texts, attending to the precise details of explanations or descriptions.

CCSS.ELA-Literacy.RST.9–10.4.

Determine the meaning of symbols, key terms, and other domain-specific words and phrases as they are used in a specific scientific or technical context relevant to grades 9–10 texts and topics.

Determining the Need

Some of the most inquisitive students Ms. Thayre had ever had were in this year's 10th-grade class, and they really wanted to know more about almost every topic they encountered (Lapp, Thayre, & Wolsey, 2014). Sometimes they struggled with the ideas because they knew they needed to learn more than what they found in the required readings in science, social studies, and so on. Ms. Thayre used the thinking map to help students recognize that they knew quite a lot about many things, but any knowledge they had naturally led to new questions and additional readings and consultation with other sources.

Ms. Thayre taught at a high school that encouraged students to explore health issues and careers in the health industry. As a result, when they found that a character in Oscar Wilde's (1890) *The Picture of Dorian Gray* appeared to have a condition called narcissistic personality disorder (NPD), they wanted to know more. Ms. Thayre asked students to read "Narcissistic Personality Disorder Is Not Harmless Behavior" (Carrasquillo, 2013) to help them understand the disorder; however, because personality disorders were an unfamiliar topic to the students, they struggled to grasp this class of disorders. It was such new terrain that they often didn't fully realize how much more there was to know; one article on the topic didn't provide a sufficient understanding. Ms. Thayre knew the graphic organizer would be instrumental in leading students out of the messy disequilibrium of first learning. They could lean on it to guide their thinking and accrue information as they researched the topic further. Her students would write an analysis of a main character from the Oscar Wilde novel, so they needed to be knowledgeable about the book, the author, and the disorder.

Introducing It

Ms. Thayre gave each student a graphic organizer. She and the students discussed whether the organizer suited their purpose (it does) because she wanted them to be metacognitive about their learning. Then she modeled how to use it. The students had already identified the topic, NPD. Together, the students filled in the first box with what they already knew about the disorder. Next, they needed to read, and read a lot, to more fully understand the disorder. The school subscribed to a database of articles in addition to Internet resources, and students logged in to start their searches for a list of databases and indexes available online (see Figure 8-3).

FIGURE 8-3
Resources for Research in Secondary Schools

EBSCO Host: http://ebscohost.com/schools

Gale apps: www.gale.cengage.com/apps/aml/SchoolLibrary

Gale InfoTrac: www.gale.cengage.com/PeriodicalSolutions/infotracStudent.htm

ProQuest: www.proquestk12.com/default.shtml

Google Scholar: http://scholar.google.com (learn more about Google Scholar at www.freetech4teachers .com/2012/02/using-google-scholar-for-education.html#.U9UqbPldWSo)

Guided Instruction and Independent Practice

Once students had done some reading, they needed to digest what they learned thus far and determine what they still had questions about. They made notes, recorded the source of the information, and looked for patterns that showed what was important and more likely to be reliable. They looked specifically for sources that discussed mental health and diseases as well as general facts. The students often worked together, but they each created their own organizers and notes.

As they worked, Ms. Thayre moved throughout the classroom, guiding instruction as needed. For example, some students needed additional help with specific types of vocabulary; three students didn't understand what the DSM-IV was or how it was used.

Ms. Thayre called this small group to work with her so she could prompt them to look back at certain sections of the text to gain this information. A few others were not sure how NPD was diagnosed. By looking together at a visual in the text, Ms. Thayre and this small group clarified their understanding. She often clustered students together for a few minutes to provide just a little more explicit instruction.

Next, she asked students to work in small groups to compare the sources they found and the patterns that emerged. They wondered what was most important to do to take care of mental health and to avoid diseases. Finally, each student used the graphic organizer to show how his or her knowledge had changed and grown. Of course, the students had new questions, and they added them to Decision 5 on the organizer.

Closure

An important part of the entire inquiry includes the opportunity to learn how to analyze characters in literature and to write cogently about them. Because students read widely, checked their sources, and identified what they did not know, they were able to write a character analysis essay that depended on sources and demonstrated their growing capacity for understanding the literature they had read.

Reading, Writing, and Discussion Extensions

Students can use the thinking map not only to track their learning and note what they need to learn, but also to prepare presentations for their peers and for online audiences as well. Building background knowledge is not just something the teacher does for students. In the age of the Common Core State Standards, students are tasked to recognize what they know and what they still need to know to be well informed about the topics and questions they encounter. Connections to the modified KWL and I-charts and I-guides are helpful as students take responsibility for their own learning.

GRAPHIC ORGANIZERS SUPPORT COLLABORATION

The point of literacy is and has to be how human beings interact one with another. In school, students are asked to work together quite frequently. Quality of interactions is vitally important if all students are to make use of the opportunities that collaboration provides. This chapter explores graphic organizers for managing larger projects.

PROJECT MANAGEMENT ORGANIZER

THIS ORGANIZER
ADDRESSES THESE
STANDARDS

CCSS.ELA-Literacy.CCRA.R.7.

Integrate and evaluate content presented in diverse media and formats, including visually and quantitatively, as well as in words.

CCSS.ELA-Literacy.CCRA.SL.6.

Adapt speech to a variety of contexts and communicative tasks, demonstrating command of formal English when indicated or appropriate.

What Is a Project Management Organizer?

In many classrooms, students work together on projects that take several days or even weeks to accomplish.[1] These projects include preparing presentations to the class, making a digital demonstration of knowledge, or engaging in various service learning activities. The Common Core State Standards in English language arts/literacy emphasize the capacity for students to work together in a variety of settings and contexts where literacy skills are necessary. As important is that such skills prepare students for college and career experiences where project management and planning skills are necessary for success.

A project management tool that has been around for more than a century is named after the man who created it, Henry Gantt (see Clark, 1923). The Gantt chart has been used in the military, in manufacturing industries, and in long-range planning just about everywhere, including schools. Gantt charts are useful because they graphically make the plan and the actual work obvious. "Work planned and work done are shown in the same space in relation to each other and in their relation to time" (p. v), Clarke (1923) wrote of this tool. Their visual nature encourages student project participants to develop a plan, stick to it, and note their progress over time. Digital tools improve Gantt charts by automating some tasks, making them easily available to project participants at any time, and being infinitely expandable. The use of color further improves the look and feel of the organizer.

Gantt project management organizers can be created with sticky notes on a whiteboard, on butcher paper, or with an 11 × 17 piece of construction paper. In this chapter, we use Excel spreadsheets (see Figure 9-1), though the Gantt chart can easily be created in a shared spreadsheet file such as those found in Google Docs or with software specifically designed for this purpose (see Figure 9-2).

Smartsheet provides organizers for students and teachers at https://chrome.google .com/webstore/detail/smartsheet-group-project/kejkalfabljbhkapdinmjdhccbmofjio?hl =en and https://chrome.google.com/webstore/detail/smartsheet-class-syllabus/bnoamk imecefacafihefokmbhcjhnlpc?hl=en. These are best accessed using the Google Chrome web browser.

Templates for Gantt project management organizers are helpful because the setup is already done. A basic template from Microsoft downloads is available at http://office.microsoft .com/en-us/templates/gantt-project-planner-TC102887601.aspx. Figure 9-3 shows a modified Gantt project management organizer for use in upper-elementary grade classrooms.

---

1 This section was adapted from a post on LiteracyBeat.com.

FIGURE 9-1

Excel Project Management Organizer

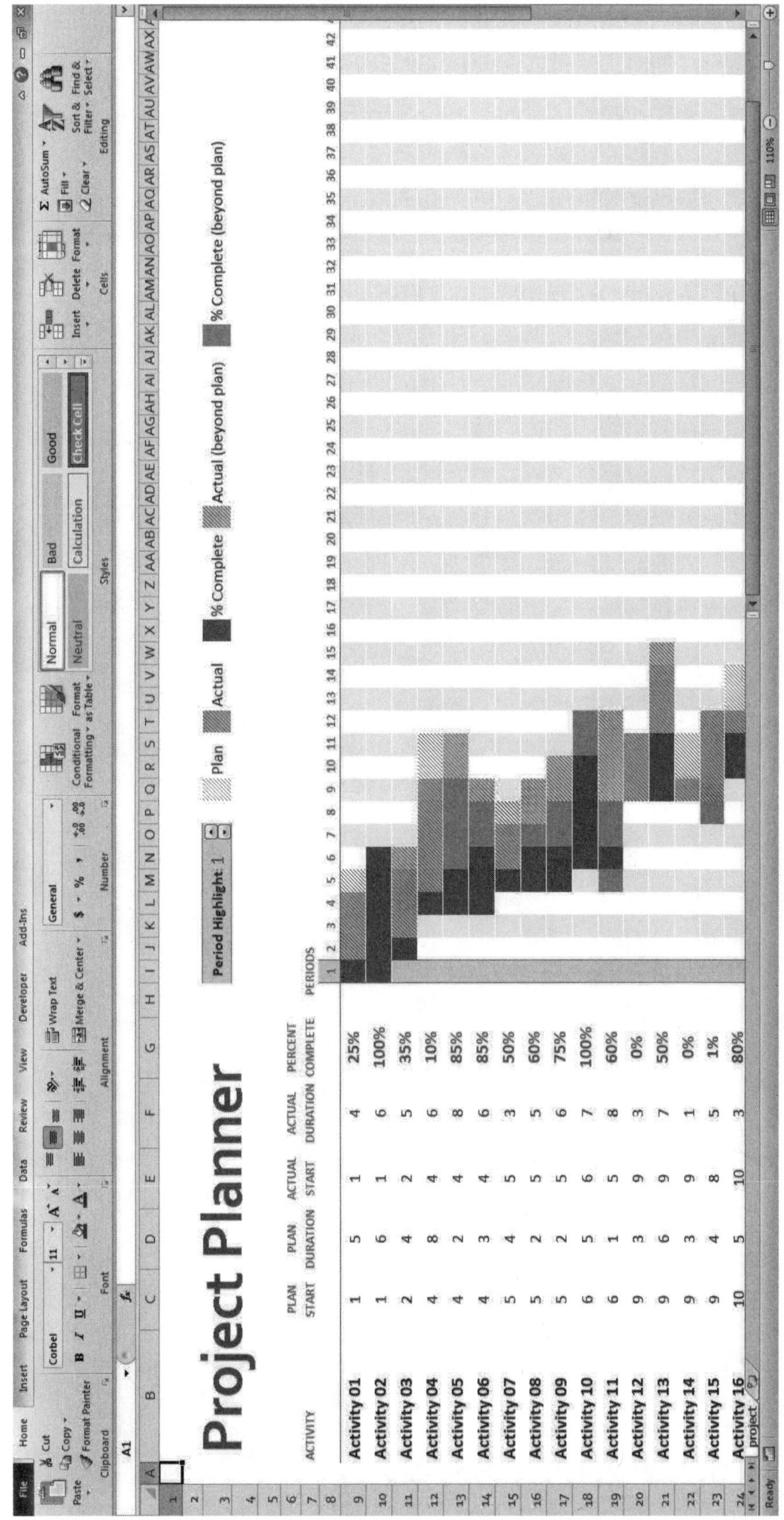

Project Planner

Period Highlight: 1

Legend: Plan | Actual | % Complete | Actual (beyond plan) | % Complete (beyond plan)

ACTIVITY	PLAN START	PLAN DURATION	ACTUAL START	ACTUAL DURATION	PERCENT COMPLETE
Activity 01	1	5	1	4	25%
Activity 02	1	6	1	6	100%
Activity 03	2	4	2	5	35%
Activity 04	4	8	4	6	10%
Activity 05	4	2	4	8	85%
Activity 06	4	3	4	6	85%
Activity 07	5	4	5	3	50%
Activity 08	5	2	5	5	60%
Activity 09	5	2	5	6	75%
Activity 10	6	5	6	7	100%
Activity 11	6	1	5	8	60%
Activity 12	9	3	9	3	0%
Activity 13	9	6	9	7	50%
Activity 14	9	3	9	1	0%
Activity 15	9	4	8	5	1%
Activity 16	10	5	10	3	80%

FIGURE 9-2
Smartsheet Project Management Organizer

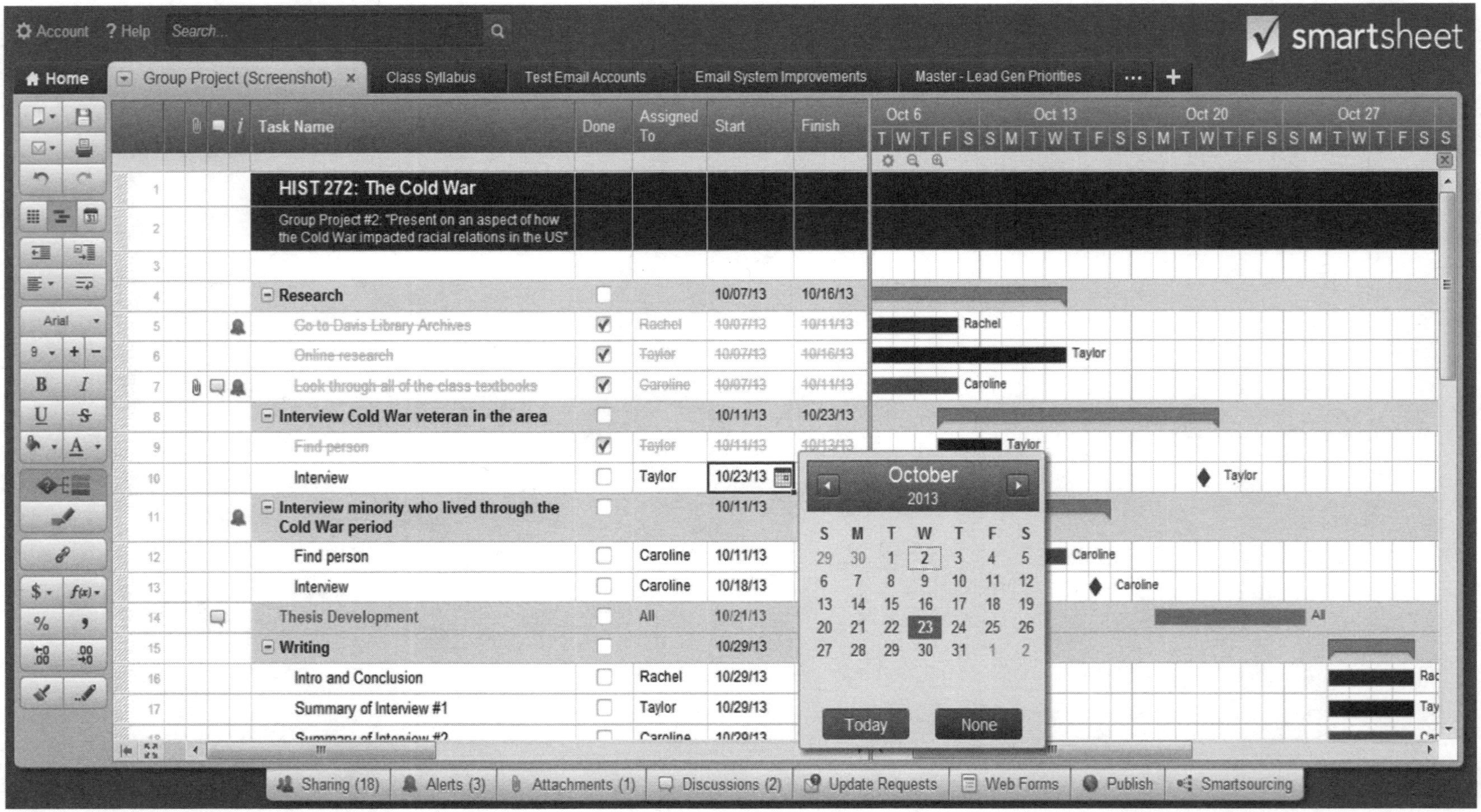

Source: Smartsheet

FIGURE 9-3
Gantt Project Management Organizer

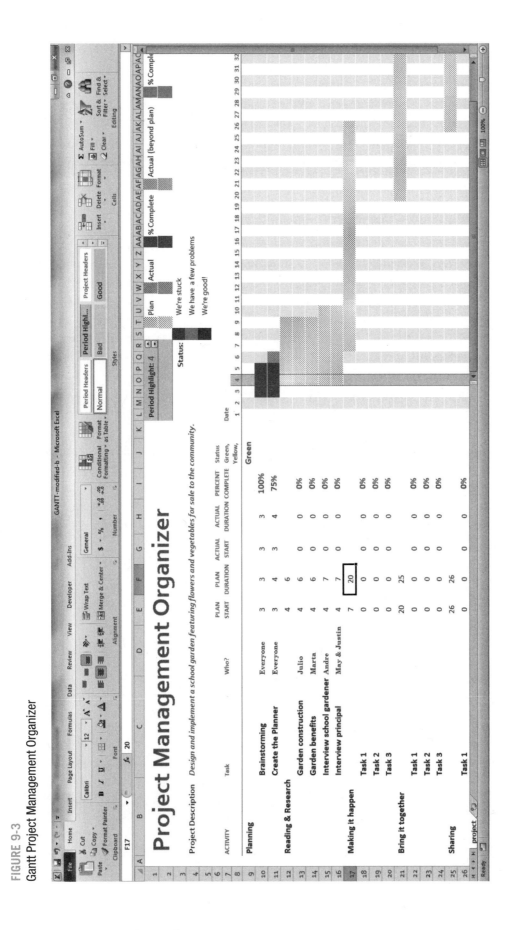

You can download this template from the Corwin website by navigating to www.corwin.com/miningcomplextext/6-12.

Both of these organizers allow students to quickly enter data about what they plan to do, how much they have accomplished, and how they are proceeding. The neat thing is that Excel and other spreadsheet software automatically create the timeline showing what is planned and what is actually accomplished. These examples show a start date for the first of the month, but teachers can create their own template by deleting columns for dates that don't match the instructional cycle.

How Do I Use a Project Management Organizer?

- As we discussed in Chapter 1, some skill development is necessary with graphic organizers. With project management organizers, students need to know why the tool will help them be successful with the project, what norms (Cohen, 1994) they will need to work in groups, and how to use the technology itself, even if that technology is paper or sticky notes! Share models based on previous small projects using a digital projector or document camera, depending on the format. Demonstrate how changing the values (usually these values are dates) in the plan, actual, and percent columns changes the timeline to the right automatically.

- Train a few students, perhaps one from each project group or team, to be the group expert on using technology. In this way, you are not the only resource for using the tool.

- Help students define the major parts of the task. In the example in Figure 9-3, the teacher defined large categories as *planning, reading and research, making it happen, bringing it together,* and *sharing.*

- Assist students with breaking down each category into specific tasks. A model will be very helpful in guiding students to decide just what the specific tasks might be.

- Start the project!

Eighth Grade—Science and Language Arts

CCSS.ELA-Literacy.RI.8.7.

Evaluate the advantages and disadvantages of using different mediums (e.g., print or digital text, video, multimedia) to present a particular topic or idea.

CCSS.ELA-Literacy.SL.8.1.

Engage effectively in a range of collaborative discussions (one-on-one, in groups, and teacher-led) with diverse partners on grade 5 topics and texts, building on others' ideas and expressing their own clearly.

CCSS.ELA-Literacy.SL.8.5.

Integrate multimedia and visual displays into presentations to clarify information, strengthen claims and evidence, and add interest.

CCSS.ELA-Literacy.SL.8.6.

Adapt speech to a variety of contexts and tasks, demonstrating command of formal English when indicated or appropriate.

THIS CLASSROOM EXAMPLE ADDRESSES THESE STANDARDS

Determining the Need

Mr. Semilla's students approached science by getting their hands right into the thick of things. They surveyed the area around the school for rock formations, modeled how waves destroy communities during particularly powerful storms, and now, one group was ready to engage in a bit of dirty work. They planned to put their spades right into the soil in a part of the schoolyard to build a garden that would be beautiful but also produce vegetables for the community. They would have to work collaboratively, read many resources, convince others of the project's value, and then make the school garden happen (see Wolsey, 2014).

The students at Cesar Chavez Middle School were very accustomed to having their voices be part of the school community. The podiums in the auditoriums were not just for the administrators and teachers; they were for any student who had something to say. The main lobby was a gathering place for students, parents, and teachers where ideas were explored and problems solved (see Uline, Tschannen-Moran, & Wolsey, 2009). Students were not surprised when Mr. Semilla asked them to think of a service learning project that would benefit the community. One group chose to focus on a school garden that would produce vegetables they might sell to the community at cost because so many families had to travel long distances by bus just to purchase fresh produce.

Introducing It

Once students decided on their projects, Mr. Semilla demonstrated how students could use Excel to organize the project so that they kept to timelines. He chose several students to serve as Excel masters to solve problems that arose; they were excused from other tasks so they could explore online tutorials and play around a bit with the project management organizer. To make sure students stayed on task, Mr. Semilla adjusted the template to show the timelines for the project, then placed it on the class web page for students to download.

Students worked together to create a plan using the project management organizer and decided just what steps they needed to take. Every 3 days, students met with Mr. Semilla to show him their organizer and ask questions about the next steps. During this time he assessed how their knowledge was developing and also provided any reteaching that was warranted. The school garden group created an organizer which you can see in Figure 9-3.

Mr. Semilla inserted the "plan dates" into the template. He knew that students would need to present this to the school board on the 26th day, and actual timelines based on the board meeting dates would be critical. Students worked through the project, and as they moved from one major category to another, they added the specific steps they would need to complete. Maria volunteered to keep the project management organizer updated and posted to the group blog so they could each review it every day. Throughout the project, students wrote letters asking for support from the community, discussed their plans, implemented those plans, made presentations to the principal and parent groups, and read extensively about school and community gardens.

Closure

At the end of the project, students had successfully designed a garden and obtained the permission of the principal and school board to make it happen. They also had created a schedule for maintaining the garden and invited other students to participate. Before long, the school garden project was in full flower—selling produce, at cost, to the parents who came to school to pick up children or participate in parent-teacher-student events.

Reading, Writing, and Discussion Extensions

Throughout any project, many opportunities exist for discussion, speech, writing, and reading. Teachers may choose to make these components explicit parts of the project depending on curricular goals. Our objective in including this project management organizer is that it is infinitely adaptable and expandable, and it gives students a way to organize how they engage in literacy tasks as they collaborate with each other. It also provides endless opportunity for them to go beyond current graphic organizers to create others that accommodate their expanding ideas. Read more about project management at http://literacybeat.com/2014/03/22/project-planning.

CONCLUSION

Throughout this book we have shared many graphic organizers that support students as they read and organize information and also as they organize ideas and information they plan to share through written or oral presentations. In the process of organizing or comprehending the organization others use, students learn to make sense of complex texts and become composers of such texts as well. As we have emphasized throughout, we encourage you to use these examples to model for students the power of using graphic organizers. But this isn't where we want you to stop. We encourage you to also help students realize that they can construct organizers to promote and share their thinking. It is through their individual construction that they will think deeply about the information they are learning or presenting. This personalization promotes their independence as thinkers.

APPENDIX

GRAPHIC ORGANIZERS AT A GLANCE: MEETING EIGHT ESSENTIAL ACADEMIC SKILLS

In the matrix on pages 148–149, we have identified eight essential skills and aligned them with the graphic organizers in this book. It is important to know that the specific tasks, students' capacities for understanding content and processes, and curricular goals may mean that each graphic organizer should be adapted by students and teachers to meet the instructional goals and standards intended.

	1. Acquire and use academic language appropriately	2. Make connections	3. Comprehend complex processes or events	4. Understand five types of informational text structures
Frayer Organizer	x			
Vocabulary Triangle	x		x	
Concept/Definition Map	x			
Word Map	x			
Freytag's Pyramid		x		
Text Search and Find Board		x		
4-Square With a Diamond		x		x
Modified KWL			x	x
Note-Card Organizer	x	x	x	
Tabbed Book Manipulative	x	x	x	x
Somebody-Wanted-But-So		x	x	
Five Text Types				x
Sequential			x	x
Descriptive				x
Cause/Effect		x		x
Compare and Contrast		x		x
Problem/Solution		x	x	x
Rereading Organizer		x	x	
I-Chart and I-Guide				
Flip Chart Manipulative				x
Text-Dependent Question/ Response Organizer		x	x	x
Seven-Part Graphic Organizer for Composing an Argument				
Thinking Map				
Project Management Organizer		x		

	5. Understand content	6. Explore a concept and determine the nature of inquiry	7. Synthesize multiple sources	8. Use reliable sources to form and write opinions
Frayer Organizer	x			
Vocabulary Triangle	x			
Concept/Definition Map	x			
Word Map	x			
Freytag's Pyramid				
Text Search and Find Board	x			
4-Square With a Diamond	x			
Modified KWL	x	x	x	
Note-Card Organizer	x	x	x	x
Tabbed Book Manipulative	x	x		
Somebody-Wanted-But-So	x			
Five Text Types				
Sequential	x			
Descriptive	x			
Cause/Effect	x			
Compare and Contrast	x			
Problem/Solution	x			
Rereading Organizer				
I-Chart and I-Guide		x	x	
Flip Chart Manipulative	x			
Text-Dependent Question/ Response Organizer	x			
Seven-Part Graphic Organizer for Composing an Argument	x	x		x
Thinking Map	x	x	x	x
Project Management Organizer		x		

FRAYER ORGANIZER

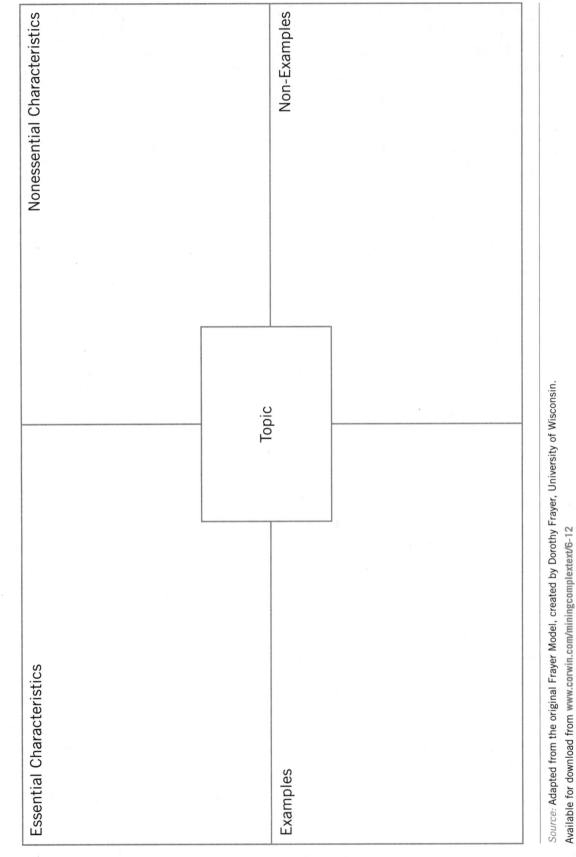

Essential Characteristics

Nonessential Characteristics

Topic

Examples

Non-Examples

Source: Adapted from the original Frayer Model, created by Dorothy Frayer, University of Wisconsin.

Available for download from **www.corwin.com/miningcomplextext/6-12**

Reprinted from *Mining Complex Text, Grades 6–12: Using and Creating Graphic Organizers to Grasp Content and Share New Understandings* by Diane Lapp, Thomas DeVere Wolsey, Karen Wood, and Kelly Johnson. Thousand Oaks, CA: Corwin, www.corwin.com. Reproduction authorized only for the local school site or nonprofit organization that has purchased this book.

VOCABULARY TRIANGLE

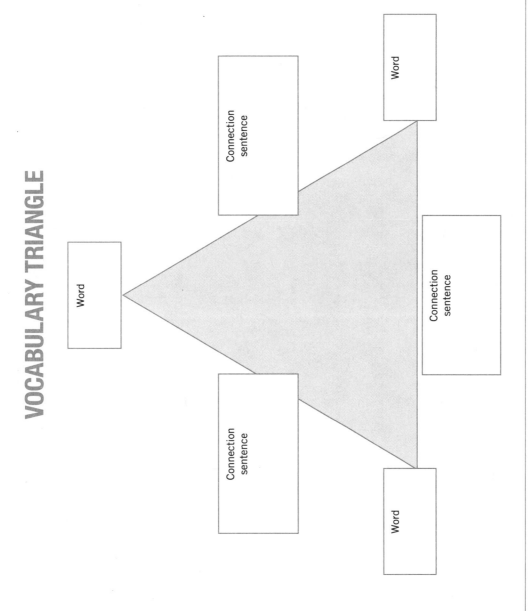

Source: Created by Kyle Kester.

Available for download from www.corwin.com/miningcomplextext/6-12

Reprinted from *Mining Complex Text, Grades 6–12: Using and Creating Graphic Organizers to Grasp Content and Share New Understandings* by Diane Lapp, Thomas DeVere Wolsey, Karen Wood, and Kelly Johnson. Thousand Oaks, CA: Corwin, www.corwin.com. Reproduction authorized only for the local school site or nonprofit organization that has purchased this book.

CONCEPT/DEFINITION MAP

Name:

Subject:

Date:

Topic, Word, or Concept:

What are non-examples?

What is it like?

The topic word or concept is:

What is it?

My explanation or definition of the word is:

WORD MAP

The word is:

Word used in the sentence from the book or lecture:

Dictionary definition:

Symbol or picture:

Synonyms and related words:

Two examples of how the word can be used in your own life:

Explanation of symbol or picture:

FREYTAG'S PYRAMID

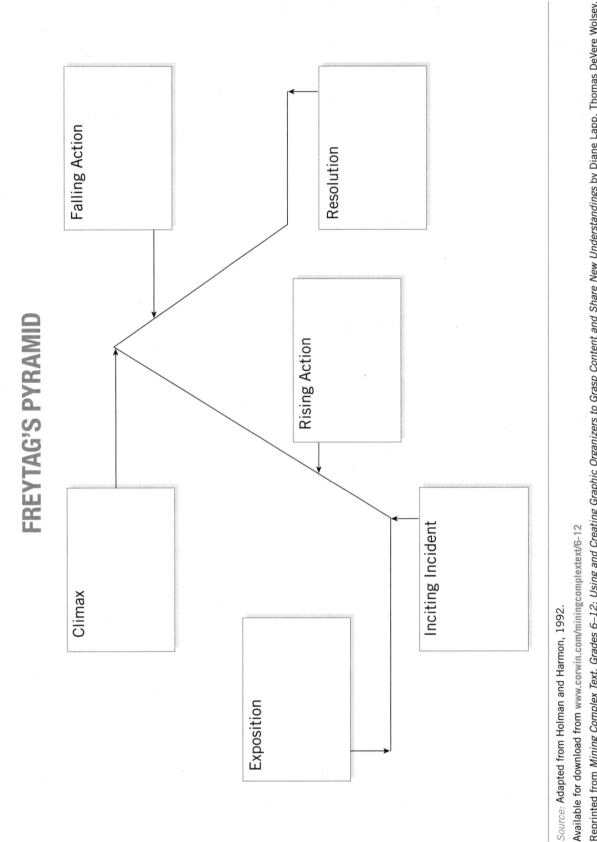

Source: Adapted from Holman and Harmon, 1992.

Available for download from www.corwin.com/miningcomplextext/6-12

Reprinted from *Mining Complex Text, Grades 6–12: Using and Creating Graphic Organizers to Grasp Content and Share New Understandings* by Diane Lapp, Thomas DeVere Wolsey, Karen Wood, and Kelly Johnson. Thousand Oaks, CA: Corwin, www.corwin.com. Reproduction authorized only for the local school site or nonprofit organization that has purchased this book.

TEXT SEARCH AND FIND BOARD

Title	Main Idea	Key Details	Vocabulary
Include the book title and your name here.	*What's the main idea? Write a complete sentence that tells the main idea.*	*Provide at least three key facts that support your main idea.*	*List and define at least three important vocabulary words from the book.*
Connections *How does this text remind you of something in your life or another text you have read?*	**Chart, Illustration, or Graph** *Create a chart, illustration, or graph to display some of the information you learned from the book.*	**Questions** *After reading your book, create questions.*	**Answers** *Choose at least one of your questions and provide an answer with supporting details from the text.*

Source: Created by Rebecca Kavel.

Available for download from **www.corwin.com/miningcomplextext/6-12**

Reprinted from *Mining Complex Text, Grades 6–12: Using and Creating Graphic Organizers to Grasp Content and Share New Understandings* by Diane Lapp, Thomas DeVere Wolsey, Karen Wood, and Kelly Johnson. Thousand Oaks, CA: Corwin, www .corwin.com. Reproduction authorized only for the local school site or nonprofit organization that has purchased this book.

4-SQUARE WITH A DIAMOND

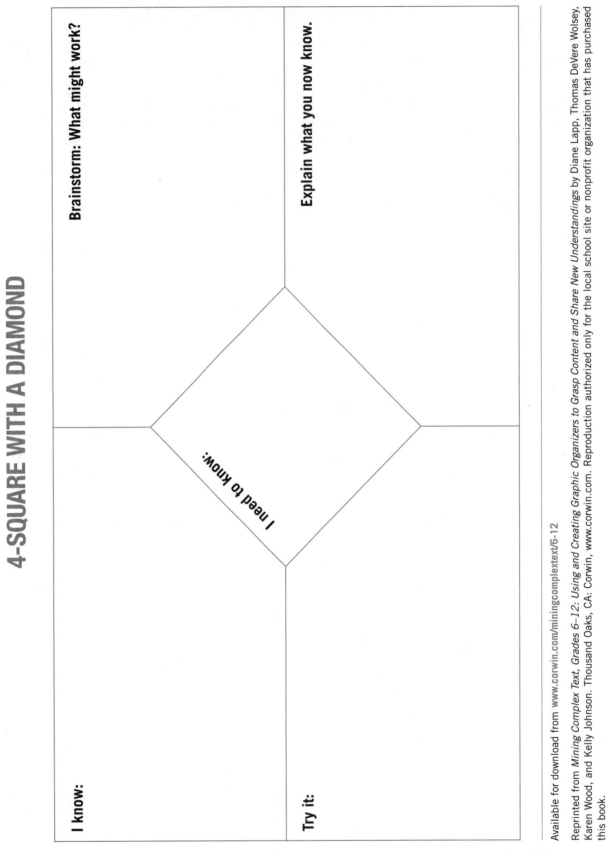

Brainstorm: What might work?

Explain what you now know.

I know:

Try it:

I need to know:

KWL

K **What do we know about the KWL instructional strategy?**	W **What do we want to know about the KWL instructional strategy?**	L **What did we learn about the KWL instructional strategy?**

Categories:

SOMEBODY-WANTED-BUT-SO

Somebody (Characters)	
Wanted (Plot motivation)	
But (Conflict)	
So (Resolution)	

COMPARE-AND-CONTRAST ATTRIBUTE CHART

Name:

Date:

Subjects:

Topic or Concepts:

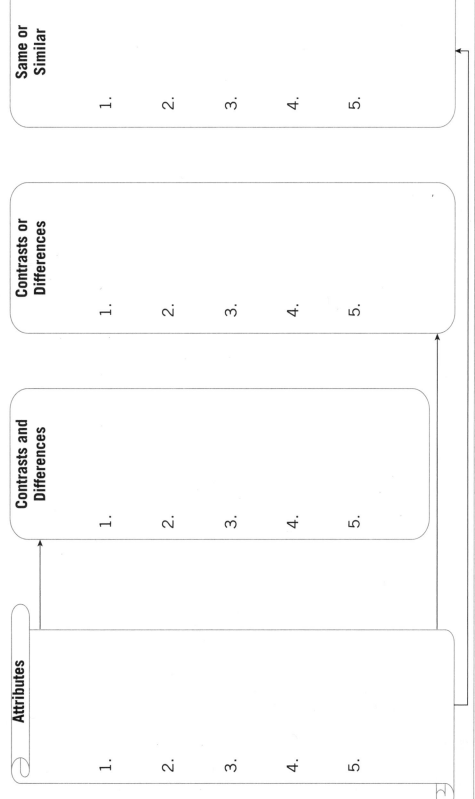

Attributes

1.

2.

3.

4.

5.

Contrasts and Differences

1.

2.

3.

4.

5.

Contrasts or Differences

1.

2.

3.

4.

5.

Same or Similar

1.

2.

3.

4.

5.

PROBLEM/SOLUTION GRAPHIC ORGANIZER

Name:

Date:

Subjects:
Topic or Concepts:

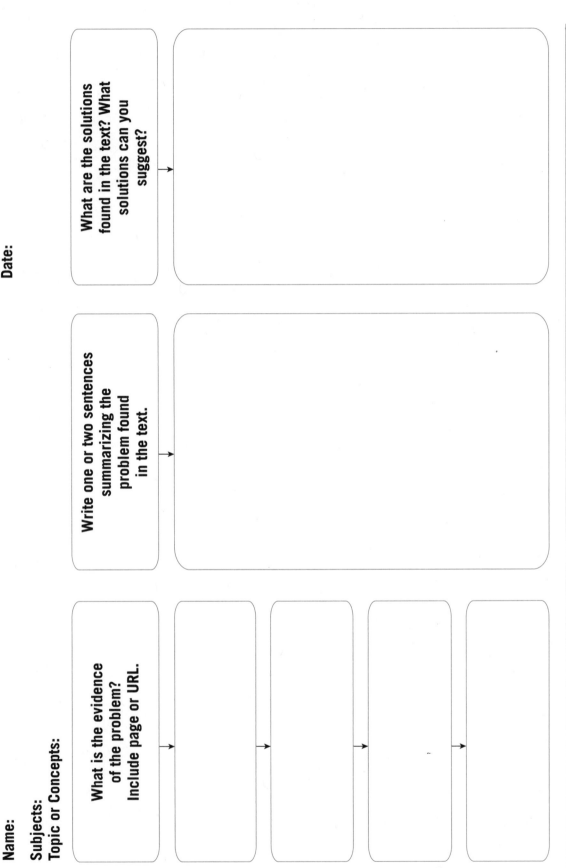

What is the evidence of the problem? Include page or URL.

Write one or two sentences summarizing the problem found in the text.

What are the solutions found in the text? What solutions can you suggest?

REREADING ORGANIZER

Name: _____   **Date:** _____   **Reread Book:** _____

List five MAJOR things that happened in your independent reading book this week.	**Explain** one thing that you noticed during your reread that you did NOT notice the first time you read the book. Write a full paragraph with as many specific details as possible.	**Describe** the protagonist (main character) in your book.	**Illustrate** a scene from your reading this week. Include a caption that tells what is happening.
1.			
2.			
3.			
4.			
5.			

Term 1: Reread Book Analysis; TESTING Words

Term 1: Reread Book Analysis; TESTING Words

I-CHART

	What We Know				
Topic	**Question**	**Question**	**Question**	**Other Interesting Facts and Figures**	**New Questions**
Sources					
Synthesis					

I-GUIDE

Topic or Question	Major Subtopics or Themes				Summary of Each Text	Importance or Relevance of the Information
Sources						
Synthesis						

What We Know

TEXT-DEPENDENT QUESTION/RESPONSE ORGANIZER

Name:

Subject: **Date:**

Circle one:

- This is my first reading
- Second reading
- Third or more readings

The text-dependent question is:

After reading the text again, I found this evidence to support my answer (with page or section numbers):

And now my response to the question is:

SEVEN-PART GRAPHIC ORGANIZER FOR COMPOSING AN ARGUMENT

Writing an Argumentative Essay

Question:

Part 1: Take a Position

State your position. My current position is:	State what you think might be positions that conflict with yours. I think the position of others might be:

Part 2: Support Your Position

These points support my position. (Identify at least three. Use multiple sources and types of sources.) • • •	These are the sources that support my position. • • •

Part 3: Present Counter-Perspectives

Counter-perspectives are positions or views that differ from yours. (Include at least two counter-perspectives.) • •	I found support for these counter-perspectives in these resources. (Match each counter-perspective with its resource.) • •

Part 4: Write Your Thesis Statement

This is the part of your essay where you explain to readers what your essay is going to talk about. This is your thesis. Your thesis is the statement that shares your position. It should be the one you identified as your position in Part 1.

Part 5: Craft Your Hook

Now add a hook that gets the attention of your readers and makes them want to read your essay. Your hook should connect to your thesis statement.

Part 6: Reflect on the Issue, Your Position, and Possible Other Positions

Think again about the issue you are addressing. Now refer back to Parts 1 and 3 to summarize your position and also the counter-perspectives. Once you've finished, it's time to write your argumentative essay.

Part 7: Writing Your Essay

Now it's time to write your essay. You can use the ideas you compiled in Parts 1–6 of this organizer to write your essay.

Paragraph 1—Introduction

Your first paragraph should begin with the hook you wrote in Part 5. Next, connect your hook to the initial question. Now look at Part 6, and use this summary of information to show all sides of the issue identified in the question. Finally, add your thesis statement from Part 4.

Body Paragraphs (2–4)

The supports you identified in Part 2 should now be added as the next paragraphs in your essay. Each support for your position should be shared as a paragraph that also includes its documentation. After discussing all of your supports, add at least one position that does not agree with yours. Remember to also add the support for this counter-perspective. This counter-perspective should also be a paragraph.

Conclusion

Now write a concluding paragraph. This paragraph should restate your main points and then end with another sentence that is as strong as your hook. Quotes work well in conclusions because they inspire your readers to keep thinking about the issue identified in the question.

Available for download from **www.corwin.com/miningcomplextext/6-12**

Reprinted from *Mining Complex Text, Grades 6–12: Using and Creating Graphic Organizers to Grasp Content and Share New Understandings* by Diane Lapp, Thomas DeVere Wolsey, Karen Wood, and Kelly Johnson. Thousand Oaks, CA: Corwin, www.corwin.com. Reproduction authorized only for the local school site or nonprofit organization that has purchased this book.

THINKING MAP

Thinking Map: What Do I Know?

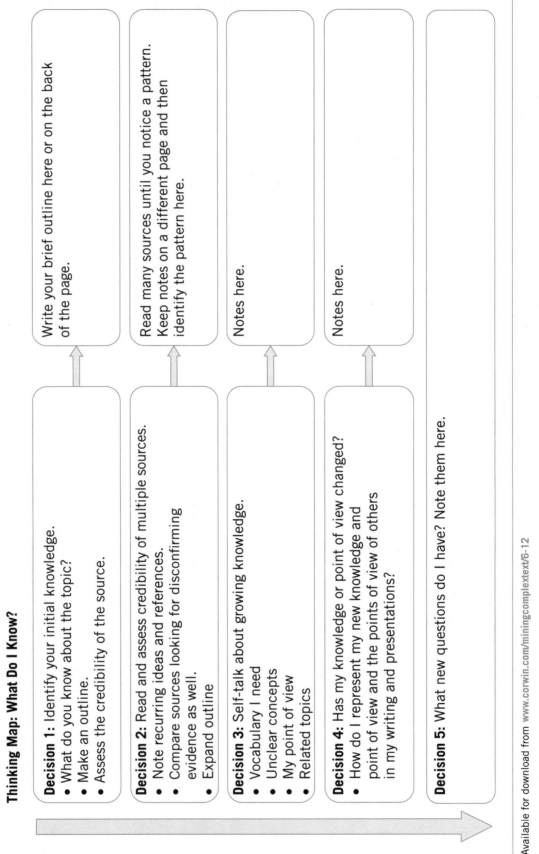

Decision 1: Identify your initial knowledge.
- What do you know about the topic?
- Make an outline.
- Assess the credibility of the source.

Write your brief outline here or on the back of the page.

Decision 2: Read and assess credibility of multiple sources.
- Note recurring ideas and references.
- Compare sources looking for disconfirming evidence as well.
- Expand outline

Read many sources until you notice a pattern. Keep notes on a different page and then identify the pattern here.

Decision 3: Self-talk about growing knowledge.
- Vocabulary I need
- Unclear concepts
- My point of view
- Related topics

Notes here.

Decision 4: Has my knowledge or point of view changed?
- How do I represent my new knowledge and point of view and the points of view of others in my writing and presentations?

Notes here.

Decision 5: What new questions do I have? Note them here.

Available for download from www.corwin.com/miningcomplextext/6–12

Reprinted from *Mining Complex Text, Grades 6–12: Using and Creating Graphic Organizers to Grasp Content and Share New Understandings* by Diane Lapp, Thomas DeVere Wolsey, Karen Wood, and Kelly Johnson. Thousand Oaks, CA: Corwin, www.corwin.com. Reproduction authorized only for the local school site or non-profit organization that has purchased this book.

GLOSSARY

Academic language is characterized by word choice (see academic vocabulary) as well as the syntactic structures that make deep connections. It is also a term used to describe the language that students and scholars might employ in their academic work.

Academic vocabulary describes the function of academic vocabulary in terms of complexity, higher-order thinking, and abstraction. The terms associated with these functions are usually thought of as they relate to a specific discipline (e.g., science, social studies) and to those that are typically used in academic environments but are used across disciplines (Coxhead, 2000). Tier two vocabulary (Beck, McKeown, & Kucan, 2002) are those terms that are mainly specific to academic environments but cut across disciplines. Tier three vocabulary, by contrast, are typically specific to a domain. We encourage you to read more about these topics by consulting Coxhead (2000) and Beck et al. (2002).

Advance organizers (Ausubel, 1960) are often thought of as synonymous with graphic organizers; however, the two terms are not interchangeable. Advance organizers are presented, as the name implies, in advance of learning. They are typically graphical in nature, but they need not be. Graphic organizers may be used throughout any learning sequence. A structured overview is a type of graphic organizer that demonstrates connections among broad topics in advance of learning.

Digital environment is a term that describes interactions between humans in an electronic environment.

Gradual release of responsibility implies a method whereby the teacher initially has responsibility for student learning, often through direct instruction (see Durkin, 1990), but students are increasingly given responsibility for understanding the processes, conditions, and tasks of the learning (Pearson & Gallagher, 1983).

Literature circles (Daniels, 2002) are designed to foster a love of reading and for students to "work together to choose literature they wish to read and explore collaboratively" (Wolsey, 2004, para. 1).

Manipulatives (including foldables such as those advanced by Zike, n.d.), for the purposes of this book, generally mean a graphic organizer that is in some way manipulated physically, such as by folding paper, by the student.

Scaffold is a term first conceived by Bruner (1978) to describe the helping interaction found in Vygotsky's (1978) theories of learning. Scaffolding is a technique by which a teacher or capable peer assists a student, often through the use of tools such as a graphic organizer, to make sense of what would otherwise be nearly incomprehensible. The principle of scaffolding rests on the notion that it is only useful if the student cannot proceed efficiently or meaningfully without the assistance. A graphic organizer, for example, that does not promote student learning independently would not be considered a scaffold.

REFERENCES

Abilock, D. (2014). Adding friction: How to design deliberate thinking into the research process. *Library Media Connection, 32*(4), 44–45. Retrieved from http://www.librarymediaconnection.com

Affirmative action banned? It's not that simple. (2014, April 23). *Los Angeles Times*, p. A12.

Akhondi, M., Malayeri, F., & Samad, A. (2011). How to teach expository text structure to facilitate reading comprehension. *Reading Teacher, 64*, 368–372. doi:10.1598/RT.64.5.9

Anderson, L. W., & Krathwohl, D. R. (Eds.). (2001). *A taxonomy for learning, teaching, and assessing: A revision of Bloom's taxonomy of educational objectives*. New York, NY: Longman.

Ausubel, D. P. (1960). The use of advance organizers in the learning and retention of meaningful verbal material. *Journal of Educational Psychology, 5*, 267–272. doi:10.1037/h0046669

Beck, I. L., McKeown, M. G., & Kucan, L. (2002). *Bringing words to life: Robust vocabulary instruction*. New York, NY: Guilford Press.

Birbili, M. (2006). Mapping knowledge: Concept maps in early childhood education. *Early childhood research and practice, 8*(2), 1–11.

Bluestein, N. A. (2013). Comprehension through characterization: Enabling readers to make personal connections with literature. *Reading Teacher, 55*, 431–434.

Braselton, S., & Decker, B. C. (1994). Using graphic organizers to improve the reading of mathematics. *Reading Teacher, 48*, 276–281.

Bruner, J. (1978). The role of dialogue in language acquisition. In A. Sinclair, R. J. Jarvelle, & W. J. M. Levelt (Eds.), *The child's concept of language* (pp. 241–256). New York, NY: Springer-Verlag.

California Department of Education. (2000). *History–Social Science content standards for California public schools, kindergarten through grade twelve*. Sacramento, CA: Author.

Candler, L. (2012). *Laura Candler's graphic organizers for reading comprehension*. Saint Johnsbury, VT: Compass Brigantine Media.

Clark, W. (1923). *The Gantt chart: A working tool of management*. New York, NY: Ronald Press. Retrieved from https://archive.org/details/ganttchartworkin00claruoft

Clarke, J. J. (1994). Sequencing graphic organizers to guide historical research. *Social Studies, 85*(2), 70–75.

Cohen, E. G. (1994). *Designing groupwork: Strategies for the heterogeneous classroom* (2nd ed.). New York, NY: Teachers College Press.

Coleman, D., & Pimentel, S. (2012). *Revised publishers' criteria for the Common Core State Standards in English Language Arts and Literacy, Grades 3–12*. Retrieved from http://achievethecore.org/content/upload/3._Publishers_Criteria_for_Literacy_for_Grades_3–12.pdf

Common Core State Standards Initiative. (2010a). Appendix A: Research supporting key elements of the standards. In *Common Core State Standards for English language arts & literacy in history/social studies, science, and technical subjects*. Retrieved from http://www.corestandards.org/assets/Appendix_A.pdf

Common Core State Standards Initiative. (2010b). *Common Core State Standards for English language arts and literacy in history/social studies, science, and technical subjects*. Retrieved from http://www.corestandards.org/assets/CCSSI_ELA%20Standards.pdf

Concept/definition maps to comprehend curriculum content. (2011). *Reading Teacher, 65*, 211–213. doi:10.1002/TRTR.01029

Coxhead, A. (2000). A new academic word list. *TESOL Quarterly, 34*, 213–238. doi:10.2307/3587951

Daines, D. (1986). Are teachers asking higher level questions? *Education, 106*, 368–374.

Daniels, H. (2002). *Literature circles: Voice and choice in book clubs and reading groups* (2nd ed.). York, ME: Stenhouse.

DiCecco, V. M., & Gleason, M. M. (2002). Using graphic organizers to attain relational knowledge from expository text. *Journal of Learning Disabilities, 35*, 306–320. doi:10.1177/00222194020350040201

Dirksen, D. J. (2011). Hitting the reset button: Using formative assessment to guide instruction. *Phi Delta Kappan, 92*(7), 26–31.

Duke, N. K., & Pearson, P. D. (2002). Effective practices for developing reading comprehension. In A. E. Farstrup & S. J. Samuels (Eds.), *What research has to say about reading instruction* (3rd ed., pp. 205–242). Newark, DE: International Reading Association.

Durkin, D. (1990). Dolores Durkin speaks on instruction. *Reading Teacher, 43*, 472–726.

Fisher, D., & Frey, N. (2012a). *Improving adolescent literacy* (3rd ed.). New York, NY: Pearson.

Fisher, D., & Frey, N. (2012b). Text dependent questions. *Principal Leadership, 13*(3), 70–73.

Fisher, D., Frey, N., & Lapp, D. (2012). *Text complexity: Raising rigor in reading.* Newark, DE: International Reading Association.

Florida Center for Reading Research. (n.d.). *Comprehension: Narrative text structure, character consideration.* Retrieved from http://www.fcrr.org/curriculum/PDF/G4–5/45CPartOne.pdf

Gaipa, M. (2004). Breaking into the conversation: How students can acquire authority for their writing. *Pedagogy, 4*, 371–381. Retrieved from http://english254.qwriting.qc.cuny.edu/files/2011/08/Gaipa.pdf

Gallagher, K. (2011). *Write like this: Teaching real-world writing through modeling and mentor texts.* Portland, ME: Stenhouse.

Gallavan, N. P., & Kottler, E. (2010). Visualizing the life and legacy of Henry VIII: Guiding students with eight types of graphic organizers. *Social Studies, 101*, 93–102. doi:10.1080/00377991003711699

Gardner, H. (2006). *Changing minds: The art and science of changing our own and other people's minds.* Boston, MA: Harvard Business School Press.

Gick, M. L., & Holyoak, K. J. (1983). Schema induction and analogical transfer. *Cognitive Psychology, 15*, 1–38. doi:10.1016/0010–0285(83)90002–6

Gill, S. (2007). Learning about word parts with Kidspiration. *Reading Teacher, 61*, 79–84. doi:10.1598/RT.61.1.8

Gould, J., & Gould, E. (1999). *Four square writing method for grades 1–3.* Carthage, IL: Teaching and Learning.

Graff, G., & Birkenstein, C. (2010). *They say/I say: The moves that matter in academic writing* (2nd ed.). New York: W. W. Norton.

Griffin, C. C., Malone, L. D., & Kameenui, E. J. (1995). Effects of graphic organizer instruction on fifth-grade. *Journal of Educational Research, 89*(2), 98–107. doi:10.1080/00220671.1995.9941200

Haggard, M. R. (1985). An interactive strategies approach to content reading. *Journal of Reading, 29*, 204–210.

Hartman, D. K. (1995). Eight readers reading: The intertextual links of proficient readers reading multiple passages. *Reading Research Quarterly, 30*, 520–561.

Harvey, S., & Goudvis, A. (2000). *Strategies that work: Teaching comprehension to enhance understanding.* Portland, ME: Stenhouse.

Hilligoss, B., & Rieh, S. Y. (2008). Developing a unifying framework of credibility assessment: Construct, heuristics, and interaction in context. *Information Processing and Management, 44*, 1467–1484. doi:10.1016/j.ipm.2007.10.001

Hoffman, J. V. (1992). Critical reading/thinking across the curriculum: Using I-charts to support learning. *Language Arts, 69*, 121–127.

Holman, C. H., & Harmon, W. (1992). *A handbook to literature* (6th ed.). New York, NY: Macmillan.

Howard, R. M. (2001a, March). *Plagiarism: What should a teacher do?* Paper presented at the Conference on College Composition and Communication, Denver, CO. Retrieved from http://wrt-howard.syr.edu/Papers/CCCC2001.html

Howard, R. M. (2001b). Plagiarism: What should a teacher do? In A. Lathrop & K. Foss, *Guiding students from cheating and plagiarism to honesty and integrity: Strategies for change* (p. 174). Retrieved from https://drive.google.com/file/d/0BzFlmiQ-tMe2TUh2WUs4dmVab1U/edit?usp=sharing

Hunter, M. (1982). *Mastery teaching.* Thousand Oaks, CA: Corwin.

Hyde, A. (2006). *Comprehending math: Adapting reading strategies to teach mathematics, K–6.* Portsmouth, NH: Heinemann.

IRIS Center. (n.d.). *What should content-area teachers know about vocabulary instruction?* Page 7: Building vocabulary and conceptual knowledge using the Frayer model. Retrieved from http://iris.peabody.vanderbilt.edu/module/sec-rdng/cresource/what-should-content-area-teachers-know-about-vocabulary-instruction/sec_rdng_07

Ives, B. (2007). Graphic organizers applied to secondary algebra instruction for students with learning disorders. *Learning Disabilities Research & Practice, 22*, 110–118. doi:10.1111/j.1540–5826.2007.00235.x

Ives, B. B., & Hoy, C. C. (2003). Graphic organizers applied to higher-level secondary mathematics. *Learning Disabilities Research & Practice, 18*, 36–51. doi:10.1111/1540–5826.00056

Kimmel, J. (2005). Web evaluation in the history classroom: Reconsidering the checklist. *Journal of the Association for History and Computing, 8*(2). Retrieved from http://hdl.handle.net/2027/spo.3310410.0008.201

Kuhlthau, C. C. (2003). *Seeking meaning: A process approach to library and information services*. Englewood, CO: Libraries Unlimited.

Lapp, D., Thayre, M., & Wolsey, T. D. (2014). *Arguments are only as credible as their sources: Teaching students to choose wisely*. Available from http://www.reading.org

Lorenz, B., Green, T., & Brown, A. (2009). Using multimedia graphic organizer software in the pre-writing activities of primary school students: What are the benefits? *Computers in the Schools, 26*, 115–129. doi:10.1080/07380560902906054

Macon, J., Bewell, D., & Vogt, M. (1991). *Responses to literature*. Newark, DE: International Reading Association.

Marzano, R. J., Pickering, D. J., & Pollock, J. E. (2001). *Classroom instruction that works: Research-based strategies for increasing student achievement*. Alexandria, VA: Association for Supervision and Curriculum Development.

McGregor, J. H., & Streitenberger, D. C. (1998). Do scribes learn? Copying and information use. *School Library Media Quarterly, 1*. Retrieved from http://www.ala.org/aasl/slr

McGregor, J. H., & Williamson, K. (2011). Generating knowledge and avoiding plagiarism: Smart information use by high school students. *School Library Research, 14*. Retrieved from http://www.ala.org/aasl/slr

McLaughlin, M., & Overturf, B. J. (2013). *The Common Core: Graphic organizers for teaching K–12 students to meet the reading standards*. Newark, DE: International Reading Association.

McMackin, M. C., & Witherell, N. L. (2005). Different routes to the same destination: Drawing conclusions with tiered graphic organizers. *Reading Teacher, 59*, 242–252. doi:10.1598/RT.59.3.4

Meola, M. (2004). Chucking the checklist: A contextual approach to teaching undergraduates web-site evaluation. *Portal: Libraries and the Academy, 4*, 331–344. Retrieved from http://www.tcnj.edu/~meolam/documents/Chucking_003.pdf

Meyer, B. J. F., Brandt, D. M., & Bluth, G. J. (1980). Use of top-level structure in text: Key for reading comprehension of ninth-grade students. *Reading Research Quarterly, 16*, 72–103. doi:10.2307/747349

Meyer, J., & Land, R. (2003). *Threshold concepts and troublesome knowledge: Linkages to ways of thinking and practising within the disciplines* (Occasional Report No. 4). Retrieved from http://www.etl.tla.ed.ac.uk/docs/ETLreport4.pdf

Moje, E. B. (2007). Developing socially just subject-matter instruction: A review of the literature on disciplinary literacy teaching. *Review of Research in Education, 31*, 1–44. doi:10.3102/0091732X07300046001

Novak, J. D., & Musonda, D. (1991). A twelve-year longitudinal study of science concept learning. *American Educational Research Journal, 28*, 117–153. doi:10.3102/00028312028001117

Ogle, D. (1986). K-W-L: A teaching model that develops active reading of expository text. *Reading Teacher, 39*, 564–570.

Olson, C. B. (1996). Integrating clustering and showing, not telling. In C. B. Olson (Ed.), *Practical ideas for teaching writing as a process at the elementary and middle school* (Rev. ed., pp. 52–54). Sacramento: California Department of Education.

Olson, P. (1968). Introduction: On myth and education. In P. Olson (Ed.), *The uses of myth: Papers relating to the Anglo-American seminar on the teaching of English at Dartmouth College, New Hampshire 1966*. Champaign IL: National Council of Teachers of English.

Pearson, P. D., & Gallagher, M. C. (1983). The instruction of reading comprehension. *Contemporary Educational Psychology, 8*, 317–344.

Raphael, T. E. (1984). Teaching learners about sources of information for answering questions. *Journal of Reading, 27*, 303–311.

Raphael, T. E. (1986). Teaching question-answer relationships, revisited. *Reading Teacher, 39*, 516–520.

Reardon, C., & Vossler, T. (2013). *The Gettysburg campaign, June–July 1863* (CMH Pub 75–10). Washington, DC: U.S. Army, Center of Military History. Retrieved from http://www.history.army.mil/html/books/075/75-10/CMH_Pub_75-10.pdf

Richardson, A. (1983). Imagery: Definitions and types. In A. A. Sheikh (Ed.), *Imagery: Current theory, research, and application* (pp. 3–42). New York, NY: John Wiley & Sons.

Rosenblatt, L. (1995). *Literature as exploration* (5th ed.). New York, NY: Modern Language Association of America.

Sadoski, M., & Paivio, A. (2004). A dual coding theoretical model of reading. In R. B. Ruddell & N. Unrau (Eds.), *Theoretical models and processes of reading* (5th ed., pp. 1329–1362). Newark, DE: International Reading Association.

Schwartz, R. M., & Raphael, T. E. (1985). Concept of definition: A key to improving students' vocabulary. *Reading Teacher, 39*, 198–205.

Shanahan, T., & Shanahan, C. (2008). Teaching disciplinary literacy to adolescents: Rethinking content-area literacy. *Harvard Educational Review, 78*(1), 40–59.

Sundeen, T. H. (2007). So what's the big idea? Using graphic organizers to guide writing for secondary students with learning and behavioral issues. *Beyond Behavior, 16*(3), 29–34.

Thiede, K. W., Dunlosky, J., Griffin, T. D., & Wiley, J. (2005). Understanding the delayed-keyword effect on metacomprehension accuracy. *Journal of Experimental Psychology: Learning, Memory, and Cognition, 31*, 1267–1280. doi:10.1037/0278–7393.31.6.1267

Tomlinson, C. A. (1999). *The differentiated classroom: Responding to the needs of all learners.* Upper Saddle River, NJ: Merrill Education.

Townsend, D. R., & Lapp. D. (2010). Academic language, discourse communities, and technology: Building students' linguistic resources. *Teacher Education Quarterly.* Retrieved from http://teqjournal .org/townsend_lapp.html

Uline, C., Tschannen-Moran, M., & Wolsey, T. D. (2009). The walls still speak: A qualitative inquiry into the effects of the built environment on student achievement. *Journal of Educational Administration, 47*, 395–420. doi:10.1108/09578230910955818

Vacca, R. T, Vacca, J. A., & Mraz, M. (2013). *Content area reading: Literacy and learning across the curriculum* (11th ed.). New York, NY: Pearson.

Vansledright, B. (2012). Learning with texts in history: Protocols for reading and practical strategies. In T. Jetton & C. Shanahan (Eds.), *Adolescent literacy in the academic disciplines: General principles and practical strategies* (pp. 199–227). New York, NY: Guilford Press.

Vygotsky, L. S. (1978). *The mind in society: The development of higher psychological processes.* Cambridge, MA: Harvard University Press.

Wallace, D. F. (1997). The string theory. In G. Plimpton (Ed.), *1997: The best American sports writing* (pp. 249–282). Boston, MA: Houghton Mifflin.

Wolsey, T. D. (2004). Literature discussion in cyberspace: Young adolescents using threaded discussion groups to talk about books. *Reading Online, 7*(4). Retrieved from http://www.readingonline.org

Wolsey, T. D. (2014). The school walls teach: Student involvement in the green school. In T. C. Chan, E. G. Mense, K. E. Lane, & M. D. Richardson (Eds.), *Marketing the green school: Form, function, and the future.* Hershey, PA: Information Science Reference/IGI.

Wolsey, T. D., & Grisham, D. L. (2012). *Transforming writing instruction in the digital age: Techniques for grades 5–12.* New York, NY: Guilford Press.

Wolsey, T. D., Grisham, D. L, & Heibert, E. (2012). *Teacher development series.* Retrieved from http:// textproject.org/professional-development/teacher-development-series

Wolsey, T. D., & Lapp, D. (2009). Discussion-based approaches for the secondary classroom. In K. Wood & B. Blanton (Eds.), *Promoting literacy with adolescent learners: Research-based instruction* (pp. 368–391). New York, NY: Guilford Press.

Wolsey, T. D., Lapp, D., & Fisher, D. (2012). Students' and teachers' perceptions: An inquiry into academic writing. *Journal of Adolescent and Adult Literacy, 55*, 714–724. doi:10.1002/JAAL.0086

Wood, K. D. (1998). Guiding readers through informational text. *Reading Teacher, 41*, 912–920.

Wood, K. D., Lapp, D., Flood, J., & Taylor, B. T. (2008). *Guiding readers through text: Strategy guides in "new times."* Newark, DE: International Reading Association.

Zike, D. (n.d.). *Dinah Zike's reading and study skills foldables.* New York, NY: McGraw-Hill Glencoe.

Zollman, A. (2009). Mathematical graphic organizers. *Teaching Children Mathematics, 16*, 222–230.

Zull, J. E. (2002). *The art of changing the brain: Enriching teaching by exploring the biology of learning.* Sterling, VA: Stylus.

Student Literature Cited:

Bradbury, R. (1962). *Something wicked this way comes.* New York, NY: Bantam.

Carrasquillo, P. (2013, November 16). Narcissistic personality disorder is not harmless behavior. *Washington Times.* Retrieved from http://communities.washingtontimes.com

Fitzgerald, F. S. (1925). *The great Gatsby.* New York, NY: Scribner.

Hand, L. (1944). *I am an American day address.* Retrieved from http://www.digitalhistory.uh.edu/disp_ textbook.cfm?smtID=3&psid=1199

Hemingway, E. (1952). *The old man and the sea.* London, UK: Jonathan Cape.

Hinton, S. E. (1967). *The outsiders.* New York, NY: Dell.

Lee, H. (1960). *To kill a mockingbird.* New York, NY: Grand Central Publishing.

L'Engle, M. (1962). *A wrinkle in time.* New York, NY: Farrar, Straus & Giroux.

McDermott, G. (1972). *Anansi the spider: A tale from the Ashanti.* New York, NY: Henry Holt.

Riggs, R. (2011). *Miss Peregrine's home for peculiar children.* Philadelphia, PA: Quirk Books.

Wallace, D. F. (1997). The string theory. In G. Plimpton (Ed.), *The best American sports writing, 1997* (pp. 249–282). Boston, MA: Houghton Mifflin.

Wilde, O. (1890). *The picture of Dorian Gray.* Retrieved from http://www.gutenberg.org/ebooks/174

INDEX

A SAGE Company

CL CORWIN LITERACY

Lapp, Wolsey & Wood

On using graphic organizers to make the complex comprehensible, 2–5

Laura Robb

On helping students tackle the biggest barrier to complex texts

Nancy Frey & Douglas Fisher

On five access points for seriously stretching students' capacity to comprehend complex text

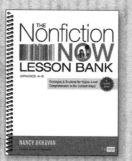

Nancy Akhavan

On top-notch nonfiction lessons and texts for maximizing students' content-area understanding

Douglas Fisher & Nancy Frey

On how text-dependent questions can inspire close and critical reading

Gretchen Bernabei & Judi Reimer

On 101 lessons and mentor texts for tackling the most persistent issues in academic writing

ISBN: 978-1508426134

Printed in the United States of America

People don't care what you know until they know you care.

– Bill Hill, owner of Bill Hill's College of Cosmetology
in Davenport, Iowa (my beauty school)

This book is dedicated to my family support system.

**In memory of
Doug Chaplin**

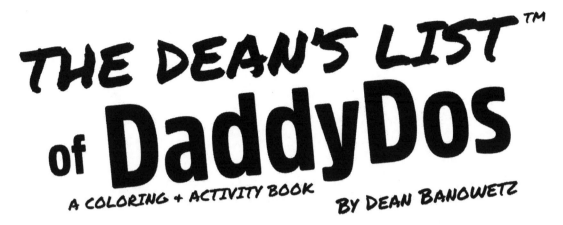

THE DEAN'S LIST™
of DaddyDos

A COLORING + ACTIVITY BOOK   BY DEAN BANOWETZ

FOR MOMMIES TOO!

TABLE OF CONTENTS

INTRODUCTION

My partner and I spent an hour and a half curling our daughter's hair and all we got was a bad attitude!

– Eric Metten, Dean's friend who was hair challenged.
Until now.

There are times in a man's life when his true mettle is tested. It's not providing money for the family, mowing the lawn or checking that strange noise in the middle of the night. The true test of any Dad is when their precious young daughter comes up to him and says in that sweet, hopeful voice, "Daddy, can you do French braids?" When a befuddled Dad looks like you just asked him to do nuclear fusion, that little girl is likely to burst into projectile tears. That is a Daddy *Don't.*

Daddy Dos is the help that you've needed for years. Creating amazing hairstyles for your daughters and sons or the little girls in your life. It's for every single time the Chief Hairstylist of the House (a.k.a. probably the woman) has left the nest and someone under five feet tall is having a

9-1-1 hair emergency. Do you want an issue with tissues? Or do you want to get the job done?

There will be no more pleading, "Wait until Mommy gets home."

There will be no more wishing, "Why can't my own mother just materialize?"

There will be no more thinking, "I can rebuild a car, but I'm afraid of a bobby-pin."

It's time to be the man I know you can be. In other words, just 'do it! This book will show you how.

I wrote this for husbands, boyfriends, fathers and even some women who are *not so gifted* in the art of hair—ladies, I know you're out there, and there is no shame in being a CEO who can't make a bun. In fact, the other day, I had a lesbian and her partner approach me with tears in their eyes. They weren't the victims of prejudice and they didn't just have one of those annoying couple's spats over which paint color goes up in the living room. One of the partners was pregnant and both confided something that rocked them to the core about having a child. College fund? Nope. "I can't even do a ponytail without the kid's head looking lopsided, or like she has a weird growth coming out of one side," said one of the women with a look of horror. That was her biggest parenting fear! Dean to the rescue. It was time for these lovely ladies to rise to an important challenge: ensuring the child has the most amazing hairstyle on the block. We're talking about a final result that prompts someone to stop you and ask, "What salon did you take little Penelope to today?" You'll be able to look back at them with equal parts smug and joy and say, "That would be the salon down the hall from the kitchen called our bathroom."

Snap! But don't get too smug just yet. We got a lot of 'dos to cover.

In this book, I will teach you over 30 basic 'dos for little girls ranging from the time they actually grow hair to those testing years of dance classes, ballet recitals, school dances (yes, those excruciating social rituals still exist), graduations, the horrible visit from Aunt Bev, and many other social occasions when you're judged by how your child looks. Most importantly, she'll experience the joy that comes with looking her best. I will also break this down to the most common questions I'm actually asked as a Hollywood hairstylist, including: "What is a bobby pin?" or "What is that @$%# French roll?" (swearing—never beautiful)

These dos are quick and easy. They'll cover your butt on the day you've got five minutes to get out of the house, while your child is looking like one of those street urchins from *Les Miz* (if you don't know the reference, Google it). No, your neighbors cannot call Child Protective Services for bangs that look like the cat cut them, but you're setting your little wonder up for tons of teasing and bullying at school, which sucks. Why not take the necessary steps to avoid the pain altogether?

I know the mommies and step-mommies will find this book useful, but the men really need the help. That's why I explain hair in "guy" lingo. Every style can be phrased in man-speak. Hair will no longer be a foreign language. Consider me your one-stop Rosetta Stone for the universal language of hair. Ready for some translations? Your brush is your tool (hold back your giggles). Your arsenal of hair products goes in your tackle box. Braiding hair is like dealing with cable wires. Three wires: white, red and yellow. I'll explain how to cross them to form the perfect braid. Defusing a bomb with a ten-second countdown, you are now Kiefer Sutherland saving the free world from impending doom. No, the bathroom won't explode, but your six-year-old might.

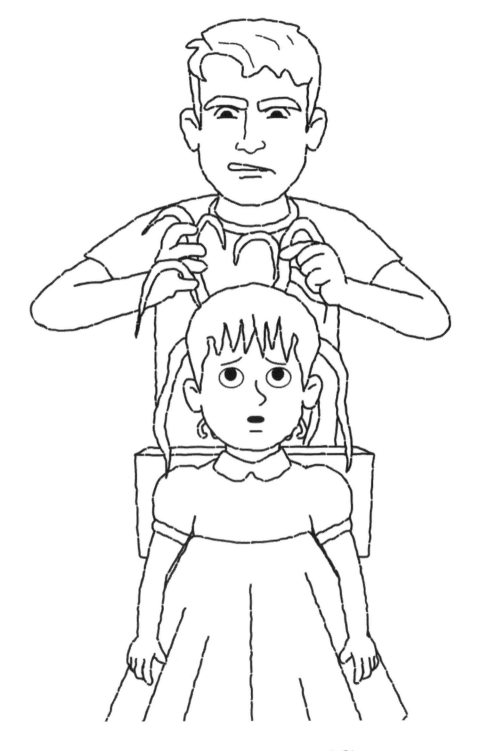

BREATHE AND FOCUS!

@DBANO @DEANBANOWETZ
#DADDYDOS

Activity Time!

Dads—you can't have all the fun. The illustration on the previous page (and throughout the book) is meant to be **colored**!

Rip it out, color away and throw it on the fridge when it's done. Better yet, snap a photo of you and little miss with your final masterpiece and share it!

Be sure to tag:

 @DBANO @DEANBANOWETZ #DADDYDOS

I bet most men never knew that hair could be this action packed and exciting. Your buddy Dean here isn't just your teacher. I'm your hair commando. And just like that Tom Hanks movie, I want you to look at that paddle brush and coated rubber bands and say, "I am the captain now!"

Let's talk intentions for a moment. Why are you doing your daughter's hair in the first place? First of all, you don't want to look like a dork in front of your kid or your significant other. From stopping a speeding train, to that damn math homework, to trimming split ends, Daddy should be able to do anything. Second, when you're a parent and caregiver, you should be the "go to" because it establishes trust. You won't always have to say, "ask Mommy" or "ask your other Daddy" or "ask that nice lady down the street. She must know how to do hair." You wouldn't run next door if your child had a fever to ask "the nice lady" what to do. It's the same thing when your daughter wants a high pony or half-up, half-down. You don't need to call in the SWAT team – **s**pecial **w**omen **a**ll **t**attling on you. Get educated on these pages. You can do it yourself!

Not to make you feel guilty, but as a Dad, you're often considered the provider, safety net, emotional resource, dog walker, driver and the person your child can turn to on a Saturday morning when gymnastics is looming. Your baby will be able to say to you, "Today, let's make it a low braid with a pink bow. Thanks, Daddy! You're the best!"

By the way, there are perks to knowing how to style your child's hair. Your frazzled partner might take one look at you doing that curled pony and, despite that ripped, nacho stained college T-shirt you're wearing from 1992 and the fact you haven't been to the gym in two weeks (or years), actually say, "Baby, you are so damn helpful with hair that it's turning me on. Let's have a 'date' tonight." You can thank me later.

Before I show you the styles and restore happiness and harmony to many households, let me tell you a bit about myself. My name is Dean and I'm the 13th of 15 kids who grew up on a farm in De Witt, Iowa. My early life can be summed up in a few words: get up at the butt crack of dawn. Wait, there are more words: walk through wet fields of corn in the middle of summer where it was only 1,000 percent humidity. The only good thing about working the fields (oh yes, I did!) was the awesome farmer's tan.

My job in those days was detasseling the corn. In case you've never detassled anything in your life, this is not a stripper's term. No, it's all about corn, which grows in stalks and there is a tassel on top that once it's pollinated changes direction. You detassel to get more corn. Or basically, I had to rip the stuff off. Detasseling was a walk in the park vs. roughing a bean field. Oh, I know that you know that means walking through a soybean field and pulling out all the weeds in that row.

Right now, the jaws of my celebrity clients are dropping and quite a few must be making plans to have a benefit in my honor. Yes, your buddy Dean worked the land and worked it from dusk until dawn. People make about $35 to $45 a day for this backbreaking work, but I worked for free and my feed.

*1st row: Annette (#11), Dee (#3), Judy (#1), Sally (mom), Alice (#2), Mary (#7) and Deb (#10) **2nd row:** Randy (#14), Alan (#6), Lloyd (#4), me (#13), Leon (#12), Steve (#5), Dick (#9) and Marvin (#8)*

Permed mullet. Eddie Murphy in Coming to
America influenced me.

That's more farm talk. By the way, please feel free to call your parents and thank them for your childhood, which might have only involved mowing the backyard.

Now, back to style. In those days, my Dad was the family hairdresser and he would buzz us, so we didn't pass out on those hot summer workdays. Even worse was my high school look, which was your basic, curly, permed mullet. Take a moment to digest. Yes, I was close to six feet tall at age 16 and wore *a permed mullet.*

I took my mullet self during one of the summer months (Mom liked to get rid of us) to our family friends Alice and Charlie's farm. Some might call this a vacation, but I'm still not so sure. They had cows, and milking them was job number one. It was hideous work and the reason why I still don't drink milk. If there were a way to make some good ice cream without milk, I'd do that in a second. Until then I refuse to drink what came out of a cow's boob. Meanwhile, they had one horse and I'd ride him around the pasture—otherwise known in farm talk as "chillin' on a horse"—and this is where the magic began. Since there was absolutely no other way to possibly entertain myself, I would do a little French braid on the horse's mane. No one was happy about it, but I got in worse trouble when I braided the cow's tail. There are some very interesting styles you can do on a tail and I think the horse appreciated a way to break out of her generic equine look. It also redefines the idea of getting some tail on summer vacay.

Back on my own farm, I used to steal my sister's oh-so-chic Barbie dolls and do their hair. Again, these weren't paying customers, but everyone needs a little practice. My punishment for stealing these Barbie dolls was more time in the field working. I think my parents tried to work the gay away, but it didn't matter one bit. Left alone with those long corn tassels, I'd simply braid them. Then I'd grab bunches of long grass and create my own special plant ponytails. It was never ending. I'm not even kidding. *Really.*

My sister Annette is the one I call #11. Most of the time, my brothers and sisters and I call each other by our birth numbers. But I digress. #11 had me French braid her hair almost every single day before she went to school. I hated that she had to go to school so much earlier, but I still dragged myself out of bed to do her hair—my job and my joy.

When I lived with her after I got out of the U.S. Army, she would still bang on my bedroom door and beg me to do her hair. I'd do a French braid from the bottom up, and then my nieces started begging, "Uncle Dean, we want to make an appointment. We hear you work for free and hugs, which are free." Who was I to say no to all these amazing women in my family?

It got serious when I started doing several nieces' weddings. But it didn't have to be a special occasion to get me to backcomb. I was the one who started saying, "Do you know what a nice pony might do for that outfit?" I wasn't talking about anything that lived in the barn.

When I went to beauty school it was on! I learned my art at Bill Hill's College of Cosmetology in Davenport, Iowa, located in the back of a tasteful carpet and furniture retail store. Sure, it wasn't exactly a gorgeous place to train and you had to look past the hideous green shag carpeting and orange lawn chairs that were often on sale. Despite these obstacles, Bill Hill took our training seriously and made his students wear lab jackets over dress pants.

I'd go a step further and wear a button-down shirt with a tie during school hours. My goal was to always look like a cross between a famous author and a mad scientist with my long assed lab coat on. My unusual garb worked on several levels. People would come in and the receptionist would say, "So, who do you want to do your hair?"

"The tall guy in the lab coat," they would say. Maybe it was because I looked so professional. Or maybe they heard a good reference from a dairy cow on our farm or #11. Or perhaps in hair it's about how you carry yourself, and I've always had high confidence levels in this area.

DADDY DO TIP

Dads, if you look like you're scared to death, your girls won't trust you to touch a strand of their hair. Wipe that terrified expression off your face – stat.

CHOICES =
GOOD

My professional training encouraged my family and soon even Judy (#1) had me cutting her bangs. My niece Cindy (#1.4 - the kids were the point whatever after their parents) made their appointments with Uncle Dean. Even Lloyd (#4) sent his wife Karry (#4.0) for a trim.

My sister Dee (#3) also went to beauty school to learn how to do hair, but only trusted me with her own personal haircuts. We'd joke about how doing hair with me was such a calm experience vs. our time spent with Dad the hair destroyer. When we were kids if Dad ever saw hair fall into our eyes (even for a second or in a tornado-like storm), he would get so pissed off that he'd line up the entire row of boys and take the clippers to us. Our hair was hostage to his moods and our ability to see to do chores while avoiding any high winds. You never wanted to see those clippers come out because for the rest of the summer, you would be a lopsided mess with origami hair patches.

Of course, his counterpart was my lovely Mom, a once-a-week shampoo and set lady, with a downtown hair appointment every Friday with Dee (#3). She looked at hair as a relaxing treat away from 14 of her kids, which was exactly the right attitude. Way to go, Mom! So what if she had her hair picked out and sprayed to death with that thick stuff that also clogs your lungs and doubles for glue during art projects. Mom had that hair cemented on her head and it never moved. It was almost like the hair was afraid. If it dared to break free, it would get another layer of shellac.

Hair was such serious business to her that I wasn't allowed to do my Mom's hair until after I graduated from beauty school. It might be good to mention here that my mom had dark brown hair that would be styled into a perfect bubble set with the curls taped to her skin around her hairline. I (#13) used that pink tape with the rickrack looking edges. She topped her hair creation off with a ton of spray and the sheer scarf tied under her chin to prevent the wind from even thinking about destroying it. Mom seemed to have made a deal with Mother Nature. Wind didn't bother her and Mom tried to only release her share of toxic spray chemicals into the ozone once a week. It was a win-win.

My Dad died when I was 15 years old, and Mom appreciated that I had direction in my life and later loved when I took over the entire family's follicles. The minute someone got engaged, I knew I'd be getting a call and I would always try to be available for the big day. It wasn't a wedding if I didn't 'do it, if you know what I mean.

I'd have my tackle box of tools with me, but more on that in a moment. At this point, I'm going to say enough about me. You can learn more later on.

In fact, just turn the page and let's get to it.

WHY THIS BOOK?

Here are the reasons why you need this book. YOU know who you are:

One: I'm sick of hearing hair horror stories from parents and children about how their day or event (dance competition, school dance, picture day) was wrecked by having sad/bad hair.

Two: I need to stop the insanity. The other day a Dad told me he cut the ponytail ties out of his daughter's hair because he was afraid of ripping out a strand. He ended up nicking her ear and wound up in the emergency room! You can't live in insane hair fear anymore when it comes to your child.

Three: I have a lot of gay friends who have adopted or have kids from a previous marriage. They are living the Number Two reason above and begged me to write this book. I feel their pain, and I'm here to serve.

Four: Straight people, and you know who you are, also don't know jack about doing their kids' hair. There are a lot of you out there, too!

Five: There is a lot of divorce. Divorce means kids with two homes and parents who quite often don't really communicate all that well anymore. If you ask your ex to do the hair in advance, it's just another thing she uses to say that you're a (insert swear word here). In each home, someone should be able to make the child look like she didn't spend the night hair-wise in a wind tunnel.

Six: It's time to realize that you can look manly and do hair. Skill is sexy! I'm somewhat butch and look like the bodyguard you want to have around you if you suddenly morphed into Beyonce overnight. And I do hair. I love doing hair. I'm great at doing hair. Enough said.

Seven: It's all about pride. I want your child to be able to say, "Yeah, my Dad did this style. He knows how to do hair. He takes care of me. Dad? I can always count on him."

Eight: I don't accept lame excuses. Don't hit me with the following: "Manly hands are too big to do hair or hold that brush." The last time I looked many brain surgeons held even smaller tools, and they're opening up a brain, not securing a bun. I have XXL-sized hands. If I can do hair with these bear paws, you *certainly* can too.

Nine: You will feel crazy accomplished. Happy! Overjoyed! There is nothing like putting a smile on the face of the one you love – and good hair equals smiles. In fact, studies show that when you feel beautiful then you have a better day. Don't you want your child to have the best day possible? Okay, I know that's a little Dean guilt and I'm sorry. (But it's true, so stop wrecking your child's day with bad hair and get on it!)

Ten: YOU CAN DO THIS. YES, YOU CAN. TURN THE PAGE! SORRY FOR YELLING AT YOU IN PRINT. If your wife/daughter doesn't trust you to do their hair, you have to practice. Grab a doll head and let's go.

SEE! I TOLD YOU TO TRUST ME.

@DBANO @DEANBANOWETZ

#DADDYDOS

CHAPTER ONE:
GETTING OVER YOUR
HAIR FEARS

There are many men who would rather hold a grenade than a tube of hair gel. They're not afraid of cutting down a forest with blades the size of airplane propellers, but the idea of cutting bangs makes them break out in hives. How can a 250-pound man be fearful around a French braid? This book is all about challenging yourself and learning to get over your hair fears.

Remember that overcoming fear is called growth. Or you can quote my motto, "If you can fight a middle of the night intruder and swing a bat or kill really big bugs or deal with your mother then you can do a bun."

It's a guy thing to be responsible for another human being. This is why you will take your daughter's hair fate into your own hands. By the way, if you don't do her hair right your daughter can and possibly will look like a trashy 'ho and no one wants that description under their yearbook photo.

HOW TO GET STARTED

The good news is you don't have to find some swanky salon to prepare yourself for what you need to do the Daddy Dos. You can buy this stuff wherever you get your groceries. Trust me that the products are there even if you've never seen them. I also guarantee you that they're not in the beer and chips aisle, which is why you might have not spotted them in the past. Perhaps you've noticed things in the grocery store that read GOODY. They don't have that label because some sports team won the big game and everyone is shouting out that word. This brand means they're good at hair, although there are so many brands out there that equally fit the bill. In the Appendix section of this book, I'll provide you with my Dean's List of favorite products and links where to find them if you want to order them online. (Online ordering means you don't have a checkout person seeing you with bows, although many single Dads could play the caring, concerned, competent parent card there and even get a hot date for the weekend. Nothing says good Dad like new headbands for spring).

Please don't be shy about stocking up. Again, there is no shame in buying bobby pins even when you have a tat of a giant eagle on your shoulder and a Harley sits in your driveway. There is no shame in purchasing hairspray either because it indicates that you believe in personal hygiene and looking good, which are two traits that should be celebrated by all. Again, I'm a 300-pound guy (okay 230 is my goal weight) and some of the most famous hairdressers in the world are bald, manly-men who could take down a building and then style the little old ladies they've just rescued. We're manly, but we still know how to stock up on a great hair mousse when it's on sale.

NOW LET'S GET THIS PARTY GOING

I believe that most men know what it means when that first bell in a boxing match is rung or the coin flip in football decides what team will send out their defensive squad. Think of this moment in the same way:

Ding, ding, ding, it's time to start on your quest of being the best Daddy on the planet – and one who handles your little girl's hair.

Perhaps you're saying, "Dean, I don't know a damn thing about hair. In fact, I shaved mine off years ago because I couldn't even be bothered to own a comb." No matter if you're bald or you have a Fabio-like mane, we will begin at the starting line. There will also be time to learn your new craft. Think of doing your daughter's hair for the first time like that magical day when you popped open the hood of your first car and started to learn what was what. It's all about practicing until perfecting.

Of course, the first time you changed the oil in your car you spilled a little oil on the floor. I expect you to make mistakes. I want you to make mistakes. It won't take long before you're making very few mistakes, and your little girl is bouncing out of the house with a high pony swinging in the breeze.

DADDY DO TIP

Doing your daughter's hair is all about responsibility. You cook and clean. Those are necessities of life. So is doing your baby's hair.

IT'S GOING TO
COST YOU SOME $

@DBANO   @DEANBANOWETZ
#DADDYDOS

The point here is you need to buck up. News flash: Women agree that one of the sexiest things a man can do is to take care of his children. I hate to bring this up so soon, but if you braid your kid's hair, your wife might be so thrilled that you'll have a very rocking evening when the kids are sleeping. In other words, you master the bun and you will master the buns later on.

I'm sorry, but I must drag sex into it. Hair is an easy thing to do in order to delight your partner and push them in the direction of having wild sex with you later as a thank you gift. I'm not even kidding here.

SIDEBAR: THE IMPORTANCE OF HAIR TO WOMEN

Time out, men! I know many of you are thinking, "Who cares about hair? Why is it such a big friggin' deal to the ladies?" As guys, we often like long, swinging, shiny locks on our ladies. With kids, isn't it enough to just have them put it in a messy pony and get on with it? No, no, no!

People ask, "Dean, why is hair so important?"

When your hair is done and you look good, you do feel better about the entire day. Even if something crappy happens (a teacher yells at you, you get a D in science), your child will still feel better about herself when she sees an amazing reflection staring back at her in the mirror. So what if she can't climb the damn rope in gym class? Who cares if that little turd Brandon told her she was stupid and has cooties. When little Amber looks in the mirror and sees a gorgeous braid, she still feels good about herself and realizes that Brandon is the sort of abusive little putz that Dr. Phil warns about on that great daytime talk show. She looks good, which makes her feel good, which equals she can take on the world.

Why is hair so important to our ladies, big and small? When you look good and feel better, you have more self-confidence and that equals success in life. There isn't a father I know who doesn't want his little girl to be a success in life and feel good about herself. We know about how life cuts you down and both females and males will be gunning for her self-confidence. Why not give her all the ammo possible to feel great on the inside, so those detractors just fall away like rain flowing down a gutter.

WHY DO YOU NEED DADDY-DAUGHTER HAIR TIME

It's all about the b-word: bonding. Many fathers and daughters don't get to spend quality time together and doing hair is a great, quiet time without anyone else around to have some private moments. Many dads aren't into doing little tea parties and sitting on the floor playing with dolls. Doing hair together is an actual activity that both of you can enjoy with amazing results.

If you're not convinced, I promise you will see joy on your little girl's face when you help her with her hair. The beautiful thing is this is a time to really chat and find out what's going on in your child's life. You might hear about how she thinks the dog is from outer space and that guy Matthew has a big crush on her. (What! The little bastard!) Hair is a way to accomplish a lot of things at one time, including actual grooming combined with touching base in our busy lives.

Many Dads wake up early and work all kinds of crazy hours. They're just not home. When you are home, it's great to have an important task to do with your daughter that guarantees some special time. Plus, there will still be some unenlightened Dads who don't read this book and who can't figure out how to get rid of one clump of frizz. You do hair now, and suddenly you're the coolest Dad on the entire block. Meanwhile, your partner doesn't resent you because he or she does most (if not all) of the child rearing duties. You've taken a task away, and have provided a much-needed break. This is a total win-win.

HAPPY KID =
HAPPY LIFE

 @DBANO 🐦 @DEANBANOWETZ

🏷️ #DADDYDOS

CHAPTER TWO:
YOUR HAIR TACKLE BOX

Just like when you fix a car, you don't just stand there empty-handed without any of your best tools. Hair is the same way.

It's all about having your arsenal of tools at the ready. I'd like you to buy a real tackle or a toolbox to keep your hair supplies in. You can find them for a few bucks at Target or Walmart in the camping section. You can also think of collecting your supplies as an interactive activity you can do with your daughter. Just say, "I've got a special mission we're going on today – together."

Imagine the shocked look on her precious little dimpled face when you say, "Saddle up, Sally! We're going to Target to get supplies so Daddy can do your hair." After you lift her gorgeous, future supermodel/ scientist chin off the ground, proceed to the driveway. This is your territory and you know what to do: get in the car, fire up the ignition, put on a manly Van Halen tune and get ready to buy the following things that I'll list below.

By the way, I'm combat trained from my years in the Army. I always believe that it's best to be prepared and keep your supplies very handy, so you can always find them before you go into battle. To that end, here is your preparedness kit:

YOUR BASIC DADDY DO TOOL KIT:

1. Vent brush. Great to use on wet hair.

2. Paddle brush. Perfect for brushing dry hair.

3. Round brush. This is for advanced dads who are blowing out hair with a hair dryer. Not an air compressor.

4. Wide toothed comb. Great for detangling wet hair.

5. Coated rubber bands. Goody has some great options.

6. Bobby pins in the same color as your daughter's hair. I always have about 15 bobby pins stashed in the glove box or on my tie if I am going out. Cyndi Bands work great too.

7. Snap barrettes to pull back the little pieces. Plus, they're so cute. You can put them in a pony to lock it all in. Think of them like changing a tie. You can't have enough in different colors.

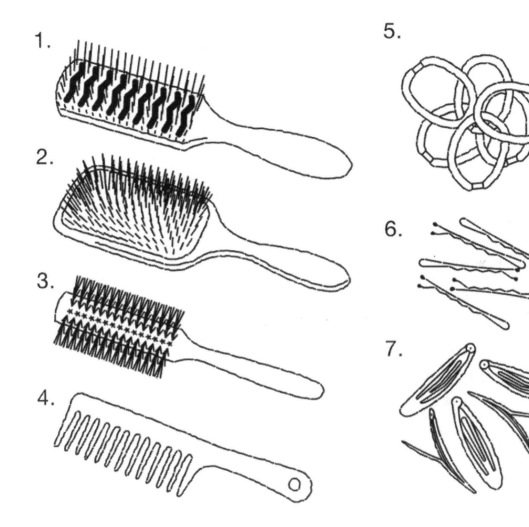

1.

2.

3.

4.

5.

6.

7.

THESE WILL SAVE YOU...

 @DBANO @DEANBANOWETZ

#DADDYDOS

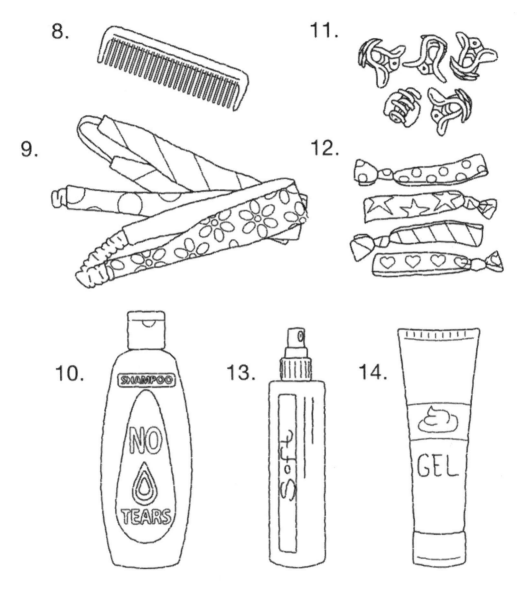

8.

11.

9.

12.

10.

13.

14.

... **BUY THEM!**

8. Standard comb. You kept this in your back pocket, remember?

9. Fabric headbands. They're quick and easy.

10. Baby shampoo and a gentle conditioner. Enough said.

11. Tiny jaw clamps. I use them on *American Idol, The X Factor* and *Dancing with the Stars* all the time. If your child is a dancer, you want to be able to lock her hair down while you style. It makes it easier.

12. Ties and colored bands. You can never have enough ponytail ties. (You'll end up finding them everywhere in the house and even on the gearshift of your car).

13. Spray leave-in conditioner. It can be a lifesaver. It tames the hair down and can help you get rid of tangles.

14. A medium-hold gel. Don't get anything too strong; it's too sticky. Gel is great to hold the little, runaway bits down.

DADDY DO TIP

People always ask me to divulge my go-to brands. Here they are in a nutshell: I love Johnson & Johnson's, Joico/Aquage products and Paul Mitchell's line. More about what I love product-wise in the Appendix of the book.

'DO DILEMMA: SHOULD YOU USE HAIR SPRAY ON KIDS?

Yes, you can use hair spray on kids, but it's not an everyday thing. This will depend upon the level of activity. If your daughter is a flower girl at a wedding use it to keep a style for a long time and for the photos. Or perhaps you'll use it for a graduation or a big dinner event.

DADDY DO TIP

When using hair spray on a child, I like to get a Kleenex and have your child hold it against their forehead. Drape the tissue down their face like a mask. You can have fun by saying they're hiding from you. Then use the spray. Remove the tissue when done. This is a great way to avoid getting the spray in the child's eyes or mouth—and it's much better than just asking them to shut their eyes. Kids love to peek!

CHAPTER THREE:
KIDS R DIRTY - CLEAN 'EM

Let's talk about kiddie hygiene for a moment or what I like to call Basic Whipper Snapper Beauty School 101. No, you can't skip this chapter and get to the styles because understanding your daughter's hair and how to get it to behave under your care is crucial. Plus, I provide advice on how to get rid of tangles and the tears that go with them.

If you want to stop the waterworks keep reading. The last thing you need is a report to the home front female/male honcho saying, "Mommy, Daddy ripped out my hair trying to get my tangles out! He made me cry". Imagine your partner giving you the death ray stare here as she/he imagines you literally ripping every strand of hair out of her precious baby's head. That is just too much hassle, so please read this entire chapter.

LITTLE PRECIOUS AND HER HAIR TYPE

Your daughter either has straight or curly hair. It will be one of the two. If it's not straight then it's curly although there can be some variations on the two themes here. You can have straight/wavy, which is your basic surfer girl hair even if you live in the middle of Iowa. You also have to consider your daughter's hair texture, which should fall into the fine or course variety.

As a rule, curly hair is usually course and a lot of times straight hair is fine, but these aren't absolutes.

Ask yourself: Does your daughter's hair naturally curl? Is it stick straight? When dry is it thinner strands that lay straight and glossy or more coarse looking and a bit less shiny? Again, you can have straight, fine hair or curly fine hair or wavy coarse hair.

You'll also want to figure out if your daughter has oily or dry hair. Does it look a little greasy if you don't wash it every single day or like it could use a little conditioner? These are pretty easy concepts, and you can figure it out if you pretend like you're *24's* Jack Bauer giving a report on a suspect to CTU (Counter Terrorism Unit). What are the particulars? Do a little detective work here, and if you just can't figure it out, you can ask a woman in your life like the woman who comes to clean once a week. Try to avoid asking your partner who will think you've lost your mind when you casually say, "What are we having for dinner and is little Ashley fine-curly or course-straight in the hair department?"

PRODUCTS FOR SHAMPOOING AND CONDITIONING

Fine, straight or curly, you just need a general shampoo and conditioner for your child. (Again, in the appendix of this book, I'll list a few personal favorites). Most likely your partner has purchased the goods, but you can do it with a little help from the Appendix section.

BEFORE YOU SHAMPOO

Before a drop of water hits little Ashley's head brush her hair out thoroughly. Don't just brush the outside layer. Get in there good and really brush all of her hair – outer and under hair. You'll want to do this with a good, vented paddle brush. After the hair is loosened, you can finish with a wide toothed comb. The rule: The curlier the hair, the wider the teeth in the comb. It follows that the thinner the hair, the smaller the teeth on the comb. Curly course hair equals a wide toothed comb. My fave is the Tangle Teezer or the Wet Brush.

NOW SHAMPOO

Getting your child's head clean is an easy task. Just wet your daughter's head in the sink or in the shower/tub and shampoo. Caution: Make sure you buy a product that doesn't burn the eyes and be careful not to use too much shampoo so it runs into the eyes. Just a glop the size of a pea will do to start. Use a little more if your child has long-long hair (past her shoulder blades).

Just rub the shampoo into your hands, rub your hands together and then start with your fingertips on the scalp of the hair and work it through. After the shampoo builds up a frothy lather, rinse it off completely. There is nothing worse than leftover caked on shampoo or conditioner. Give it an extra 30 seconds in the water if you're not sure and look down to make sure the water is running clean and not soapy. If you still see soapy then make sure to keep rinsing.

Prior to rinsing, make sure to get in there and shampoo the scalp, which should feel good and gets rid of sweat, dirt and even chlorine from the pool. It will also get rid of old products that are still there such as hair spray for special events.

Judge if your child needs one or two shampoo treatments. How? If your child hasn't had their hair washed in three days, two shampoo treatments would be necessary. Finish by using a quarter-sized amount of conditioner, which you will rub into your hands to emulsify. Start at the ends and work your way up with the conditioner. Never just glop it out of the bottle onto your child's head, which doesn't feel good. Work it upward and then allow it to sit for a minute or two – or until your child becomes a bit unglued. Then rinse completely. Quick tip: Get the shampoo halo or the baby pour cup. It will make your life so much easier.

DADDY DO TIP
Rinse with lukewarm water.

DADDY DON'T TIP
Rinse with cold water. Your child will hate you.

By the way, you need conditioner. When you skip it, most kids get crazy tangles, which you then have to rip out with a brush. Conditioner gets rid of that painful activity and all the dirty looks that go with the fact that tangles, like homework and rain, are your fault as a parent.

A NOTE ABOUT SPECIALTY SHAMPOOS

There are times when you need a more specialized shampoo. I have friends with multi-racial kids, and they're constantly asking me for advice. I love a site called mixedchicks.net where they sell a product line specially developed for mixed race children. What makes their hair different is that it's a natural texture. If you use the wrong shampoo on natural textured hair, it will dry it out and make it even more difficult to manage. It also helps to use a leave-in conditioner (you don't wash it out, but this only works for brands that say leave in; you can't just leave *anything* in).

TIME TO DRY YOUR LITTLE PRINCESS' HAIR

Here's a good golden rule: Use a bath towel to dry the body; use a hand towel to dry the hair. You don't want to get oils from the body on her hair and vice versa. In older kids, including pre-teens, using the hair towel with the corresponding hair oils on their faces can even cause acne. I like to give the hair towel to the child. Let them learn how to dry their own hair with a towel, which is a worthwhile learning activity. You dry your own hair; they work on their own hair. They feel like they're participating, which makes them enjoy the activity. Your goal is to get 80 percent of the water out.

DADDY DO TIP

If you have a child with really long hair, towel dry first then go section by section starting at the nape of the neck and then comb from the roots to the end. Then take another section and go roots to the end. You keep doing each section until all of the hair is smooth and tangle free. You can also take all the hair and wrap it in a Bounty paper towel to really suck the water out. If you don't have a Bounty, I use a Kleenex. Use anything that's absorbent and quick.

To make it extra fun, I have my nieces scrunch their hair up when they get out of the shower just to see how much water is coming out. Got a shop cloth? Use it on your daughter's hair providing you didn't use it on your greasy car. A shop cloth really gets the moisture out.

VERY BIG DADDY DON'T TIP

IF YOU BLOW DRY SUPER WET HAIR, YOU ARE BOILING IT. Plus, it will take a LOT longer to dry. Take the time to dry it with a towel before you blow-dry it. When you blow it just make sure you use low heat and high air speed to help rough dry the hair. Check out my new InBlu Turbo Ionic Hair Dryer www.instyler.com

ICE CREAM +
HAIR DON'T MIX!

@DBANO   @DEANBANOWETZ
#DADDYDOS

> ## DADDY DO TIP
>
> If you want to try a great wavy style you will do a braid (see next chapter) and let your child sleep in the braid. In the morning, your daughter will have the most amazing wavy hair once you take the braids out. It's minimal effort and it looks like you did something major! The key to this is making sure the hair is 99% dry before you braid. Another tip is you can leave about 1 ½ of the section out of the braid. The straight ends will help make it look more trendy.
> #itlooksgreatwithaheadbandalso

TROUBLESHOOT THE TANGLES

Most kids have to deal with a terror called tangles. What I always do is find the tangle and "push it up." This means I grab the ends and slide the tangle toward the scalp, which helps to loosen it up. Then I push it through again, which you may have to do two or three times. It unlocks whatever is happening that's causing your daughter's hair to look like some sort of cemented together spaghetti dish. What do you do about a tangle that's stubborn and just not coming out? Despite your daughter's tears, because tangles are a very serious issue when you're eight or nine, you have to give the tangle special attention.

Here are my tips for getting rid of the most stubborn tangle. I call this tangle troubleshooting:

▫ **Make short, calming strokes through the tangle to break it up.** Do this with a gentle brush or a wide toothed comb. I love using the tangle teaser brush or the wet brush (see page 20).

□ **Still no relief? Actually put your fingers into the tangle and slide them around.** Make a motion inside that tangle with your fingers like you're opening an umbrella. Now that you've tried your fingers, go back to using the brush to try to break it up or comb it through to get rid of it.

□ **You can use a leave-in conditioner (a few small sprays) to soften it up and thus break it up.** I like the BioMega Volumizing Moisture Spray.

□ **I do love Paul Mitchell conditioner as a product to avoid tangles.** If your daughter has tangle-prone hair, you might want to make this one of your staples. Yes, man up and go buy it, keep it in the shower or on the tub and tell your child to use it. Your partner won't question you and think that he or she bought it in the first place.

Once you break up the tangled mess and the hair is smooth again, call your sister, wife or the gay down the street and reveal the big news. You're not just a Daddy and an accountant/CPA/ cop, but also a de-tangler. Well done!

OH, THE DRAMA OF IT ALL

One quick word when it comes to the emotional drama caused by hair tangles. As I said before—but it bears repeating—most little girls will go into either gales of tears or true hysteria when you even talk about getting the tangles out: Why? Probably they know it can hurt or someone has made it hurt in the past. Don't take this lightly because this is a serious emotional drama for your child. Even if your girl is upset, don't raise your voice because it just elevates the drama. And please don't burst into tears with her. Dr. Dean the hair doctor is here to help you get past the emotional soap opera of the tangle.

Use this script:

Your Little Girl (snot running, short hiccup-y breaths):
"Daddy, I have a tangle and you're not taking it out! I want Mommy!"

You (in a calm voice like you would use with your boss):
"Honey, let me help you. No, really, I'm pretty good at getting rid of tangles. You see how I untangle all the cords by the TV, right? And the TV isn't broken."

YLG (tears flowing):
"I still want Mommy!"

You (in your best never-say-die mode):
"Baby, we have to do this together. Maybe you could help me. Could you work on one section and I'll work on the other one."

YLG (somewhat intrigued):
"Help you?"

You (avoiding a desire to ditch this and clean the garage):
"Yes, Daddy needs tons of help here. Let's do this together. You can even be in charge."

By the way, do not resort to bribes. It doesn't help if you promise 31 Flavors for allowing you to get rid of tangles. This sets up sugary carbs as a treat for basic grooming. When in doubt, educate your daughter. If they still aren't sure you're a master de-tangler, simply say, "Honey, we have no choice. We have to get this tangle out. We want your hair to be super beautiful. If this tangle is there, it will bug us all day. So, let's get this tangle out, so we have a really amazing day." You're doing so much talking that most kids will throw in the towel at this point and allow you to just get to work.

#FAIL

NOW LET'S PART THE HAIR

It's easy to make a great part in your child's hair. How do you do it? I take a comb and slide it down the scalp using my free hand to separate the hair. You can do these parts:

– Part down the middle
– Part on either side
– A diagonal or zigzag part

I have used a capped or upside down pen to create a part, sliding it through like you're writing a note. This is especially helpful when creating a zigzag look. Create the zigzag and use your other hand to separate it. You can even use a chopstick or a straw. Just make sure you're not using something sharp. This means no screwdriver or power tools.

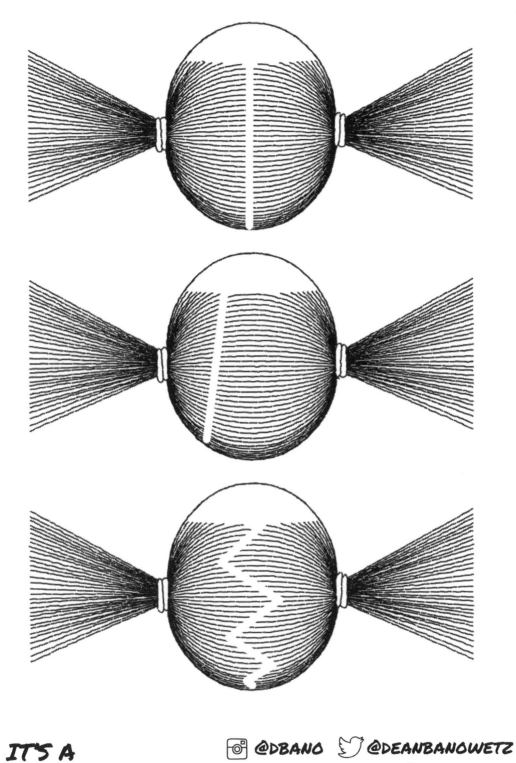

IT'S A
PART-Y!

[instagram] @DBANO   [twitter] @DEANBANOWETZ

[tag] #DADDYDOS

CHAPTER FOUR: MY LITTLE PONY(TAIL)

I'm proud that you're practicing your de-tangling, but first things first: You have to master a ponytail. This is not only easy and soul building, but also a staple style for little girls across the globe. You wake up and your little girl's hair is a mess? Put it in a pony! You want a polished look, but are running super late for school? Pony time! You want to look like a hero who can do hair? Pony, pony, pony!

The trick with the ponytail is two fold: You want it to stay in, and you also want it to look symmetrical, so it doesn't appear as if your child tried to make a ponytail and now looks like she is auditioning as one of the orphans in a revival of *Annie*.

GET READY FOR YOUR PONY

The ponytail just requires your basic hair supplies—a brush or comb and some kind of tie for the top of the pony. Be sure you have secured the ponytail with a basic ponytail holder.

DADDY DO TIP

You can use plain old string if there is nothing else around, although in a pinch I prefer packing string. Dip the string in some water and squeegee it out. Finally, just tie it in a knot around the ponytail tie. As it dries, it will shrink and thus really lock in the ponytail. Of course, you can also invest in a big packet of coated ponytail holders, so the hair doesn't rip out. Remember that your girl will leave these everywhere, so buy an extra pack because it's easy to lose them. Goody Ouchless bands are great for this.

Please don't use that horrid rubber band that holds your Sunday paper together. Yes, it will hold your pony, but it will also rip your daughter's hair out when you try to take it out. Avoid future tears and find an alternative.

DADDY DO TIP

Make sure you also have some bobby pins on hand to secure any loose strands while doing a pony. If you have old bobby pins with the end worn off and If you want to go to the next level buy some clear nail polish and coat the ends of any old bobby pins. This way the little tip of the bobby pin won't scratch your girl's noggin.

YOU CAN DO IT

Remember that a ponytail is as basic as checking your tires before you go on a long drive. Keep in mind that if you can't properly fix your car, it won't work. It will break down and your life will become miserable. The same thing goes for a ponytail. If you don't do it properly, it will fall out or sag and your kid will be miserable until you fix it. The point is: Get it right the first time and avoid any whining or tears. Again, it just takes a little bit of practice. #practicepeople

WHAT KIND OF PONY

The first thing you'll do with your little girl is to determine where the pony should rest. Is it going to be a high pony, middle pony or low, side pony? There are so many variations and like picking the right lettuce there really is no absolute or perfect thing. Just determine your pony goal, which is the first step.

WE HAVE PONY OPTIONS!

@DBANO @DEANBANOWETZ

#DADDYDOS

For rookies, I'd suggest the basic middle pony. It's pretty, and pretty foolproof. If it's your first time, you might want to avoid the middle pony because you don't have the experience to center it. It will save a lot of embarrassment if you just start small until you get this pony thing down. Ready for a tutorial? Thought so.

DADDY DO IT!
THE PERFECT MIDDLE PONY

□ Take a regular paddle brush and start at the side of the head.

□ Brush a big portion of hair into your open hand.

□ Let the hair fall gently into your hand. Brush it straight. Keep it in your hand.

□ Take hair from the other side and brush it back to rest it in your hand.

□ Now take the hair from the forehead, pull it back and let it join its friends.

□ Make sure you haven't missed a spot. If so, scoop it up and put it into the pony.

□ Group the strands in the upper middle of your daughter's head. Secure with ponytail holder.

VIDEO TUTORIAL!
See it at <u>daddy.do/middle-pony-perfection</u>

Note: If your daughter has short bangs, you can leave them alone as bangs with a pony is super cute. FYI: They also belong outside of the pony.

PONY TROUBLESHOOTING

Q: What if some of the hairs keep falling out and refuse to go into the pony?

A: Lightly mist them with water. It will help you keep them together and get rid of annoying fly-aways or use a bobby pin or a snap barrette depending on the length of the hair.

Q: What if my daughter seems like she's in pain when I make a pony?

A: This isn't good and you're pulling too hard. Don't pull too tightly. You don't want her hair plastered against her head. Save plastering for the walls in the dining room. You don't want to cut off her brain circulation either. It absolutely shouldn't hurt. If she says "ouch" then relax the pony a bit.

Q: I found tangles when I went to make the pony. Should I give up and join the Merchant Marines?

A: You must remove the tangles first. Go back to the tangle chapter, take action, and then when de-tangles. Start over from Pony step one.

Q: Do you personally prefer using a brush or a comb when making a pony?

A: I like to use a brush; it's more manageable.

Q: How do I secure the pony?

A: Get out your coated hairband and go over it two or three times to make sure it's secure. Then you're good to go! Whenever I do live TV shows I ALWAYS use ponytail ties just to make sure it is secure.

ACCESSORIZING YOUR PONY

After you secure your pony, your job might not be done. I know you're thinking, "Dean, you lied because you said this would be fast and easy." First, I'm hurt that you think this of me because I did not lie. Accessorizing a pony can take less than a minute. Think of it this way: You will spend less time accessorizing that pony than you do trying to adjust the seat in your car. Don't you have less than a minute for your child? I'm sorry, but I'm pulling out the big guilt here because an accessorized pony is a true dream come true. You can thank me later. It will take your pony esthetic to the next LEVEL!

DEAN'S RULE FOR DADDY DOING:

▫ **When using an accessory, the key to remember is that less is NOT more.** More is actually better.

▫ **Start small and add colorful or glittery bows to the pony.** Or you can tie the bottom of the pony with a pretty ribbon.

▫ **You might want to color coordinate the ribbon with the outfit.** There's nothing cuter than a polka dot dress with a matching polka dot ribbon.

▫ **You can make your own bows.** Buy the metal clasps and take a bit of fabric or tulle and make a pretty knot. Need help? Go to Michael's and ask for help.

▫ **You can buy adorable little pom-pom bows to put back there.** Girls love pom- poms and your Daddy coolness factor will quadruple.
▫ **Fourth of July time?** Buy one of those bouncy ponytail holders with streamers and stars coming out of it.

▫ **Glitter is great.** The more glitter on a bow the better. It's *bougie* which is my word, which means fancy. Now, let's try it in a sentence: "You are so bougie."

☐ **Christmas? New Year's? How about a bigger, glittery star on the pony?** Holidays mean you can go literally crazy with the accessories.

☐ **For Dads into sports, listen to Dean. I don't know JACK about sports;** however, I do know that if Dad is a Bears fan there is nothing wrong with an orange and blue ribbon on your daughter's pony on game day. Nothing says bonding like sharing the team's colors. You can also do your school's colors.

☐ **Do not raid your wife's hair accessory drawer for your daughter.** Your wife likes her stuff where it is and not in foreign drawers where she will never find these accessories again. (Kids have a rule that when they take out a bow, it falls to the ground and they leave it there or behind a bed where the dog starts to eat it.) Go to Target or Justice or Claires or anywhere and buy a few bows to surprise your daughter when you do her hair. You have gone from hero to King.

Enough with the ponytail for a second.

THE RAG ROLL SET THE NIGHT BEFORE

How about another option for going out hair? This requires a little more practice. If you want more *bougie* and you're going to an event, it's great to do a little hair project with your daughter. You can do a rag roll set the night before. At this point you might be saying, "Dean, are you speaking a foreign language here?" To do this, all you need to do is go into your manly workshop (or the store) and get shop cloth or regular strips of thin cotton fabric. Roll up the hair and tie it. Start at the ends making sure they are even on the cloth BEFORE you roll up the hair to the scalp. Then tie the ends in a bow. No one likes fishhook ends on hair. They only like it when they are BASS fishing. Make sure hair is 95% dry first.

DADDY DO IT!
THE RAG ROLL SET THE NIGHT BEFORE

□ Split the hair in small sections.

□ To secure, wrap hair around the fabric rolling it up to the scalp.

□ Take the two ends of fabric and tie together to create the rag roll set.

□ This will create amazing and erratic curls because in the morning you will take out the fabric and your child will have instant curls. Over the course of the day, the curls will loosen up. Secure with ponytail holder.

DOUBLE OR NOTHING

You can easily make double ponies, which is a great style if your daughter is going to day camp or even a swim class and needs her hair out of her face. Maybe she's a cheerleader or in dance class. It's a cute look that's also functional. If you want to be a cutting edge Dad, try it this way:

DADDY DO IT!
DOUBLE OR NOTHING

▢ Make one pony at the crown by grabbing the hair from halfway up the head.

▢ Secure with elastic band.

▢ Take the hair underneath (or bottom half) and make a second pony.

▢ The key is to add the tail of the top pony to your hand for the second pony so they are now attached. It looks like the first pony is going right into the second pony. instant curls. Over the course of the day, the curls will loosen up.. Secure with ponytail holder.

Is it okay to do a Pebbles pony? In my world, the Pebbles Flintstone top of the head pony is still okay. In fact, it's a great way to really deal with her long hair on a hot day.

DADDY DO TIP
There is no need to use hair spray on a ponytail. You want to have that swing factor. HOWEVER, a little blast of hairspray will lay down any fly aways that didn't make it into the pony.

DOUBLE OR NOTHING!

 @DBANO @DEANBANOWETZ

#DADDYDOS

DEAN'S DIY RECIPE FOR A SILKY PONY

I have absolutely no problem with DIY beauty recipes if they work. If you want your daughter to have a sleek pony, you can grab a dime-sized dot of hair gel and run it over the pony. Let's say you live in a "gel-less" house. Go into the kitchen and put a ¼ of a teaspoon of real sugar (not fake) in your hand and about six small drops of water. Swirl with your other finger to break down the sugar until it's a bit syrupy. Swirl as you go along, so you don't drown the sugar in too much water. You want the consistency of a runny maple syrup. Rub the mixture between your hands and the over the hair that is on the scalp by the roots to create a sleek, shining look. This is the best homemade gel ever and works great on vacation if you forget your gel. The end of the ponytail should be free to move.

DADDY DO TIP

Stop, in the name of good hair. You can also get way ahead of yourself and make a bun with the pony. But first master your pony and that can only be done with practice. Make sure it's perfection before we move onto topknots and buns in the following chapters.

GETTING THE PONY TAIL THINGY OUT

I hear horror stories of giant tangles that start when a ponytail tie gets stuck in the hair. Dads will try to maneuver the little rubber band out while the kid stands there doing a crying jig. There is no need to have all this angst in your home. Let's say it's bedtime, a tired kid and a ponytail tie that won't come out, find a tiny pair of sewing scissors in the house (or other small scissors). Cut the tie so the hair will come right out. You're done. Avoid the ocean of tears.

IT'S GETTING HOT IN HERE

Since I want to talk about curling the ponytail – and this is the first time I've mentioned using actual powered tools on hair (sort of like power tools, but not really) -- it's time to talk turkey about how to stay safe around children and heat. First of all your daughter has young, silky hair that hasn't been colored (unless she lives in Hollywood and works in the motion picture industry…and then who knows?)

The first rule when using a curling iron or any other heat product on your child is to spray her hair with a thermal setting spray before you use the hot tool. I love the Aquage Thermal setting spray. You don't want to actually burn her hair, which would cause tears that might last weeks, and your better half locking you out of the house––perhaps permanently. Don't be afraid of using these tools. They can be very dangerous if not used in the right way.

First things first: You never want your child to touch them in any way. Little hands can easily get burned. Hot hair tools are not toys and you need to be firm with your child. The last thing you want EVER is for your child to plug one in and try it on a friend. Keep these tools out of the reach of your younger children. Tell your kids that they are not allowed to touch these things, as they are adult tools, much like the Chevy Tahoe parked in the driveway. Other tips for using hot tools:

☐ **Never use them in the tub or shower even if it says the product is a wet and dry tool.** Never ever ever! Someone could get electrocuted.

☐ **Don't leave the tool in the hair for too long.** Use it for a couple of seconds. Don't freak out if you see a little steam when you are using a hot tool. It is simple excess product on the hair. If you see smoke and HEAR sizzle then you are literally burning the hair. Get that heated tool away from her hair – stat!

☐ **If you smell the hair, it's burning.** That's a horrible smell and you'll know it. The smell always reminds me of butchering chickens on the farm and singeing the little hairs off. GAY-ROSS!

▢ **If your child's hair is thicker or course, you will leave the heated tool in for a second or two longer.** A second or two… not longer.

▢ **The finer the hair, the less time you leave in a hot tool.** This type of hair will burn easier. You don't want to see her hair stuck to the heated hair tool.

▢ **Remember that the first time you curl your daughter's hair it doesn't have to be perfect.** She's not in a Miss USA pageant. She doesn't even know Donald Trump. Just do a few curls to practice. As you feel more comfortable you can do more with hot tools. #MissAmericaRequiresTalent

▢ **Remember that hairdryers get so hot these days that they are also hot tools.** Dry your child's hair on a cooler setting even if it takes longer. It's easy to burn their hair, scalps and even their necks if you use Mom's salon professional hairdryer on a little head.

▢ **Use common sense and caution here.** You don't want to be known for the rest of your life as the "Burn Daddy."

▢ **Always read the users manual included for any heated tool.** #usecommonsense

You're going to be careful, but the more practice you get, the more comfortable you'll become.

I LOVE USING
THE #INSTYLER!

@DBANO @DEANBANOWETZ

#DADDYDOS

A FEW LAST WORDS ABOUT HOT TOOLS

As you're mastering hot tools, remember this rule: the longer you keep the heat on *doesn't* mean a better curl. If you really want to lock the curl in, drop the curl out of the curling iron after a few seconds. (This is how I get curls to stay longer when I am working on *Dancing with the Stars*). Put down the hot tool in a safe spot where you're not dropping it on your own leg. Now, take your fingers and wrap the curl around your fingers. Clip it with a bobby pin.

Let the curls stay clipped for several minutes until they are cool to the touch and then take out the pins. You'll have amazing curls and they will last much longer after trying this technique. Plus, the next time Mommy curls her hair and she asks about the pin trick, the female parent here might say, "What pin trick?" Big points for Daddy!

In summary:

□ **Use a thermal protector on the hair before you use hot tools including blow dryers.** I love Biolage Thermal Spray.

□ **Smell hair? You've left the hot tool in too long.** Not good.

□ **Explore rag curls or even try sponge rollers (both are a whole lot safer) before going to hot tools.** It will make everyone's life much safer.

□ **If you are looking for a hot tool I would suggest looking into purchasing an InStyler to lock in some curls.** It will become your new favorite tool.

CHAPTER FIVE: THE BEST BRAIDS EVER!

It's time to let your fingers do the talking. Before you try the actual braiding in this book, it's time to go to rookie hair camp where your head counselor Dean will take you through a few training exercises.

This might sound crazy, but I want you to try the following in your spare time – and you can do this in private without prying eyes. If someone catches you doing this exercise then simply put it away in your tackle box and talk about fishing hooks with worm guts attached to them or the films of Arnold Schwarzenegger. When in doubt, get macho. Nothing makes ladies run out of the room during inopportune moments like the mention of worm innards or quoting *The Terminator*.

LET'S START BRAIDING

Here is the great news: It's very easy to braid your daughter's hair. Men, it's important to wipe the entire idea of hair out of the picture here. Just imagine that you're dealing with the cables of a TV or stereo system. In your mind, you're fixing the cables so you get a great picture for the big game. Feeling motivated now? Let's go!

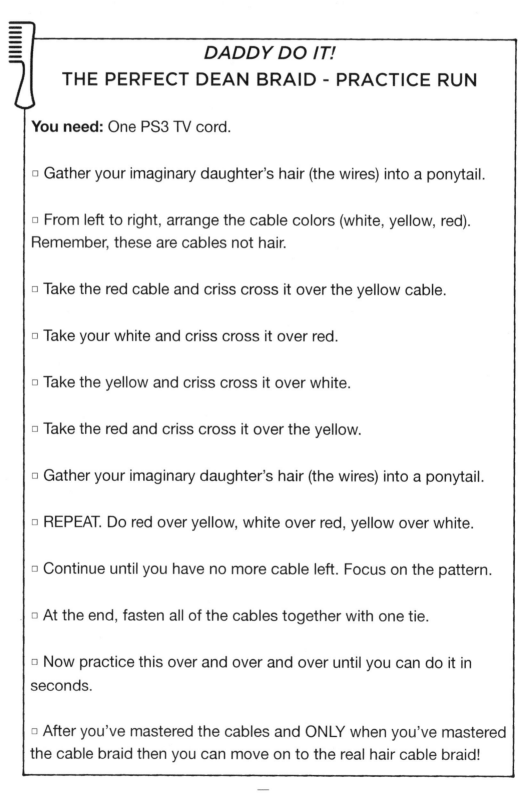

DADDY DO IT!
THE PERFECT DEAN BRAID - PRACTICE RUN

You need: One PS3 TV cord.

□ Gather your imaginary daughter's hair (the wires) into a ponytail.

□ From left to right, arrange the cable colors (white, yellow, red). Remember, these are cables not hair.

□ Take the red cable and criss cross it over the yellow cable.

□ Take your white and criss cross it over red.

□ Take the yellow and criss cross it over white.

□ Take the red and criss cross it over the yellow.

□ Gather your imaginary daughter's hair (the wires) into a ponytail.

□ REPEAT. Do red over yellow, white over red, yellow over white.

□ Continue until you have no more cable left. Focus on the pattern.

□ At the end, fasten all of the cables together with one tie.

□ Now practice this over and over and over until you can do it in seconds.

□ After you've mastered the cables and ONLY when you've mastered the cable braid then you can move on to the real hair cable braid!

DADDY DO IT!
THE PERFECT DEAN BRAID - THE REAL DEAL

You need: Take the following out of your tackle box: Yellow, red, two black and white ponytail ties and your brush.

□ Gather your daughter's hair into a ponytail with a black hair tie. Within that pony, break it into three sections.

□ At the end of section one, put a white ponytail tie. Use a yellow pony tie for the second section, and a red pony tie for the thirds. Remember, these are no longer strands of hair. They are cables (in your mind). Now, breathe. Smile. Your kid is nervous.

□ Take the red cable and criss cross it over the yellow cable.

□ Take your white and criss cross it over red.

□ Take the yellow and criss cross it over white.

□ Take the red and criss cross it over the yellow.

□ Now... go red over yellow, white over red, yellow over white. Continue until you have no more cable left.

□ Stay focused on the pattern. At the end, put all of the cables together and take a black ponytail tie and put it just above the red, yellow and white ties.

□ Take the colored ties out. Save them in your tackle box for your next training.

□ Drink a beer. You earned it.

VIDEO TUTORIAL!
See it at daddy.do/perfect-dean-braid

Imaginary conversation after you make this perfect braid:

Wife (to you):
"Did Sally braid her own hair?"

You:
"No, I did."

Wife (look of shock registering while she wonders if you were kidnapped by aliens who gave you a hairdresser probe while experimenting on you):
"How did you do it?"

You:
"It was easy. Go relax, honey."

Bonus: You are having sex tonight.

It's safe to say here—after you've broken your braiding cherry—that this hairstyle is beyond huge. Now you have a basic braid in your trick bag and you should be feeling confident. I'm sure your daughter looks adorable. Extra points if your girl has really long hair. I'm proud of you because you've done a whole braid without f-ing it up.

Now, it's time to get a bit more advanced in our braiding. Turn the page for your next adventure.

DADDY DO IT!
ADVANCED MANLY BRAID TRAINING

☐ Take 20 pieces of yarn and cut identical 8 to 10 inch strips.

☐ On your workbench counter, tape the strands down in a neat row using duct tape to make sure they are secured.

☐ Start in the middle and grab three strands of yarn.

☐ Pick them up and crisscross them over each other.

☐ Pick up the next strands and crisscross them. You are learning how to braid. Breathe. This is not brain surgery.

☐ Continue to work on your crisscross technique.

☐ The key is to pick up another string as you go from side to side

VIDEO TUTORIAL!
See it at daddy.do/manly-braid-training

Do this when your daughter or partner is not around, so you don't look like a total freak.

Spoiler: This is the beginning training for a French braid.

BRAIDED PIG TAILS!

 @DBANO  @DEANBANOWETZ

#DADDYDOS

If you want to do really great hair then put the time in with this exercise. When you feel confident enough go find one of your daughter's dolls—the one with the long hair. When you're all alone and everyone is out of the house practice braiding on the creepy doll.

Take this seriously. It is your pre-game.

I know this isn't how you usually spend your weekend, but this is a worthwhile way to kill 15 to 20 minutes. If someone walks in on you while you're playing with the doll's hair then simply call your daughter over and finish the story. Just say, "And then the prince marries the princess and all is happy in the end." Lie to your wife and say you're perfecting your storytelling abilities. She'll be so shocked that she won't even remember that the guy who tosses her over his shoulder has actually braided that American Girl doll's hair.

Kids are often too smart for this lie. It follows that if a kid actually walks in on you just say, "Honey, her neck was kind of squeaky and I wanted to make sure your brother didn't rip her head off. These dolls are expensive and money doesn't grow on trees." The minute you mention money, your daughter's eyes will glaze over and she will want to leave the room without any more nosy questions asked.

Your daughter's Barbie is also a great tool here during your practice sessions. Split her hair into four sections and make a quick ponytail. Think of your work with Barbie like taking the back off of your TV or defusing a bomb during any action film. Pretend you actually are Liam Neeson in any one of his later-in-life films where bombs and babes over 30 are involved. Think to yourself that this isn't Barbie hair, but yellow, red and white cables. You will pull the safest cable (section of hair) into a pony and thus are defusing a bomb (in your mind).

Now that you've practiced, it's time to get to some of the real styles that you will perfect.

ADDING ACCESSORIES TO YOUR BRAID
(OH YES YOU CAN!)

Braids were made for accessories including cute, decorative hairpins and even bows. It's all about placing it where you want this tool to hold the actual hair. Why settle for a plain ponytail tie at the end of your braid? Learning what to do with the braid you created is a lot of fun. Think of your original braid as the foundation for slightly more complex (but truly easy) things you can do with your daughter's hair.

DADDY DO IT!
A BASIC BRAID

□ Brush the hair smooth and put the hair into a ponytail with a hair band (any color)

□ Section that ponytail into three different ponytails this time using the **red**, **white** and **yellow** hair bands

□ Take **yellow** and move it to the center crossing OVER the **white**

□ Take **red** and move it to the center crossing OVER the **yellow**

□ Take **white** and move it to the center crossing OVER the **red**

□ Take **yellow** and move it to the center crossing OVER the **white**

□ Take **red** and move it to the center crossing OVER the **yellow**

□ Repeat this pattern continuing all the way down the hair and tie off the end with a **black** band (remove **red**, **white** and **yellow** bands)

VIDEO TUTORIAL!
See it at daddy.do/basic-braid-by-dean

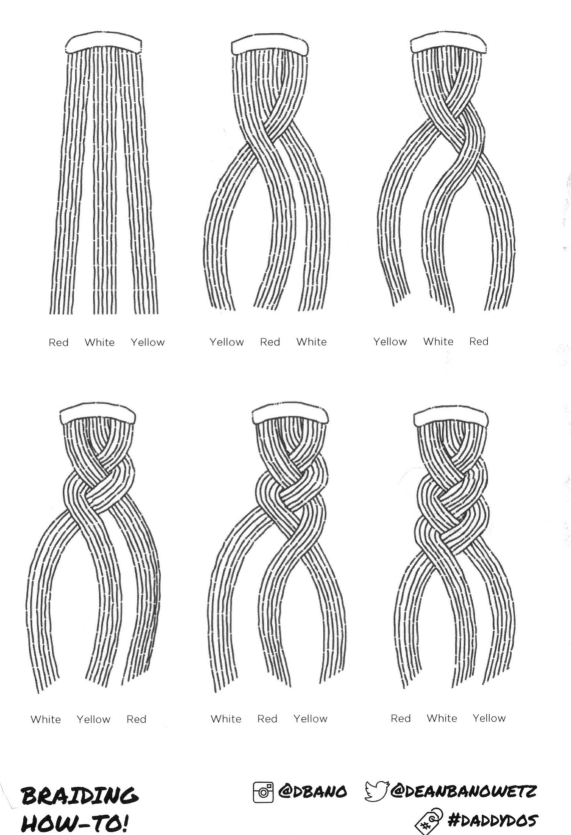

Red   White   Yellow

Yellow   Red   White

Yellow   White   Red

White   Yellow   Red

White   Red   Yellow

Red   White   Yellow

BRAIDING HOW-TO!

@DBANO   @DEANBANOWETZ

#DADDYDOS

DADDY DO IT!
A FRENCH BRAID

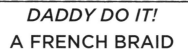

☐ Before braiding, brush hair smooth. Take a section at the top of the head and divide the hair into three equal strands.

☐ Cross the **yellow** strand over the **white** section, and then repeat this action with the **red** side, smoothing hair as you go.

☐ Before repeating the crossover action with the **right** section, gather some of the additional hair from the head's **right** side, and adding it to this section.

☐ Cross this larger strand of hair over the **middle** stand of hair.

☐ Gather a section of hair the same size as the **right** side from the head's **left** side, and then add to strand and cross over middle strand.

☐ Repeat steps 4 and 5 all the way down the head until you've gathered all additional strands. Finish at the bottom with a regular braid.

☐ Tie off the end with a hair band.

VIDEO TUTORIAL!
See it at daddy.do/a-very-french-braid

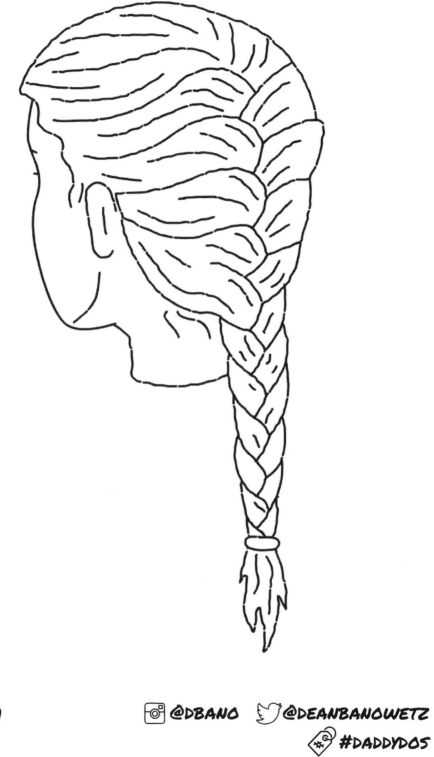

FRENCH BRAID!

 @DBANO   @DEANBANOWETZ

 #DADDYDOS

DADDY DO IT!
A FISHTAIL BRAID

☐ Before braiding, brush hair smooth.

☐ Divide hair into two large sections, parting straight down the middle.

☐ Pull a thin strand of hair from the outside of the **left** section. Pull it over the top of the **left** section, and add it to the **right** section. Try to use the same thickness for each strand throughout or your braid will look uneven.

☐ Repeat on the **right** side. Pull a skinny strand of hair from the outside of the **right** section, pull it over the **right** section, and then add it to the **left** section.

☐ Keep alternating sides, weaving over and under, until you reach the bottom of the braid.

☐ Tie off the end with a hair band.

☐ The smaller the section, the more it will look like a fishbone; the larger the section, the less time it will take and the less it will look like a true fishbone. Start with larger sections. When you have it down, start taking smaller and smaller sections.

VIDEO TUTORIAL!
See it at daddy.do/a-fishtail-braid

FISHTAIL BRAID!

 @DBANO @DEANBANOWETZ
#DADDYDOS

DADDY DO IT!
A ROPE BRAID

□ Before braiding, brush hair smooth.

□ For a tighter, more structured rope braid, start by putting the hair in a ponytail. For a messier look, skip to the next step and start the braid at the nape of her neck.

□ Separate the hair into two equal sections. Now, twirl each section around your fingers, or pinch the top of the section, twist, move down another inch, twist again, and so on. Both sections should be twisted in a clockwise or rightward motion.

□ Cross the **right** section over the left section.

□ Keep braiding all the way down the hair.

□ Tie off the end with a hair band.

DADDY DO TIP
Take the braid and use bobby pins to fasten it up. Use the same color pins as your daughter's hair. There is nothing worse than blonde hair and black pins. #ThanksKimiMessina

DADDY DO TIP
It is easier to braid with slightly dirty hair because it has less "slip." So, let your child skip a hair washing the night before you know you're going to braid.

DADDY DO IT!
A FRENCH ROPE BRAID

☐ Before braiding, brush hair smooth.

☐ Gather a small section at the front hairline and divide into two equal sections.

☐ Twist each strand to the right, or clockwise. For a French Rope, you'll twist the hair, as you go, so don't worry if you only have the base of the strand twisted for now.

☐ Cross the twisted **right** strand over the twisted left strand.

☐ Grab the section of hair directly beneath where you started the braid. Then twist the new section around the strand on the **right**. It might take a few twirls for you to get them into one cohesive twist.

☐ Cross the larger **right** section over the smaller **left** section.

☐ Grab the section of hair directly beneath the last one you took.

☐ Add the new section around the strand on the **right**. Again, it might take a few twirls for you to get them into one, cohesive twist. Repeat adding new sections and twisting until you reach the desired length.

☐ Tie off the end with a hair band.

☐ Practice over and over.

VIDEO TUTORIAL!
See it at <u>daddy.do/french-rope-by-dean</u>

Let's say your daughter has her big dance recital and your partner (the one who does good hair) has to go out of town. This is not the time to pack up the kids and move to Alaska. They still have dance recitals in the tundra. If you want to be a really cool Dad, master the basic braid and then take a glance at the dress your daughter will wear for her dance routine.

If her outfit is purple, go out and buy a big purple ribbon and even some thinner ribbons (about a quarter of an inch wide), too. You can often find these ribbons at stores including Target, Walmart and Justice. Note: If you go to Justice, prepare yourself to hear so many boy band songs that you will feel as if you should form a boy band. Suddenly, you're answering your cell phone humming, 'Baby, baby baby....'" But we digress.)

When you put the pony in, clip the thinner ribbon to a safety pin and close the safety pin. In the center of that pony, you will stick the safety pin through and pull the ribbon through the ponytail tie. Now, take the safety pin off and pull it through to the end. You've literally created another strand to braid here. Instead of letting that new purple ribbon strand hang, incorporate it into one of the red, yellow OR white cable sections. Pretend it's just another part of that section of hair – I mean, another cable. Continue to braid as you bring this ribbon into the braid. When you reach the end of the section, tie with an elastic hair tie. Then tie the ribbon ends together in a bow. It will give it a cute ribbon braided loop. (If you choose to do a braided bun – and more on buns later – you can work it through the bun). After this not-so-complex move, you might have to call your buddies and go to the local bar for some wings. I mean, you color coordinated the ribbon to go with an actual dance outfit. This is major! I think you should do a shot or go shoot hoops!

CHAPTER SIX:
BANG YOUR HEAD

There are times when any father is tempted to take a scissors to their child's hair, and most of the time as a top hairdresser to the stars, I want to scream, "Little child, run fast, run far, run to your Uncle Dean's house where there will be milk, cookies, and tastefully cut, perfect 'dos!" We've come to the point in the book, however, where I believe I'll have to let go and allow you Dads to cut your child's bangs. I'm not letting you cut her entire head of hair! The bangs are quite enough.

I do have to say that I love bangs on girls and they even help to conceal any irregular hairlines. Bangs also disguise high and low foreheads. If you have one of those high Christina Ricci foreheads and want to cover it up, just cut some bangs. Another great reason to cut bangs is that they keep the hair out of your girl's face when she's dancing, playing soccer, riding bikes, or chasing down bullies or boys. Bangs are great for kids who swim or do gymnastics, as they're a way to manage to have long hair that doesn't interrupt the activity at hand.

Are you considering bangs for your child? The first thing I tell adults is to think long and hard about it before doing it. I know I just said I love bangs, but they are a hair commitment. In other words, it will take FOREVER to grow them out. If your child hates them on day one, FOREVER will seem like forever plus eternity. Bangs are a decision that requires a consultation with your partner. You don't just "do bangs." You talk about getting bangs first with everyone involved and all parties get a vote. There might even be a lengthy period of debate. Go with the flow. You've only got one vote.

It also helps to remember that bangs require frequent trims, so you must commit to the idea of keeping her bangs fresh and exciting. One note: When you're a kid, face shape really doesn't matter when it comes to bangs. If your child has a round face, you can frame it with bangs and that will look super cute as well.

DADDY DO TIP

Make sure to get your bangs cut first by a qualified hairdresser. You don't want your child sitting in your bathroom or kitchen upset as her long hair hits the floor. And you don't want to start out with bad bangs that become shorter and shorter and weirder and weirder as you try to fix them. Get professional help. As a hairdresser, I'm happy to take the five minutes to cut a child's bangs. You could probably just take your child into your hairdresser and ask if during a break he or she will do some bangs. A hairdresser will also shape or thin out bangs so they look gorgeous. Later on, if the bangs need a trim you can probably pop back into your hairdresser for a quick reshaping. Or I'll allow you to trim them at home if you pay close attention in this chapter.

WANT TO DO BANGS AT HOME OR TRIM THE BANGS YOU ALREADY HAVE?

Then listen up. The first step is to determine what kind of bang you want it to be… shorter, longer, wispy or perhaps fuller. You'll want to clip the hair from the other areas out of the way. Remember that less IS more when trimming your child's bangs. In other words, don't get cray-cray here. Just do a little trim, and for God's sake leave enough hair for your hairdresser to fix it if this becomes a 911 moment.

DADDY DO IT!
CUTTING CUTE BANGS

Before you begin:

☐ Don't use your household scissors, which I'm sure are dull. Go to the drugstore and get professional hair cutting scissors. They only cost about ten bucks.

☐ Do not use tape. Tape stretches the hair.

☐ I would never EVER cut bangs when they're wet. They will shrink up and you'll end up with some wacko, hack job bangs. In fact, they could snap up about an inch, depending on the tension (how tight you pull the bangs down) when cutting

Here we go:

☐ Hold 100% dry hair in a comb.

☐ Pull hair away from the face with your hand. Make tiny cuts.

⟶

▢ Don't cut straight across. Those tiny chipping cuts (angling your scissors) are more forgiving.

▢ Use the eyebrows as a guideline.

VIDEO TUTORIAL!
See it at <u>daddy.do/bang-trim</u>

DADDY DO TIP

If bangs are so long they're falling into the eyes, they need a trim. But let me remind you, baby steps. Less is more. You can cut more tomorrow.

DADDY DON'T TIP

NEVER GO ABOVE THE EYEBROWS. I'M SCREAMING THIS TO YOU! You're going much too short if you go above the brows. If your child wants those cute short-short bangs, go see a pro. Remind your child it will take forever and another forever to grow those out.

Let's say, hypothetically, of course, you didn't listen to any of the above and started hacking at your daughter's bangs. Now they're way too short and you're afraid to tell her to open her eyes. You know at that moment when she sees your creepy short bangs, she will ask to be put up for adoption. If you went too short, STOP! Put down your tools. Take a step away from the child. Grab the car keys. Get in the car. Go see a real hairdresser for a fix. The more hair you leave, the easier the fix. The more you keep cutting, the worse it gets.

ANOTHER THOUGHT ON BANGS

Many adults have had professional photos taken of themselves at the local J.C. Penney when we were kids (and often victims of botched bangs). Many of these photos could double for prison pictures. I do believe our parents took us for these photos after cutting our bangs as a way to blackmail us when we were older. Now that there's Facebook, Twitter, Snapchat, Instagram, Vine, YouTube and Periscope, the blackmail options never go away. Blackmail for life. In fact, our parents often pull out those pictures when we get engaged, when we get our doctorate in nuclear science or at our weddings or various family holidays. Be a progressive parent. Don't let bangs become your future blackmail over your own child.

If you jack up your kid's bangs, it might even cause a divorce or you'll sit in the hair penalty box or the "THINK ABOUT IT" corner for a few weeks. If you're bad at hair cutting just don't do it. It's not a learning experience that you need.

If the bangs you have cut came out cute, then your wife might even want you to trim her bangs. You will definitely get lucky that night. She might even let you take a couple of buddies to a strip club. There might even be a NASCAR weekend in your future. So if you're handy with a scissors, it is worth a try. Just remember if you screw up your partner's bangs, you will be living an existence I call botched hair hell on earth. It might be easier to just drive him or her to the hairdresser and avoid total relationship banishment.

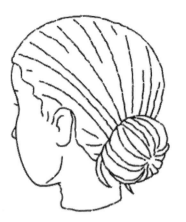

CHAPTER SEVEN:
BUNS OF STEEL AND
CINNAMON

Congratulations! You've reached this part of the book without having any kind of nervous breakdown. I'm guessing that your little daughter is running out of the house looking cuter than the average second grader while insisting, "My Dad totally rocks." Your partner's jaw has repeatedly been picked up off the floor as you've commanded the bathroom to create the world's most adorable ponytails and have even trimmed her bangs when in a pinch. When you braided, you actually had to tell your partner to lay down with a cold compress. He or she was in shock.

There have been no projectile tears from either partner or child, which is a plus. You're ready to take Uncle Dean out for a beer, which is appreciated, but not necessary. Now it's time to really butch up and get creative with hair. You're going to get off your buns and learn how to make a bun.

I know that many of you are shaking your heads, thinking I have lost my mind, but that's hardly the case. Making a bun is actually easier than jumpstarting a car or making one of those complicated Boy Scout knots. Plus, there is nothing that looks clean and classic like a wonderful bun. Let's get to work!

There are several kinds of buns, and I'll detail them in order of what you should try first. Just remember that your crowning achievement is putting smiles on your little girl's face.

DADDY DO IT!
A MESSY BUN

▢ Brush hair smooth to prep for bun.

▢ Pull hair back using just your hands. Hold the hair where you want to have the bun.

▢ Make a ponytail with a hair band.

▢ Create the messy bun by taking the tail and wrapping it around the base of the ponytail, covering the band. Use two or three bobby pins or whatever is needed to secure the tail around the base.

▢ Finish the bun by spraying a bit of hairspray.

VIDEO TUTORIAL!
See it at daddy.do/sexy-messy-bun

**A MESSY
BUN!**

@DBANO @DEANBANOWETZ
#DADDYDOS

DADDY DO IT!
A SLEEK BUN

☐ Brush hair smooth to prep for Topknot.

☐ Pull hair up high into a high ponytail

Twist hair into a knot. Take the handful of hair and twist it in the same direction, creating a rope-like piece. Then, wrap it onto itself to make a knot-like spiral.

☐ Wrap a hair band around topknot.

☐ Finish the bun by spraying a bit of hairspray.

VIDEO TUTORIAL!
See it at daddy.do/sleek-bun-by-dean

Turn the page for an example (you can also color, of course).

KEEPIN' IT SLEEK!

@DBANO @DEANBANOWETZ
#DADDYDOS

DADDY DO IT!
A TOPKNOT

☐ Brush hair smooth to prep for topknot.

☐ Pull hair up high into a high ponytail.

Twist hair into a knot. Take the handful of hair and twist it in the same direction, creating a rope-like piece. Then, wrap it onto itself to make a knot-like spiral.

☐ Wrap a hair band around topknot.

☐ Finish the bun by spraying a bit of hairspray.

VIDEO TUTORIAL!
See it at daddy.do/top-knots

Can't visualize it? I've got you covered on the next page, boo.

A KNOT ON THE TOP!

 @DBANO  @DEANBANOWETZ
#DADDYDOS

Word on the street is that you've become a bun master. In that case, feel free to have fun with these more advanced techniques:

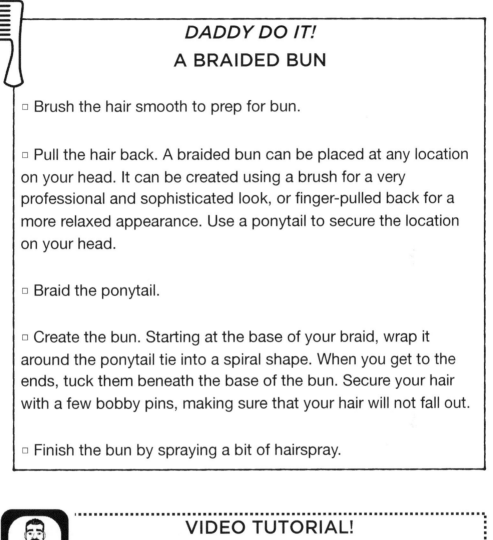

DADDY DO IT!
A BRAIDED BUN

▢ Brush the hair smooth to prep for bun.

▢ Pull the hair back. A braided bun can be placed at any location on your head. It can be created using a brush for a very professional and sophisticated look, or finger-pulled back for a more relaxed appearance. Use a ponytail to secure the location on your head.

▢ Braid the ponytail.

▢ Create the bun. Starting at the base of your braid, wrap it around the ponytail tie into a spiral shape. When you get to the ends, tuck them beneath the base of the bun. Secure your hair with a few bobby pins, making sure that your hair will not fall out.

▢ Finish the bun by spraying a bit of hairspray.

VIDEO TUTORIAL!
See it at daddy.do/a-braided-bun

BRAIDED BUN MAGIC!

@DBANO @DEANBANOWETZ
#DADDYDOS

DADDY DO IT!
A SOCK BUN

☐ Brush the hair smooth to prep for bun.

☐ Pull the hair back. Select the place on your head you would like to create your sock bun and make a ponytail.

☐ Prep the hair sock by cutting a hole in the toe end of a sock and rolling it up into a doughnut shape.

☐ Take the sock and slide it onto your ponytail all the way to the base.

☐ Spread the hair over the doughnut, making sure the sock is fully covered, and then wrap a hair band around the base of the bun.

☐ Wrap the ends around the base of the bun, then tuck them under and pin them in place.

☐ Finish the bun by spraying a bit of hairspray.

☐ Make sure if you're working with dark hair to use a dark sock.

VIDEO TUTORIAL!
See it at <u>daddy.do/sock-bun-by-dean</u>

You know the drill. See it on the next page!

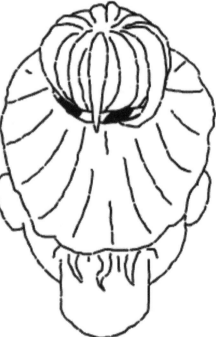

SOCK BUN RIGHT HERE!

@DBANO @DEANBANOWETZ

#DADDYDOS

BRO YOU
DID IT!

@DBANO @DEANBANOWETZ
#DADDYDOS

CHAPTER EIGHT:
EXTRA CREDIT
DADDY DOS

Think of this chapter like grad school. You've mastered the pony, the braid and the bun. Now it's time to explore some other options to make your little girl look fabulous.

HAIR LENGTH AND TRIMS

Let's start with how long you want your daughter's hair to grow. Just remember that the longer it gets the more tangled it will be over time. It's crucial to not just allow your daughter's hair to grow and grow. Have your child's hair cut every four weeks. Remember that their hair grows faster than adults, just another perk of youth. You can trim the ends, or take them in to a quick cut place to keep them trimmed. Those ends get really dry and that can become a split-ends nightmare.

Remember, if you go to a regular hairdresser, you can ask them to do a "bang drive-by" or "ends drive-by" on your child, which basically means you bring them in for about five minutes for a quick trim. It's a real lifesaver and will help your child develop great habits, while also looking neat and clean. Regular trims will also make styling much easier for you.

WHAT IF YOUR KID PITCHES A FIT?

There are girls (and boys) who love pampering and others who toss a hissy when it's time for a haircut. The whole thing about haircutting (in my opinion—back off Dr. Phil) is that you gotta pull out the bribes. Of course, there are levels of bribes. You might choose ice cream, a new Barbie or a trip to the islands. It just depends on how your family does bribes. If you do the trip then please adopt me. I'm available.

First and foremost, you need to have a hairdresser the kid likes and trusts. You might not want to take your child to that crazy Led Zeppelin rocker dude. There are a lot of different salons these days that cater to kids, and make it fun with funky chairs and kiddie music, plus candy as a treat. It makes me sad that I didn't get to go to one of them when I was younger. My dad just lined all of us up and buzzed our hair GONE. You never cried or you got a spanking. I hate spankings. Just take your kid to a cool place, smile, and bribe them. Easy! A trip to Yellow Balloon for a no drama haircut? It's a small price to pay.

Remember that you're going to be hair cutting every four weeks, so make sure these bribes are affordable. Also let your hairdresser know the deal, especially if the child is afraid or hates going there. When I worked at my salon in Iowa, I'd keep little toys and treats for the kids in a special drawer. Or the parent can give the hairdresser a treat to bestow on the child for being good during their haircut. I remember a little boy, Kenny, who hated going for haircuts. His mom gave me a plastic plane to hide in one of my drawers. I promised Kenny if he didn't cry and sat still, I'd have a special treat for him after I was done. Kenny behaved and then became my new best friend after I gave him that plane. He even started asking Mom when we were going to see his new buddy Dean again. Last week, I gave Kenny a Toyota Prius and Taylor Swift's home phone number—just kidding. But you get the idea.

YOUR HAIRDRESSER AND YOUR CHILD

The one gripe kids have when it comes to hairdressers is when they go silent. Kids don't feel comfortable around silent people. I talk to kids the entire time when we're doing a cut. Some kids talk to me, but many will just sit there and feel good that I'm talking. Other kids don't give a rat's ass about the gibberish, but I'm sure they would be a little freaked if I was just this silent big guy hovering over them with a scissors.

I will ask the kids what celeb they want to look like—if there is one. One little girl in my chair was obsessed with Pink's haircut and her mom gave the A-OK to cut the child's hair like the famous rocker. We shaved the sides and kept it longer on the top. Adorable doesn't begin to describe it because this little girl had great 'tude. The cut made her feel even more empowered. The next time, the mom told me, "My daughter is beyond sassy now." Both Mom and I were so glad, because this girl wasn't just connected to her true self, she was empowered by her beauty at this young age. Now, that's a great feeling!

If your kid starts crying in the hairdresser's chair (and I've seen it all), I keep talking to them. I'll even talk slowly like a teacher. With boys, a lot of times the clippers freak them out. I'll pretend the clippers have transformed into an airplane landing on their heads. The thing is, your hairdresser should make the entire situation seem less intimidating. If he or she doesn't do that, it might be time to find someone new for your child.

DADDY DO TIP

It's really helpful to bring a photo of EXACTLY what you want to your hairdresser. This includes bringing in a photo for what you want your child's hair to look like because hairdressers aren't mind readers!

SHOULD I COLOR MY KID'S HAIR?

I'd never do all-over color on a child. Some parents prefer to do a few highlights, but I'd say never more than a few foils. Kids have a lifetime to dye their hair, and there is no point of ruining the natural shine of their beautiful youthful locks. And you don't want your six-year-old to look like a Goth princess with roots as it grows out – even if you are a Goth princess and want people to know this is your child. The point is, hair color and children don't usually mix. Sure, a little hint of pink or purple that washes out in a few weeks as a quick highlight can be fun. Just make sure your child won't hate it in 24 hours.

COMPLICATED CUTS

I'm so sick of the Bieber cut for boys. You can tell he was counseled on the haircut by a committee who thought, "This is cool hair." Don't be hell-bent on a certain celeb style. Those people have hairstylists at their beckon call. You don't want your child to have a complicated cut that will probably soon go out of fashion. Then you're stuck with the complex growing out period. Believe me, it's better to have a real person hairstyle that's easy to do. Kids need to be quick and easy when it comes to hair care. If daily hair care takes more than 5 to 10 minutes, it's too complex.

HOT WEATHER HELP

In the summer, I like to give boys a fresh buzz cut and girls can do little bobs. It's great to get the hair away for all the summer activities like sports and swimming. By the way, the bob is also a great year round style for girls with finer hair. It will look thicker shorter. If your child is upset about getting shorter hair then do it gradually with several smaller cuts, which helps them get used to it. If your little girl is still married to the long hair then spend the summer up in a pony or a braid and call it a day.

FUN WITH BANDANAS

I love a little bandana on girls, which is s great way to pull all of her hair up. Think of it like doing a high pony. Swoop the bandana around the nape of her neck and pull upwards into a pony. Tie it yourself. A square knot that you learned as a kid works great and looks fantastic.

HEADBANDS R US

A headband is also a great, quick and easy fix. Just slide it back and allow your daughter to find the best spot. When it comes to headbands, girls know what to do. I'd suggest pulling the bangs out for an uber cute look. But if the bangs are annoying her, pull them back, too.

DADDY DO TIP
Many Dads think that headbands are just for girls with long hair, but not true. They look adorable on super short hair too.

NO PONYTAIL TIE!

Let's say you're a camping family and you forgot your Dad hair toolbox. Shame, shame, shame, but the day is not lost. Your daughter is sick of her hair in her face, but you don't have anything out there to secure a ponytail. Just take an old T-shirt and cut a strip off the bottom. Tie up that pony! If you rip the strip of T-shirt off with your bare hands then you really are Superman Dad.

DADDY DO IT! HALF UP/HALF DOWN

One style I love on girls if half up, half down. Start at the top of her ears and with your fingers work your way back, separating the hair. Take this top portion and put in a ponytail tie to anchor it. Add any accessory like a flower bow or a pretty barrette over the tie. If you're camping (again) or need a fast 'do in a pinch, I love this style to get the hair out of the face. Again, if faced with no ponytail holder, a zip tie from a food bag will work in a pinch.

TRY A MULTIPLE PONY

Start with the half up, half down do. And then go back to the middle of the ear and slide in another ponytail. Put that ponytail in with the second. Do the exact same thing under the ear. You can take the rest of the hair and put it into a pony.

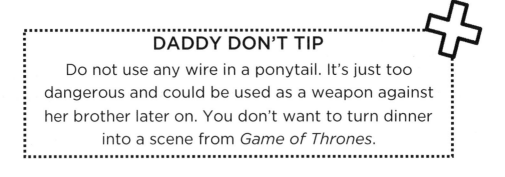

DADDY DON'T TIP

Do not use any wire in a ponytail. It's just too dangerous and could be used as a weapon against her brother later on. You don't want to turn dinner into a scene from *Game of Thrones*.

LOW PIGTAILS

If the hair is short, I love a high ponytail. Low pigtails are cute if you wrap them with little bows You can even do that with a younger toddler, but make sure they don't eat the ponytail holders or bows. I've found that bows are cute for baby pictures, but take them out before they can choke on them.

TRY A PONY FLIP

You can do a pony flip with a loose pony. I usually like medium to low pony flips. You reach down through the ponytail between the scalp and the ponytail tie and grab the pony. Pull it up all the way through and twist the pony. The pony flip is great. You can make it as dressy as you want and put a beautiful bow on it. It will look amazing.

DO A PUSH BACK

This is a nice, kicky little style. Just push some hair back around the temple areas and clip on both sides with a snap barrette. This is a quick fix at the soccer game when you need that hair immediately out of the face. This is also popular when the hair is growing out including when you want to turn growing bangs into all one-length hair.

STYLES FOR THE LITTLE GUYS IN YOUR LIFE

Now that you've become the hair master in your household, your partner is going to look at you and say, "Can you cut Tommy's hair too?" It's true that your work is NEVER done. These are some styles I'm going to suggest to my friend Simon Cowell once his little boy is old enough to have enough hair. Or maybe I'll just tell Simon that I'll come over to do the job. Since I can't go to every household in America, it's up to you Dads to learn how to give your little boys a great haircut. It's simple. It's easy. And your son will be glad to get it over with! In a pinch, you could try, or better yet just take them to a professional. Just take this handy book with you to the salon for the hairstylist.

DADDY DO IT! FOR HIM
"TEXTURED TOM"

▫ Use a #4 sized clipper on the back and sides.

▫ Use a #6 or #7 on the top then blend. (AKA scissor-over-comb on sides and back and finger length on top)

▫ Apply flexible to firm hold hair wax or pomade by using your fingers to the of the head and piece it up.

DADDY DO IT! FOR HIM
"DASHING DOUG"

□ Taper the neck up and around the ears into about an inch and a half on the top of the head.

□ When hair is still wet part it to the side with a comb and then style with a product that has some hold.

DADDY DO IT! FOR HIM
"SPIKEY SCOTT"

□ Use a #2 sized clipper on the sides and back, a #3 or #4 on top, and then blend.

□ Apply firm hold gel when hair is wet if needed.

DADDY DO IT! FOR HIM
"MESSY MARV"

□ Tapered up around the ears and neck and the top left long.

□ While hair is still wet arrange hair into place with fingers.

□ Let air dry.

□ Spray texturizing spray throughout if wanted.

DADDY DO IT! FOR HIM
"PIECE-Y PAUL"

□ Keep interior layers short for texture. Leave bangs and perimeter longer.

□ Apply light hold foam throughout hair when wet.

□ Let air-dry.

See these styles for yourself. Flip over!

Textured Tom

Dashing Doug

Spikey Scott

Messy Marv

Piece-y Paul

DADDY DOS FOR HIM!

@DBANO @DEANBANOWETZ
#DADDYDOS

Textured Tom

Dashing Doug

Spikey Scott

Messy Marv

Piece-y Paul

YOUR TURN TO
DRAW SOME DOs!

@DBANO   @DEANBANOWETZ   #DADDYDOS

DADDY DO IT! FOR HIM
"BEACHY BRODY"

☐ Use a razor to cut the shape (early Justin Bieber haircut)

☐ While still wet use fingers to arrange hair by pushing top hair forwards and bangs to the side.

☐ Let air-dry.

☐ Apply light-hold pomade and pinch the tips of hair.

DADDY DO IT! FOR HIM
"SURFER STEVE"

☐ Keep the nape and ear area clean but leave the sides around and inch and the top around two to three inches long

☐ Towel dry then air dry.

☐ Apply wax throughout hair with fingers and spike the hair on top back.

DADDY DO IT! FOR HIM
"WHISPY WESTON"

□ Use clippers with a low guard size around neck and ears; then blend to longer pieces on top.

□ Apply a little pomade on dry hair.

DADDY DO IT! FOR HIM
"CURLY CURTIS"

□ Keep hair a couple inches long all over to show natural curl.

□ Apply soft hold gel when wet and comb hair forward.

□ Scrunch with fingers.

DADDY DO IT! FOR HIM
"MOHAWK MATT"

□ Keep hair short around the temples and ears and blend to long down the middle of the head.

□ Let air-dry.

□ Spray some hairspray for texture.

Now, let's get back to the girls . . .

GREAT STYLES FOR MULTI-CULTURAL HAIR

DADDY DO IT!
BANTU KNOTS

□ Prep the hair by wetting and brushing through hair.

□ While still partially wet, separate hair into multiple sections. The exact width will vary depending on how short or long your hair is, as well as the look you want to go for if you plan to do knot-outs. Typically speaking, if you have short hair, you should use smaller sections, while women with long hair can opt for larger sections.

□ Apply a curl cream or similar setting product. Stick with a product that has light to medium hold to create knots and knot-outs that hold their form without becoming stiff. Twist the product into each section of hair.

□ Twist a small coil at the base of your scalp. Twist each section of hair for a few turns in between your fingertips, as though screwing in a screw or turning a doorknob. Only wind the hair enough to create a short spring-like coil against your scalp.

□ Wrap the rest of the hair around this section. Gradually wind the remaining hair in the section around the base coil, bringing the hair closer to your head with each wrapped layer.

→

▫ Set in place. If the coils are tight enough, you can usually tuck the ends under the coil to hold them in place. If the coils feel a little too loose, however, you can use hairpins or small elastic ponytail holders to hold the end of the knots in place.

▫ Repeat the knotting procedure on the remaining sections. Each section of hair needs to be twisted into a small coil. Wrap the remainder of each section around its corresponding coil and tuck or pin the ends in place.

VIDEO TUTORIAL!

See it at <u>daddy.do/bantu-knots-by-dean</u>

BANTU
BABY!

@DBANO @DEANBANOWETZ

#DADDYDOS

DADDY DO IT!
STRAND TWIST (ROPE BRAID)

☐ Before braiding, brush hair smooth.

☐ For a tighter, more structured rope braid, start by putting the hair in a ponytail.

☐ For a messier look, skip to the next step and start the braid at the nape of your neck.

☐ Separate the hair into two equal sections. Now twirl each section around your fingers, or pinch the top of the section, twist, move down another inch, twist again, and so on. Both sections should be twisted in a clockwise or rightward motion.

☐ Cross the right section over the left section.

☐ Keep braiding all the way down the hair.

☐ Tie off the end with a hair band.

VIDEO TUTORIAL!
See it at <u>daddy.do/strand-twist-by-dean</u>

DADDY DO IT!
BRAID OUT

▢ Prep hair by brushing and washing hair.

▢ Part the hair in four quarters. First, part down the middle of the head, so there are two big halves. Secondly, part across, horizontally, so that there are two sections in each half part, four total on the head.

▢ Clip each section.

▢ Apply leave-in moisturizer to each of the four, separated sections. I find that combing the product through works best on very, very, VERY thick hair. Be sure to pay attention to the roots and the ends.

▢ When all parts of the hair are amply moisturized, grab oil and rub it on the hands as if rubbing someone down. LOL! Just kidding. Anyway, rub the oil on the hands and in between fingers. Greasy hands make for even distribution when braiding the hair.

▢ Loosen each of the four sections (one by one) and put four or five braids in each.

▢ Do Step 4 as needed for each section.

▢ When all sections are plaited up, slap on a satin bonnet.

VIDEO TUTORIAL!
See it at <u>daddy.do/braid-out-by-dean</u>

BRAID IT
OUT!

 @DBANO   @DEANBANOWETZ

 #DADDYDOS

CHAPTER NINE: BEAUTY SCHOOL

People are always asking me for my best beauty tips for both adults and the kids. Here are some of my top suggestions:

□ **Learning the structure of your hair is important.** Remember that when their hair is wet, it is fragile. Don't pull on it hard or it will rip and snap. I tell all of my clients, big and small, to always use a wide toothed comb to detangle wet hair. Proceed carefully. Comb and do not rip.

□ **The basic hair care regime is to wash and then condition.** I think the real first step to successful hair is to make sure you comb hair out prior to ever getting it wet. It will be so much better and easier to wash.

□ **You should wash your hair in water that's never too hot or too cold.** Tepid is the best. Kids basically hate hot water and you could burn them. Make sure to test the water in the shower before you tell them to get in. Remember that a child's sensitivity to heat is much greater than ours. You can stand that hot shower; she cannot. Yes, it does burn her.

☐ **It's great to buy a baby shampoo.** Kids will turn savage if they have burning shampoo in their eyes and they will blame you forever.

☐ **There are all sorts of DIY hair care recipes out there for both kids and adults.** I've heard of using egg white and even mayo or baby powder to absorb the oil if you can't wash. Remember that eggs can be dangerous if residue is left in the tub because they're slippery. They can even turn into salmonella poisoning, so I'd avoid using eggs. Mayo just seems messy. A sprinkle of baby powder will help dry up oil. Make sure to brush it out, so you don't walk around with white fluff in your hair.

AND NOW A FEW DADDY GROOMING TIPS:

I can't help it, but I want to spread beauty everywhere. Since you've taken such great care of your little girl, it's time for a little papa pampering. A few last words for you fabulous daddies from your best friend Dean:

☐ **When you cut your hair have the hairdresser cut your eyebrows.** You don't want to braid them.

☐ **You wouldn't be happy if your little daughter had hair growing out of her ears.** She feels the same way about the fur in your lobes and nose. Removing that hair is basic grooming 101. You don't have to be Beckham, but good grooming is a must for all men.

☐ **Get your hair cut every four weeks.** You will always look good. Some men prefer more regular cuts. I cut Simon Cowell's hair every ten days. The point is, if you wait too long you will get split ends. And you don't want to look like a shaggy mess.

☐ **You don't have to blow dry your hair.** Just towel dry it out dry. You can also use a dime-sized drop of gel to control it. Just air dry and call it a day.

☐ **Don't use too much product.** You don't want to be an oil slick. The same goes for not washing your hair every single day. Remember, you don't want hands to glide off your head.

☐ **The three products I believe every man needs are a basic hair gel, a finishing pomade or putty, and hair spray.** That's what I use on men whose hair I cut.

☐ **Spend three more minutes in the shower and use conditioner.** Also use it to soften your beard. It will make shaving so much easier for you. Plus, I hate shaving cream. I just use shampoo and conditioner in the shower to shave. It's so much easier on your facial skin than some harsh shaving cream with menthol.

☐ **Guys, wash your hair well after a workout.** After a workout, you release hormones that can even clog your pores and cause balding. So don't just jump into a shower and avoid your hair. It's stinky, plus you could become a baldie over time – and not that much time. Wash out what is clogging your scalp and thus causing your hair to fall out.

☐ **If you are balding, I recommend getting a shorter cut, which will conceal it.** You can also explore other options. I've had four hair transplants done on my head (shoutout to bosley.com). Most say that transplants look horrible. Do I look horrible? No! It's really important to get an initial consultation. If you can't afford transplants or don't want to do it, you can also look into a hairpiece. Some pieces do an amazing job. This is not the time to skimp on price. A cheap piece looks like a cheap piece. In other words, you get what you pay for here.

☐ **To avoid baldness, do a nightly scalp massage.** Even Jon Bon Jovi reportedly does it. Just rub your fingers in circular motions gently on your scalp. Don't do it on wet hair because that is fragile hair. Do it when your hair is dry. A scalp massage increases oxygen rich blood and brings it to the surface to feed the hair. There are also drugs that help retain your hair. Ask your doc. If you use the shampoos to cope with balding make sure you're consistent. You can't use them "sometimes" because they won't work that way. Check out Bosley Professional Strength Shampoo and Conditioner.

▢ **Take Vitamin A, D and E, which are crucial for skin, hair and nail health.** I'm always really aware of my vitamins.

▢ **By the way, bald is really hot on a lot of guys.** Embrace it. Love it. Get rid of all the hair and don't just leave a '70s patch. So get rid of that horseshoe of hair and commit to bald. My favorite product is the Headblade. A little shadow however looks hot. Remember to put sunscreen on your shaved head because nasty burns happen fast. Or wear a hat.

▢ **Have fun with hair**—your own, and the hair you create for you daughter!

Until next time,
Your Do Master, Dean

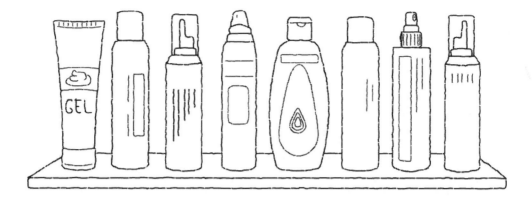

APPENDIX:
TOP PRODUCTS FOR THE KIDS

JOHNSON'S BABY SHAMPOO

Baby's delicate eyes need special care during bath time. JOHNSON'S® baby shampoo is as gentle and mild to the eyes as pure water. This baby shampoo's NO MORE TEARS® formula cleanses gently and rinses easily, leaving your baby's hair soft, shiny, manageable and clean while smelling baby-fresh.

MIXED CHICKS KID'S TANGLE-TAMER

Worried about what to do the next day with your little one's nest? Mixed Chicks Kid's Tangle-Tamer light, moisturizing formula revives bedhead and gives wild hair a fresh look.

WEN KIDS™ APPLE CLEANSING CONDITIONER

This menthol-free formula is made exclusively with rice protein and contains no nuts, no wheat and no soy ingredients, making it safe to use even for those with many common allergies.

TANGLE TEEZER FLOWER POT PRINCESS PINK

A pretty flower-shaped Tangle Teezer brush which is easy to hold and perfect for children. Comes with a flower pot case that can be used to store hair clips and bands.

PAUL MITCHELL BABY DON'T CRY® SHAMPOO

Gently cleanses and soothes hair and scalp. Mild cleansers and a neutral pH create a tearless formula. A unique blend of extracts helps to hydrate and prevent moisture loss, while chamomile and cornflower extract calm and soothe.

PAUL MITCHELL TAMING SPRAY® OUCH-FREE DETANGLER

Easily detangles dry or damp hair. Leaves hair fresh and full of body. Smoothes static and helps control children's "morning hair."

NUBY TEAR FREE RINSE PAIL

The Tear Free Rinse Pail is designed to make bath time easier and more enjoyable. It features a comfortable grip for Mom or Dad, a deep base for easy filling in shallow water and a unique tear free edge that can be gently placed against your baby's skin to help prevent water from running into your baby's eyes.

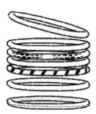

GOODY OUCHLESS ELASTICS

Only Goody Ouchless elastics are made with SmartStretch Core™. This improvement helps each one hold its shape longer without stretching out while giving you the same gentle and comfortable hold.

OUIDAD KRLY KIDS NO TIME FOR TEARS SHAMPOO

KRLY Kids No Time for Tears Shampoo is a super-gentle, tear-free formula that cleanses while helping delicate curls retain moisture. Proteins and amino acids restore internal weight so curls are moisturized, tangle-free, manageable, and healthy.

OUIDAD KRLY KIDS NO MORE KNOTS CONDITIONER

KRLY Kids No More Knots Conditioner is a detangler and nourishing conditioner that softens curls and protects against frizz and split ends. A gentle duo of proteins and amino acids penetrate hair strands, giving curls substance and encouraging separation and easy detangling.

SUNDAY AFTERNOON SUN HATS

The need for children's sun protection is unprecedented; early education and use of natural sun care, including sun protective wear is critical for their future health. Sunday Afternoon Sun Hats offer a wide down sloping brim, excellent ventilation.

WAHL LITHIUM ION CLIPPERS FOR KIDS CUTS

Powered by Lithium Ion technology, the clipper outperforms standard Wahl rechargeable clippers by providing up to two times the run time, clocking in at one hour and forty minutes on a full charge.

BIOMEGA MOISTURE MIST CONDITIONER

Revitalizes fine, limp or thinning hair with a volumizing infusion of lightweight Omega-nutrients and Gugo Bark Extract. It detangles and conditions hair without weighing it down.

JOICO K-PAK INTENSE HYDRATOR

There's dry hair... and there's hair that's so parched, so thirsty, so starved for moisture that only a serious drink could bring it back to life. Intense Hydrator is the cocktail of choice: a profoundly nourishing treatment (at a gentle 3.5 PH level) offering immediate hydration to hair that's gasping for air.

HASK ESSENTIALS 5 IN 1 HAIR RESCUE

Repair That Hair is formulated with a specialty blend of ingredients developed to pack your hair with moisturizing agents that are lost due to environmental and styling damage.

HASK PURIFYING CHARCOAL SHAMPOO

Charcoal, derived from coconut shells, combined with lemon and grapefruit oils, thoroughly cleanses and clarifies while helping to eliminate impurities from your hair and scalp. Gentle enough for daily use and safe for color-treated hair.

THANK YOU!!!!

A very special thanks goes to a few people. Here they are:

▫ My mom Marcella, #SallyorSal, who always encouraged me when I was in beauty school and still does with everything I do in my life.

▫ All of my siblings Judy (#1), Alice (#2), Dee (#3), Lloyd (#4), Steve (#5), Allan (#6), Mary (#7), Marv (#8), Dick (#9), Debra (#10), Annette (#11), Leon (#12), (I'm #13), Randy (#14) and Patti (#15).

▫ Kyle Assenmacher, #10.2, my one and only godson, and all my nieces and nephews...

▫ A special thanks to #12 for telling me to go to beauty school and giving me pep talks of encouragement. He has always been who I look up to and want to be like.

▫ I look to a lot of my celebrity clients who I admire for their constant support and loyalty:

▫ Leeza Gibbons who has always told me I am the perfect husband because I anticipate what is needed and I know when to embrace the silence. She inspires me to try new and different things regardless of fear. She is my #1 fan and the woman who, just by knowing her, makes me want to be a better person.

▫ Simon Cowell who is one of the most amazing men I have met who has taught me the importance of loyalty in the business. He has allowed me to explore the globe going to new and beautiful places; something I never thought would happen to a farm boy from Iowa.

▫ Melanie Griffith is one of the kindest and most generous people I know. I love her passion for life and adventure.

▫ Lori Greiner for her constant friendship and encouragement to take the leap and make it happen. She is always ready to chat about what I want to do with my life and how I can change the world around us with hair.

▫ Noah Galloway, who I instantly bonded with on the set of *DWTS*. As a U.S. vet who has overcome so much in his life, I admire how he lives his life to the fullest and inspires others daily!

▫ Ryan Seacrest, who I styled and groomed for 10 years, has taught me more about being an incredibly hard worker, a meticulous thinker about my business, and how to make sure everything fits together in perfect harmony.

▫ Carlos and Alexa Pena-Vega—this amazing couple have been a constant source of joy in my life since meeting them years ago. They are always encouraging me to take the leap to my next adventure and are always super supportive. I have learned valuable traits from them, live your life with love and compassion tackle life with a positive attitude and kind intensions. All things are possible with hard work and guidance from above.

▫ All my hair people who I have worked with over the years who have taught me to see the world a little differently through hair: Meagan Herrera-Schaaf, Cory Rotenberg, Don Wismer, Luis Alverez, Suzanne Weerts, Ryan Randall, Roni Roehlk, Linda Flowers, Sydell Miller, Mitch

Stone, Ann Bray, Milton Buras, Mary Guerrero, Kimi Messina, Jen Guerrero, Sean Smith, Gail Ryan, Sharon Blain, Vivienne Mackinder, Nicolas French, Sara Jones, Vince Davis, Ann Mincey, Michael Maron, Joe Santy, Stephanie Wiley, Maren Lonergan, Yuko Koach, Melissa Jaqua, Melanie Verkins, Nancy Stimac, Cheryl Marks, Jerilynn Stephens, Dev Rice, Pat O'Keefe, Ralph Abalos, Rachel Dowling, Alyn Topper, Kay Majuerus, Lotus Corricelli, Sallie Nicole, Cortney Ajamian, Lyndsey Palumbo, Keyonna Tillman, Karen Kaalberg, Lawrence Davis, Derrick Spruill, Renee Vaca, Miss Deb, Margaret Dempsey, Kear Lonergan, Okyo Sthair, Trista Bremer, all my 706 Union hair and make up friends I get to work with everyday, and many, many more.

▫ My core group of non-doing-hair friends who don't judge me and make my world a better, happier, safer place to be: Scott Carter, Leann Donovan, James Aquilina, Doug Rago, Glenn Soukesian, Dave Lawrence, Mike Catlett, Mark Keppy, Julie Kozak, Keith Crary, Amy Scribner, Stacie Krajchir, Kamy Bruder, Trish Suhr, Heidi Clements, Kyle Kleibeoker, Phil Pallen, Jeff Hall, Charles F. Reidelbach, Hillary Bibicoff, Cindy Pearlman, Arline Kramer, Doloras Cardelucci, Rhonda Roeder Evans, Deaquinita Hill, Sean Nadeau, Robin Radin and many more.

▫ My heart and soul are one with Claire Kaye, the best beauty PR person I've ever met. Claire has believed in me more than I have believed in myself. She is a constant source of knowledge and wisdom; the 1st person I call whenever something is happening in my life. Claire, I love you and am so happy you are in my life.

▫ My manager Cat Josell who has been my biggest cheerleader and supporter in life. I appreciate all you do and look forward to doing so much more in the future. Get me my own show!!!!!! :)

▫ Lisa Gregorisch Dempsey, a prolific TV executive I met at "EXTRA" who has always encouraged me to think big and jump in feet first! It is all about the Four Agreements!

▢ Winn Claybaugh and all the Paul Mitchell Schools throughout the United States. I love being a part of this learning culture! Winn thank you for always being there to listen to my ideas and helping me fulfill my dreams. You are amazing and I love and appreciate you very much! Everyone needs a hair daddy!! Thanks for being a great mentor!

▢ Sara Jones for believing in me from the beginning. She hired me for my first professional hair gig. She has been a personal and professional friend ever since #Joico

▢ My Instyler leaders Dave, Mark, Karl, Marty Jon, Stephanie and everyone on the team, thank you for having faith in me its a pleasure to collaborate with all of you.

LOOK FOR DEAN'S NEXT BOOKS

THE DEAN'S LIST OF...

Made in the USA
Middletown, DE
18 March 2017